Hackforth, Hornby, Langthorne
East & West Appleton and Arrathorne

~

A Brief Contemporary History

Copyright Hackforth Millennium Committee 2004 ©

Edited and Produced by
Blaisdon Publishing
3 Park Chase, Hornby, Bedale
North Yorkshire DL8 1PR

Binding: Remploy Ltd

ISBN 1 90283819 X

These accounts, photographs, pictures, cuttings and sketches relate to actual events and memories, and nothing is intended to vitiate, or misrepresent any persons, alive or dead.

The cover picture of Hornby Castle is an engraving by B Fawcett.
It comes from the book "The Country Seats of Noblemen and Gentlemen of Great Britain and Ireland" (Volume 4). Edited by Rev F O Morris B.A. Published by William McKenzie, 69 Ludgate Hill, London.   *(Betty Burke)*

Introduction

It was suggested at an early Hackforth Millennium Committee meeting that a sub Committee be given the job of looking into the possibility of producing a book of facts and memories of the local community, to be based around the old Duke of Leeds Estate. Now four years on, that sub Committee is beginning to realise what it let itself in for – collecting photographs, paper cuttings, and diaries, minute books and peoples' memories of years gone by. We would like to take this opportunity to thank all the contributors.

The Duke of Leeds Estate covered Hornby, Hackforth, Langthorne, Arrathorne, East and West Appleton and parts of Patrick Brompton. The Estate was self sufficient, with its own sawmill, corn mill, blacksmith's shop, dairy, ice house and museum. Most of the farms on the estate were similar in build i.e. a fold yard surrounded by stable, loose boxes, calf house, pig sties and cow byres with granary and hay loft above. Hornby with a Castle and Church were central, with a school at Hackforth and a Church and Chapel at Langthorne.

In the following pages, we hope to show maps, sketches and photographs of the surrounding areas of how things have changed over the last hundred years. It has taken some considerable time to get it all together and no doubt some will question dates and facts, but they are as we have been given them, so we hope you will read and enjoy our efforts.

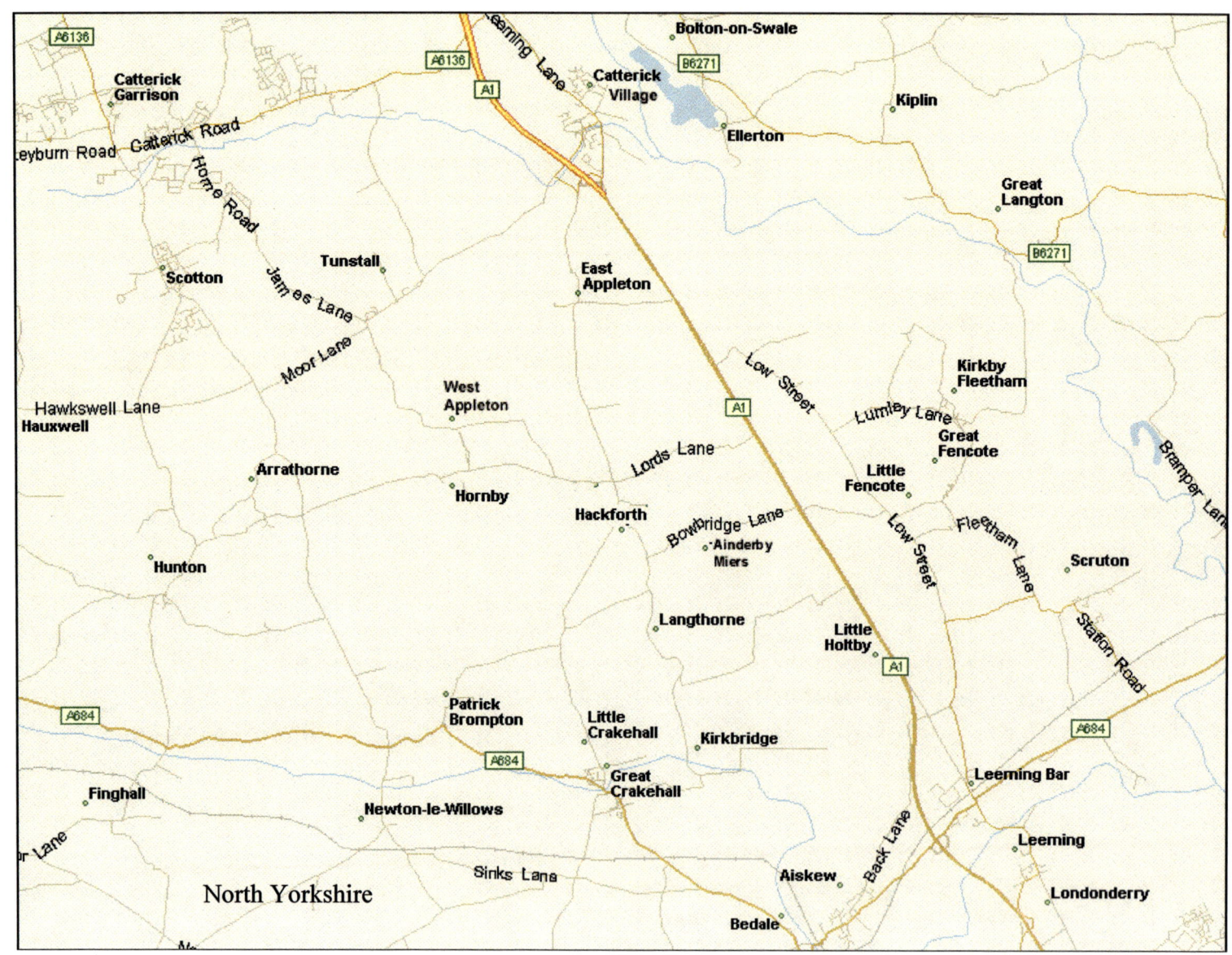

Name Derivations

Hackforth: 1086 Domesday Book – *ACHEFORD*
"Ford with a hatch or by a bend."

Old English – hæcc or haca + ford.

Hornby: 1086 Domesday book – *HORNEBI*
Farmstead or Village on a horn-shaped piece of land, or of a man called 'Horn ', or 'Horni'.

Old Scandinavian – 'Horn' or personal name + bý.

Langthorne: 1086 Domesday Book – *LANGETORP*

C.1100 Langthorn – Tall thorn-tree

Old English – lang + thorn.

Appleton: 1086 Domesday Book – *APELTON*

Farmstead where apples grow, apple orchard

Old English – æppel + tũn.

Ainderby: 1086 Domesday Book – *EINDREBI*

Farmstead or village of a man called 'Eindrithi'.

Old Scandinavian – personal name + bý.

With thanks to A D Mills
A Dictionary of English Place Names

List of Contents

Introduction 3
Name Derivations 5
Hornby Castle Estate 11
    Hornby Castle 13
    St Mary's Church, Hornby 20
    The Estate Villages 25
1900-1910 37
    The Hornby Castle Kennels & Hounds 38
    The Duke of Leeds 43
    The Duck Decoy 45
    Gamekeepers on the Hornby Estate 48
    Hackforth School 50
    Langthorne 1900-1910 ~ Horse and cart unattended 51
    Street House Farm Tenancy Agreement 53
1910-1920 57
    The School 59
    The Great War 1914 –1918 62
    War Memorial 63
1920 - 1930 65
    Remembrance Day 66
    School & Village Life 66
    The School 67
    Sports Teams 70
    The Castle and Dukes of Leeds 73

1930 - 1940 .... **75**
    Hornby Castle Auction 77
    Mr Prime's Memories 89
    Hackforth School 91
    Farming 95
    St Mary's Church 104
    The Village Hall 111
    Women's Institute (W.I.) 117
    Life in Hackforth Village in the 1930s 118
    Royal Occasions 122

1940 – 1950 .... **125**
    The War Years (1939 – 1945) **126**
    Home Guard Memories 132
    Hackforth Camp 134
    The Village Hall 137
    Land Army Girls 138
    End of War Celebrations 141
    The Wedding of Miss Joan Heeley and Mr. Donald Chapman 144
    Stars of the Plough 145
    1940s Farming 147
    Transport 154

East Appleton 1920s – 1940s **157**
    Childhood memories of East Appleton – Jim Pearson 158

1950-1960 .... **163**
    St Mary's Church, Hornby 164
    Royal Occasions 167
    Coronation Leaflet 168
    Hackforth Celebrations 169

Farming ~ 1950s 172
Point to Point at Hornby Castle ~ 1954 175
The Women's Institute...176
Hackforth School 179

1960-1970 ....**183**
Hackforth School 184
The Post Office 187
Bus Service 188
Langthorne's Last Stand 190
The W.I. and their families at Hornby Castle (3-7-68)..192

1970-1980 ....**193**
St Mary's Church Anniversary 194
Church Concert 196
The Bedale Hunt was active in the area in the 1970s 198
Farming 199
Hackforth School 203
Queen's Silver Jubilee ~ 1977 204
Hackforth School 207
Village Day ~ 1979 209
The Women's Institute...211
Hornby Park Chase 212

1980-1990 ....**215**
Summer 1980 216
Diana Day ~ 1981 217
Hornby Fête ~ 1982 220
Hackforth School 221
Medieval Banquet at Richmond Castle ~1985 227
Rudd Hall Fire..232

    Rutex 233
    The Village Hall 234
    The W.I. 234

1990-2000 ....**237**
    The Village Hall 239
    Delight as Village Hall gets face lift 240
    Hackforth Village School 242
    The Women's Institute (W.I.) 249

The Millennium **251**
    The Fundraising Events in 1999 253
    2000 Events: 263
    Bulb Planting outside Hackforth 269
    Hornby Yew 270
    Village Millennium Projects 271
    Hello 2000! 273
    After 2000 275

Appendix 1 ~ Domesday 1985 ....**277**
Appendix 2 ~ 19th Century Census **289**
Index **295**

Hornby Castle Estate

Hornby Castle

Fig.1 – From the south-east. Hornby was sadly reduced in the 1930s after its sale by the Duke of Leeds. Only the south range, rebuilt by John Carr for the 4th Earl of Holdernesse, and adjacent tower survived.

ENLIGHTENED landowners were key figures in the agricultural revolution of the 18th century, and their spirit lives on in the Royal Show. But, sadly, today's agricultural improvers do not share the architectural eye of their forbears. Nothing in modern farm-building compares with the delights of the Georgian model farm, especially those built for the 4th Earl of Holdernesse at Hornby.

Robert Darcy, 4th Earl of Holdernesse, inherited the great medieval seat of the Conyers family in 1722 as a boy of three. Its appearance then can be judged from Samuel Buck's sketch (Fig 2), which must have been made about that year. Despite its name and its four towers, Hornby had always been a fortified house rather than a castle, and owed most of its appearance to William Conyers, who was created Baron Conyers in 1509.

The failure of William's son to produce a male heir spelled the end of the Conyers line, and Hornby passed through one of his daughters to Thomas Danby, whose grandson was created Earl of Holdernesse in 1682. His great-grandson was the 4th Earl.

Holdernesse is an attractive figure, a keen promoter of opera in his youth and an important member of the Dilettanti Society. In 1740, the year after he came of age, he was appointed Lord Lieutenant of the North Riding, a notable sign of the esteem in which his family was held, and a post that he held until 1777.

Fig.2 – Samuel Buck's sketch of the castle, made in the 1720s, shows the late-medieval seat of the Conyers family essentially intact, but with later windows.

The following year he was made a lord of the king's bedchamber. Although young, he was twice an ambassador before being made a Secretary of State in 1751

After being dismissed on the accession of George III in 1761, Holdernesse held no further office, but was consoled by a pension on the post office and the reversion of the wardenship of the Cinque Ports, to which he succeeded in 1765. Instead he turned to the improvement of his estates, financed by this extra income, as a summary of his finances drawn up in 1768 shows. His total income was £8,191 after expenses, of which £4,200 was the net profit from the Cinque Ports and his pension. The rental of his Hornby estate was £3,578 and that of his Aston estate £2,678, but against that had to be set interest at 4.5% on debts of £27,000.

Buck's sketch (Fig 2), and an early COUNTRY LIFE photograph (Fig 3) – taken before the castle was sadly reduced in the 1930s after its sale by the Dukes of Leeds' heirs to the Holdernesses – show that it may have been modernised not long before Holdernesse succeeded. Sash windows had been inserted and a photograph in the sales particulars of 1930 shows that the dining room had early 18th-century panelling. This was probably the work of Holdernesse's predecessor, the 3rd Earl, who succeeded in 1692 and came of age in 1702.

Fig.3 – The courtyard from a photograph of 1906. The main wall was probably refenestrated in the early 18th century, although traces of medieval windows remain.

But by the time Holdernesse came of age the castle had probably not been lived in for 20 years. Work was soon put in hand to make it habitable, and in 1745 Lady Oxford remarked that it was being painted and repaired. Lady Oxford's remarks do not suggest any new work, and it is not clear which architect was involved. Holdernesse personal accounts among the Holderness papers in the British Library show that the Venetian architect Giacomo Leoni was paid £260 "on account of the building" in 1710, but Howard Colvin has suggested that payment for alterations carried Holdernesse's London house, 4 Whitehall Yard. However, Holdernesse was later to embark on a much more ambitious programme of restoration.

We know from Arthur Young who visited the castle in the summer of 1768 that major improvements were then under way and from Theophilus Lindsey, writing to the Earl of Huntingdon, that Holdernesse and his family had moved back into the castle by September 1770. This ties in with a lone estate account for March 1766 to March 1767, which shows that £221 was spent on building work at the castle in that year. What we do not know is when work began.

Working out his building campaign is complicated by the fact that Holdernesse was a keen architectural patron who employed at least three architects – Leoni, James Stuart and John Carr – on three different houses besides Hornby. Despite the work done on 4 Whitehall Yard, Stuart designed a new London house, Holdernesse House, in about 1760 to 1765. Holdernesse is also said to have rebuilt Sion Hill near Isleworth, which he bought in 1755. And in Yorkshire, Carr was employed to rebuild Aston Hall near Rotherham after a fire in about 1767. This was completed by 1772, but then sold in 1775.

Thus it is difficult to be certain that a reference to an architect or builder is connected with Hornby Castle. Furthermore, Holdernesse's papers are confused and scattered, with some personal accounts and papers in the British Library, and some even more partial estate accounts in the Leeds' papers held by the Yorkshire Archaeological Society in Leeds.

Holdernesse may have been at work at Hornby in the early 1750s, for I S 1754 has been scratched on the side of the main entrance to the courtyard. Although this is not a formal datestone, it could be the mark of a mason engaged in restoration. This might tie in with a payment in his accounts of £50 to Mr Carr on July 2, 1753. It is unclear if this is the architect John Carr, who had just begun his practice. Another account book records the payment of £280 to Mr Carr on February 14, 1757. As there are also payments of £100 to the mason John Devall in 1755, with further payments of £80 in 1756, £142 and £425 in 1758, £200 in 1759, and £186 and £530 in 1760, this may well be a payment for architectural services. But the two may not be connected, and the payments to Deval may be for work at Sion Hill. A letter from William Mason to Holdernesse dated August 1, 1760, discusses major building work at Hornby, apparently at the castle, but in terms too ambiguous to be certain. But whatever the building, Mason makes it clear that he advised Holdernesse on its restoration. In the same year Mr Carr and Co. were paid £68. However, it is only on May 30, 1763, when Mr John Carr was paid £120, that we can be fairly confident that it is the architect being referred to. Thereafter the account, which ends in 1768, refers frequently to Mr Carr and to Mr John Carr. So it is probable that building work started early in the 1760s and perhaps even in the 1750s.

Fig.4 – The east range of the castle was entirely rebuilt by John Carr with Gothick detail but Georgian proportions.

Carr's main work was to rebuild the south and east ranges between the medieval towers (Figs 1 and 4). He chose a simple Gothick vocabulary to fit the castle's medieval aspect, with crenellations, hoodmoulds to the windows, delightful ogee arches to the tops of the window frames and a blank quatrefoil cross above the bow on the east front. Even so, the proportions remain Classical. Practicality may have argued against the expense of demolishing the solid masonry of the towers, but family piety was probably a more important reason. By retaining them, Holdernesse would have reminded all comers that he was not only an earl of relatively recent vintage, but also the heir of the ancient baronies of Darcy and Conyers.

Lindsey's letter, in which he compares the Duke of Northumberland at Alnwick with Holdernesse, is revealing about the reasons for rebuilding: "I do not think that his Grace so good a levee-man as my neighbour Lord Holdernesse, who has now got into his castle with his family, and has his public day, the honours of which he does with great ease and affability to everyone." The importance in the late 18th century of the public day, when great aristocrats held a levee in a quasi-regal fashion, has been little studied, but its influence on the rebuilding of Hornby is clear.

From an inventory of 1778 and another of about 1839, and from the sale plan of 1930, we can see that the two ranges served different roles. The south range was largely given over to the three large rooms on the first floor, with the ground-floor rooms having lower ceilings. These were clearly the public rooms. On the east range, however, the two floors were of equal heights and were for private use.

Little is known about the interior of the castle, as it was entirely gutted in the 1930s, but the staircase and the Great Hall (Fig 5) were illustrated by COUNTRY LIFE in 1906. Of these, the hall is the more fascinating, for it does not seem to be the work of Carr. Could it be by James Stuart?

If Holdernesse began his alterations at Hornby in the mid 1750s, as seems possible, then the fashionable Stuart, newly returned from Greece, was the obvious architect for him to employ. Carr, who had only recently moved from being a builder to an architect, could have begun as executant architect. Holdernesse was a keen Dilettante, subscribed to Stuart's *Antiquities of Athens,* and employed Stuart at Holdernesse House. Stuart's architectural style is something of an enigma, for it not only combines Greek and Roman motifs in a manner that is often novel, but also includes elements of Palladian and even Rococo design.

The Great Hall is a difficult room to understand. The coving of the ceiling may be evidence of earlier work by the 3rd Earl, as it is reminiscent of early-18th-century Yorkshire houses such as Gilling Castle or Beningbrough. But the rest of the decoration central door is clearly mid-18th-century, and the whole room, including furniture, was designed as a single decorative scheme.

Fig.5 – The Great Hall, in a photograph of 1906. The unity of the design, including the pier table to the right of the door, suggests that it may be the work of James Stuart.

Although the basic framework of the room is Palladian, with a bracketed cornice, doors with architraves (and in the case of the central door pediment), and a heavily architectural chimneypiece, the general effect is not Palladian.

The chimneypiece frieze is one of Stuart's favourite motifs – it derives from the Incan-tada in Thessalonica – and the dominant motif of the fluted band is repeated in the doorcases, the cornice, the chimneypiece and (most telling of all) the pier table.

. It is the pier table to the right of the central door (it was clearly designed for that position and appears in the 1778 inventory) that makes the attribution to Stuart plausible. With its triple-fluted legs, lions' claw feet and mask, and repeated motif of the triple rosette, it is a classic example of Stuart furniture design. Holdernesse had a similar, but not identical, pier table at Holdernesse House.

In the centre of his state apartment at Hornby Lord Holdernesse set a bay window in place of an earlier oriel. When it was built, it looked out over ordinary farmland, but it was part of Holdernesse's plan to give his house the landscaped setting now favoured by his peers, and he called in the greatest practitioner of the day to do it, "Capability" Brown. Arthur Young was probably aware that he was about to start work when he described "the environs abounding with capabilities of all kinds."

Fig.6 – Hornby Park viewed from the castle.

Like most great late-medieval houses, Hornby Castle had a deer park set away from the house, in this case to the south-west. The palisaded enclosure of the park can be seen on a 17th-century survey, and its extent can also be traced on another survey of 1766, but this shows the park divided into fields. Holdernesse turned all the former deer park over to farming and imparked in its place a smaller block of land to the south and east of the castle to give it a suitable setting.

Arthur Young notes Lord Holdernesse's interest in agricultural improvements, but also that his methods were rather extravagant. Commenting on grassland that was more level than was usual, he discovered that it was Lord Holdernesse's doing and was achieved by leaving the field fallow for two years and then sowing with grass but leaving the first crop to rot on the ground. As Young wryly notes, "such methods are much too expensive to be imitated."

The series of model farms that are Holdernesse's chief legacy confirm Young's analysis of his approach to agricultural improvement. Turrets, dressed stone and arcading make them handsome buildings, but grossly extravagant for what they are. Arbour Hill (Fig 7) and Street Farm (Fig 8) are identical in design, and both are clearly intended to be eyecatchers, Arbour Hill from the first floor of the castle, Street Farm from the Great North Road. They differ only in that one is in stone, while the other, which was not part of Lord Holdernesse's view, was in brick.

More restrained in its design is Home Farm, which has an ashlar façade but rubble walls (Fig 9). Its giant arcaded front may be modelled Thorpe Farm, designed by Sir Thomas Robinson at Gretabridge to the north.

The 1766 survey seems to have been made to record the enclosure of the deer park and shows that Arbour Hill and the Home Farm, which are within its area, had yet to be built. However, the estate accounts for 1766-67 record £40 being spent on building New High Street House, almost certainly Street Farm, and £36 on John Swale's New Park House, which could be Arbour Hill.

Although the architect of the farms is mentioned, the consistent payments to Carr make it most unlikely that any other architect was involved. Knowledge of Carr's farm buildings is limited, but Arbour Hilland Street Farm are consistent with his style.

Little attention has been paid to the park at Hornby. The description made for the Department of the Environment when the park buildings were listed suggests that the lakes were formed for the 6th Duke of Leeds in about 1790-1805, and the rustic bridge built in about 1806. In fact, Hornby Park is the unnoticed work of "Capability" Brown.

It is surprising that Brown's work here should have gone unremarked for Holdernesse was one of the 13 peers who petitioned the Duke of Newcastle in March 1758 to make Brown royal gardener, "being well-wishers of Mr Browne, whose Abilities and Merit are fully acquainted with." Holderness's accounts in the British Library show that Lancelot Brown was paid £1,525 between September 14, 1756, and April 27, 1762. This does not seem to have been for work at Hornby, and was probably either for Sion Hill, which Holdernesse bought in 1755, or Aston Hall.

Among the estate accounts for Hornby is a reference to £100 being paid to "Lanet Brown" on November 3, 1768. This is clearly for Hornby, and coincides with extensive payments for improvements to the house, the park and estate buildings.

Fig.7 Arbour Hill, built of dressed stone, is the most elaborate of the model farms. Its south and north facades are symmetrical. It has just been restored by Mr and Mrs Nigel Stourton.

Fig. 8 – Street Farm

Fig. 9 – Home Farm

Work had already begun, with £53 17s being spent on the garden and plantations from March 1766 to March 1767, and £60 in 1768. Estate accounts are fragmentary, but those from March 1777 to March 1778 show that major landscaping was going on right up to the end of Holdernesse's life; work was nearing completion, with £237 being spent on the first serpentine river. This included lowering a hill in the new park and filling the piece of water below the bridge; digging and wheeling away 1339 cubic yards of earth at the river below the bridge; laying turf and gravel for walks; digging out the end of the second piece of water and smoothing the hill away; digging the ha-ha on the south-west side of the first river and walling the west side of the river.

The sum of £25.19s. was paid for fencing woods and plantations, and money was also spent on trees, shrubs and garden seeds. £87.17s.6d. went to labourers in the garden and plantations. Work was almost equally extensive the following year, but tailed off in 1780 and 1781.

It is clear from this account and Lord Holdernesse, presumably following Brown's plan, was responsible for all the significant landscaping at Hornby today, including all three of the lakes which curl round like a river, and probably most of the planting too.

This is best seen in the survey of the park made in 1806 (fig.10). Only the duck decoy is later *(see 1900-1910)*. The need for water at Hornby had been noticed by Lord Harley in 1725. Compared with the effort to put into the creation of the lakes, planting was limited, being restricted to a substantial plantation beyond the first lake and a narrow belt beyond the third, together with ornamental planting round the castle. Scattered trees in the park would probably be left from earlier days when it had been the sheep closes. It is also clear from the accounts that the remarkable bridge, with its tula-like appearance had been built by it 1777 (figures 11 and 12). The architect is unknown but could have been Brown or Carr.

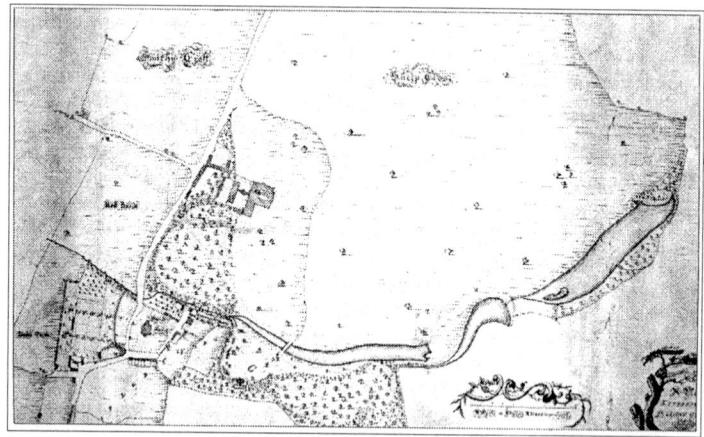

Fig.10 – Survey of 1806 shows the park laid out by "Capability" Brown, with the sequence of three lakes, and the Castle on the left.

Happily, the 1930s reduction of the castle left the south front and its tower, which were the focus of Brown's landscape. Despite some replanting with poplars, his planting is largely intact, as are his lakes. The farms, too, have survived and Arbour Hill has recently been restored. Hornby may no longer be a great estate, but the work of the 4th Earl of Holdernesse remains.

With permission of Roger Clutterbuck
Article by Giles Worsley
Country Life June 29,1989

(Right and bottom) Figs 11 and *12* – The park bridge had been built by 1777 as part of the landscape laid out by "Capability" Brown. It may have been designed by John Carr who had great experience as surveyor of bridges to the North Riding or by Brown himself.

St Mary's Church, Hornby

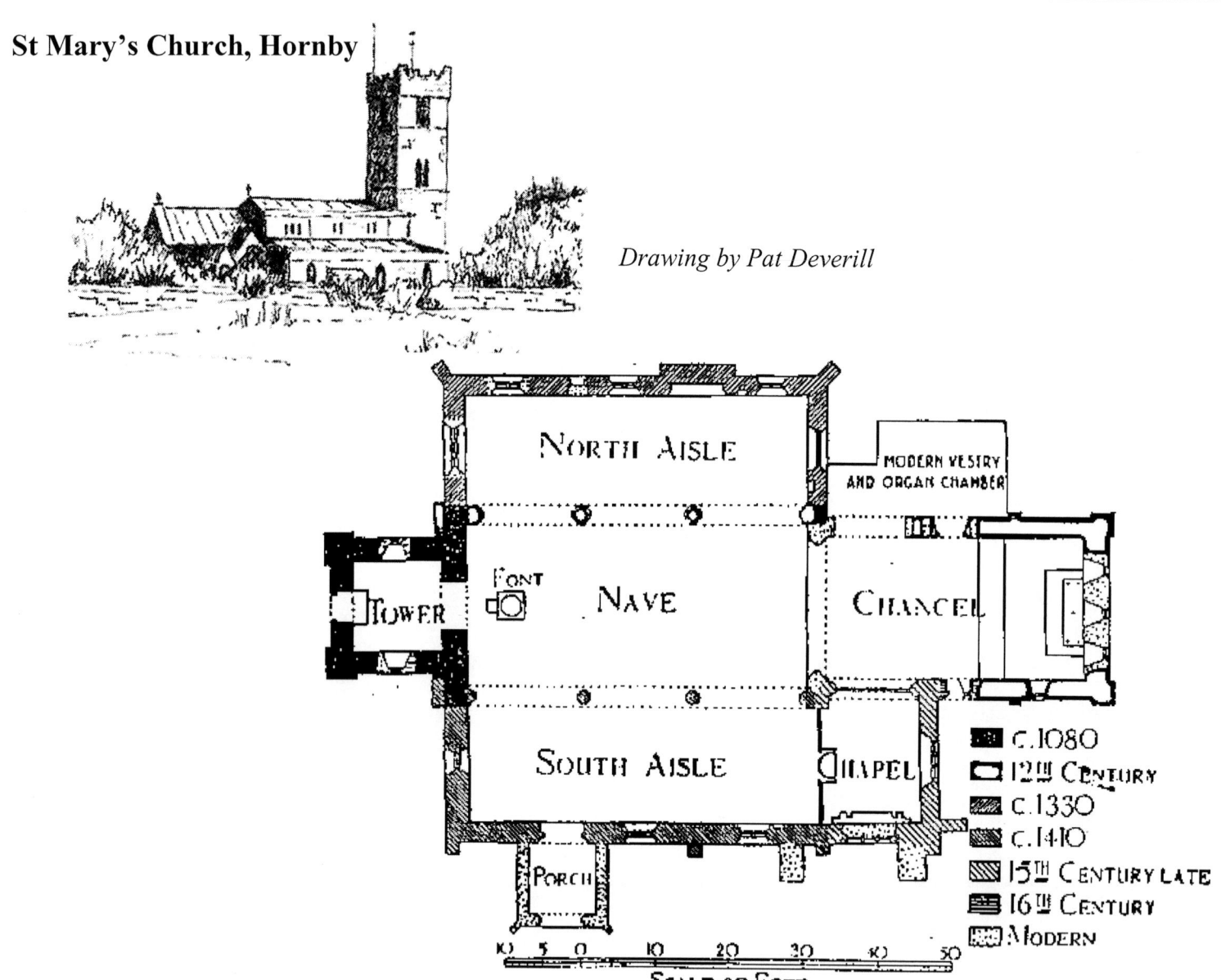

Drawing by Pat Deverill

FOUNDED IN THE 11TH CENTURY AND RESTORED IN THE 19TH and 20TH CENTURIES

The earliest part of the present structure is the tower, dating from about 1080 and built on the site of a pre-Conquest Saxon church, and which was evidently attached to a small church consisting of a chancel and nave. The present chancel and nave was rebuilt about 1170-80 and a north aisle (which was widened in 1330) added. The south aisle was built in 1410 and the tower raised one stage further. The church was thoroughly restored in 1878-79, with the chancel arch and east wall being rebuilt as well. The vestry, organ chamber and porch are modern.

During the 1990s, a huge effort was made by the local parishioners to raise money for the restoration of the tower, a total refurbishment of the organ, loft and other essential maintenance. This work was completed.

THE PARISH OF SAINT MARY, HORNBY

In the early 12th century the church and manor were in the possession of Wigan, son of Landric, who was known to have held lands at Ainderby Miers in 1086. During his lifetime Wigan bestowed *'the church of Hornabi with one carucate of land'* upon Saint Mary's Abbey at York; this gift is known to have been confirmed by Stephen, Earl of Richmond from 1093 to 1137.

On the nones (5th) of September 1220, it was granted by the Abbott and Convent of the Abbey to Archbishop Walter de Grey, who gave it to the common fund of the Cathedral of York by deed in the *'sixth year of his pontificate'* (22nd May 1221). It was thus appropriated by the Dean and Chapter of York and a 'Vicarage' was ordained (that is provision for a regular vicar of the church as distinct from chantry priests). The first recorded occupant of the VICARAGE is RICHARD DE MILEFORD who is mentioned as Vicar of Hornby in October 1274 during Archbishop Giffard's Visitation.

THE CHURCH AND PARISH OF SAINT MARY, Hornby thus became one of the 'Peculiars' or privileges of the Dean and Chapter of York, who are still patrons of the living.

THE PARISH REGISTERS

The Parish Registers commence in 1582 and the Churchwarden's Accounts in 1703, although items of expenditure appear amongst the records-of Baptisms etc., from 1587 onwards. The registers were kept in an old iron box in the vestry until recently, when they were transferred for safekeeping and preservation to the County Archivist at County Hall, Northallerton.

Hornby Castle Estate

1900

2000

(Tom Pace)

THE TOWER

It is evident that a western tower of Saxon character was added towards the close of the eleventh century to a pre-conquest church, which consisted of a nave and chancel of narrow proportions.

The oldest part of the present church is best seen from the outside in the three lower stages of the tower, which shows a combination of Saxon and Norman styles. The Saxon influence is most noticeable in the third stage, the original belfry, where the windows are divided into openings by recessed shafts surmounted by crude capitals. The lowest stage has wide shallow clasping buttresses at its corners and shallow buttresses against the nave walls, though these are obscured by the later western buttresses of the nave; this stage is lighted in the north and south walls by small round headed lights inserted at a much later date. On the western side is a door with a big stone lintel and blank tympanum or relieving arch. The second stage carries the clock faces and has one small window to the south.

The walling of the three lower stages is of irregular rubble with thick mortar joints and fairly uneven quoins, or corner stones; the clasping buttresses are of rubble in their lower halves and ashlar in the upper.

The fourth stage of the tower has a centre-pillared double belfry window, with the windows in perpendicular style of curious construction, and it is thought that the pillar might even be of Saxon origin. This stage was added in the late fifteenth century and is contemporary with the nave clerestory and south chapel. It is walled with squared, coarse rubble with quoin stones. The embattled parapet is a nineteenth century addition, as were the corner pinnacles, removed after storm damage in the 1980s.

THE BELFRY

The fourth stage of the tower is now the belfry and contains four bells. The treble is inscribed *'Veni Exultemus Domino 1695'*.

The second has the name *'The Reverend Thomas Kirkby, Vicar'* indicating a date between 1783 and 1800.

The third was originally provided by William, Lord Conyers (1468-1524) and was recast in 1656; the original bell had the inscription *'When I do rung, God's praises sing. When I do tole, pray heart and soul'*.

The fourth bell was cast in 1793.

In 1793, the bells were dispatched to Barton-on-Humber to be recast again. Undaunted by lack of modern transport facilities, those responsible ensured that they got there just the same, first by cart to Boroughbridge, thence by boat via York down the Ouse, and so on by river to Hull and Barton.

THE CLOCK

In the second stage of the tower is the clock, some 250 years old; in recent years it has been equipped with an electrically operated mechanism.

FURNISHINGS

The NAVE PEWS were provided when the church was restored in the 1870s, as were the chancel stalls and pulpit. Prior to this time the interior of the church contained a gallery at the west end and high backed pews, the chief of which was the great ducal pew raised high above the others, all being overshadowed by a three-decker pulpit. The church possesses two fine silver CHALICES bearing the London hallmark and dated 1729, with the arms of D'Arcy impaling those of Sutton engraved upon them with the inscription *'For ye use of Hornby Parish'*. There is also a FLAGON by Robert Cox of London dated 1758 and a PATEN made in London in 1782.

THE CHURCHYARD

Extended in the early 1930s, the original churchyard contains some interesting monuments, some of which are listed for preservation. Note particularly the chest tombs, also the medieval effigy, apparently with crossed legs, some 5 metres west of the south aisle and the early 19th Century sarcophagus commemorating Stephen Walton and Martha Greaves, *'Good and faithful servants at Hornby Castle',* to the north-east of the chancel.

The **SUNDIAL** near to the porch is mounted on a much earlier (late medieval) cross shaft.

The Estate Villages

The villages of Hackforth, Hornby and Langthorne are situated in a pleasantly rural area, near the market town of Bedale and only a few miles from Catterick. Nearby is the A1 London to Edinburgh Road, which for some distance follows the old Roman Road, Dere Street.

Hornby

Originally the manor was held by the St. Quintin family whose ancestors were rewarded by William the Conqueror for services rendered at the time of the Norman Conquest. The St. Quintins built a castle at Hornby of which only the tower named after them survives. The castle stands on a small hill in wooded parkland, and surrounded by lakes and streams. Whatever the requirements of the St. Quintins, for most of its life the castle was never a strongly fortified building, but a castellated mansion, which even today, as it rises out of the morning mist, could have come straight out of a book of fairy tales.

When the male line of the family died out, the estate passed through the female line to a branch of the Conyers family and during their tenure, portions of the castle were rebuilt. Towards the end of the 16th Century, however, again lacking a male heir, the entire estate was conveyed by marriage to the D'Arcys, who assumed the additional name of Conyers and later became Earls of Holdernesse. It was the last Earl's daughter and heiress who married the Fifth Duke of Leeds (of the Osborne family), and Hornby eventually became their principle seat.

As with previous owners, they did what they could, and many exterior walls of the castle were rebuilt and enlarged about the mid-1800s. But inevitably, change is an on-going process. The Estate continued to influence much of the development of the area until it was put up for sale in the 1930s.

In 1930 the Duke sold his estates at Hornby and Hackforth, and after some demolition, the castle became a private residence.

The small but ancient church of St. Mary nearby was first erected in the Norman period, but again, through the ages there have been substantial alterations and additions – even discoveries.

Indeed, it was during restoration work carried out by the Duchess of Leeds in the mid-1880s that hitherto uncovered Norman carvings came to light.

However, it is human beings who add flesh to the bare bones of buildings, and for some knowledge of them we are indebted to Mary, wife of the Revd. H.T. Boultbee, who in the late 19th Century used her enforced 'idleness', when recovering from an illness, to delve deep into the Parish Chest. The registers date from 1592, and her findings were published in a little book, *'Gleanings from an Iron Chest'*, which illuminates the lives of former inhabitants.

Cottages that cluster around the ancient church were intended to house workers on the estate. They vary in age, as is to be expected in a village of continuous occupation. Some are very old; others were built in 1923.

Workers cottages in Church View, Hornby with The Vicarage in the background, built in 1828.

Longevity, for instance, is not a prerogative of modern living. The First Earl of Holdernesse died at the ripe old age of 94, and one couple, Sophia and John Hutchinson living at Diamond Hill, clocked up no fewer than 75 years of marriage, and died aged 94 and 96 respectively.

Others were not so lucky, consigned to an anonymous grave. Who, for example, was the 'poor stranger', buried 1689, and where was he or she going?

Long-forgotten occupations are also recorded, such as the 'dog-whipper' employed to rid the church of the sheep dogs that arrived with their masters, causing havoc during divine service.

We have good reason to be grateful to Mary Boultbee and her delightful recordings, but what you gain upon the roundabouts you lose upon the swings, for as recently as the 1940s, a vicar with little sense of history but a passion for spring-cleaning, burnt many invaluable old records. Those that survive are now in the Record Office at Northallerton.

Hornby Castle Estate

In the 1800s, two lodges, one in Hornby and one in Hackforth, were built to control entry into the Castle and Hornby Park, which would have been unfenced at the time.

The Ice House (Hornby) was built in 1815.

Emily Ramsay

Ice was collected from a frozen lake and stored in an underground chamber with a domed lead roof, covered with soil. In summer, the icehouse was used for preserving food, cooling drinks, and medicinal purposes. A drain allowed the water out, and by autumn the icehouse would be cleared out and then refilled with ice.

Hornby Castle Estate

Laundry Cottage

Laundry Cottage was built in 1852 to serve the castle and local village. Five laundry maids had the use of 2 coppers, 5 sinks, a drying and an airing room, and access to the garden enclosed by a high stone wall. Once the railway system was established, clean laundry was sent by train to the Duke's London house, and dirty laundry sent back.

The Estate included many farms, a large walled garden, kennels, a dairy, a maggot house and the gas works. Gas was produced from 1878 and piped to the castle for heating and lighting. Coal brought from Jervaulx station (Newton le Willows) was put in an oven, heated up to produce gas, then stored. The coke left over was sold, while the waste ash was used to fill a gravel hole nearby. The building had a vented roof and was maintained by the man who lived in the bungalow next door. Gas production stopped in 1930, and during the war, the iron was melted down and sold.

Several amenities were added to the Castle Estate: A 9-hole golf course, a bowling green, and a box hedge maze in 1778. Later, a museum and a cow house were built in 1790, a riding school in 1841, a boat house in 1890 – and the museum was restored in 1878. A proper water supply was installed in 1896. Water fed from a spring in front of the vicarage was pumped by a hydram about half a mile to West Appleton (height 129 feet). The water then flowed to the Castle and gardens, the laundry, West Appleton, and houses along the road to Winterfield.

The Vicarage

(Rosemary Marston)

The picture (postcard) taken in about 1911 also shows Nursery Gardens Cottage and Hornby Spring. In the War years, the somewhat eccentric Vicar took up the floorboards on the ground floor in the hope that it would prevent the Army from requisitioning the property. The idea did not work – the Army replaced the boards and moved in! He was last Vicar to occupy the Vicarage.

Hackforth

Hackforth comprises mainly of a few cottages and farms, with a total population of approximately 120. Until 1930 the most recent sole owner was the Duke of Leeds, but in earlier times other well-known land-owning families had been associated with the village, notably the Burghs, and the Montfors who married into the Girlington family. The Tunstalls of Thurland Castle, Lancaster, also held land here. One, Cuthbert Tunstall, born 1475, became the pious Bishop of Durham, but falling foul of Elizabeth I for refusing to sign the Oath of Supremacy, he died a captive and beggar in 1559. It is thought that Gyll House was once the seat of the Tunstall family.

Though small, one cannot escape the sense of history, which surfaces from time to time: It is recorded that in the 18th Century a resident told how his father unearthed a silver collar in the vicinity of Hornby Castle which was assumed once to have graced the neck of a stag, for it bore the inscription: "Whoever doth me take, Let me go, for Julius Caesar's sake."

The village stands on the main Bedale to Catterick Road and consists mainly of two roads which branch off it, like the arms of a letter F. One road, Silver Street (was there once an old Mint in this locality?) was the location of the sub-Post Office/shop and ends in Manor Farmyard. The other nameless road leads to the Al and on this road stand the village hall and village school.

It is in the Village Hall, built in 1937, that the local W.I. hold their monthly meetings. The Post Office, School and Inn also serve the local community. The school in Hackforth is mentioned in the earlier part of the 19th Century, but was rebuilt by the Duke of Leeds in 1871, and supported by him until the end of the 19th Century. 82 pupils were registered at one time, but attendance was often affected by illness, poor weather, and the older pupils being required to work on the farms. An extra classroom has since been added, and several improvements made over the years. More recently, reduced numbers on the school register has meant that only concerted action from the school governors has prevented its closure. By 2000, pupil numbers had risen to 44, with 3 teachers and 2 support staff.

A small brook runs across the southern end of Hackforth, past the old mill near the Greyhound Inn; so called because greyhound racing took place on the green in front. Since the Second World War, several houses, flats and bungalows have been built along the main road. The surrounding farms, with their beautifully proportioned houses and buildings, reflect the fact that they were once part of a large estate. Two houses worthy of note are Arbour Hill and Street House Farm, built almost like miniature stately homes by John Carr of York, who designed Harewood House.

Most of the houses built in Hackforth for the estate workers had their own back yard, a cow byre or pig sty and an allotment. Pre-1926, locals could pay 1 penny a month to graze cattle on the estate.

Manor House Farm is one of the oldest, about 500 years old, having at one time moved to higher ground from a site nearer the beck, but utilising stone and timber from the old building.

The farm was built around three sides of a courtyard and the walls are one-metre thick in places. Aerial photographs suggest formal terraced gardens, and even a moat.

In the mid 19th Century a fire destroyed two wings of the house, and the stone salvaged from the fire was used to rebuild both the school in 1871 and parts of Hornby Castle.

Left:
Cottages in Silver Street – included a blacksmith, with 2 furnaces and an area to shoe the horses.

The Post Office (left) was situated at No.1 North Road, Hackforth.

The Greyhound Inn (below), so named from the greyhound racing held locally, was built in 1740. The Inn was originally used as a stopover for travellers and their horses. The mounting block, which is still at the front of the Inn allowed people to get on their horse without assistance.

In their hey-day the estates were self-contained, with their own water supply, sewage, gas house, ice house, saw mill, blacksmiths, laundry and market garden, and traces of these still survive for us to see.

The Saw Mill

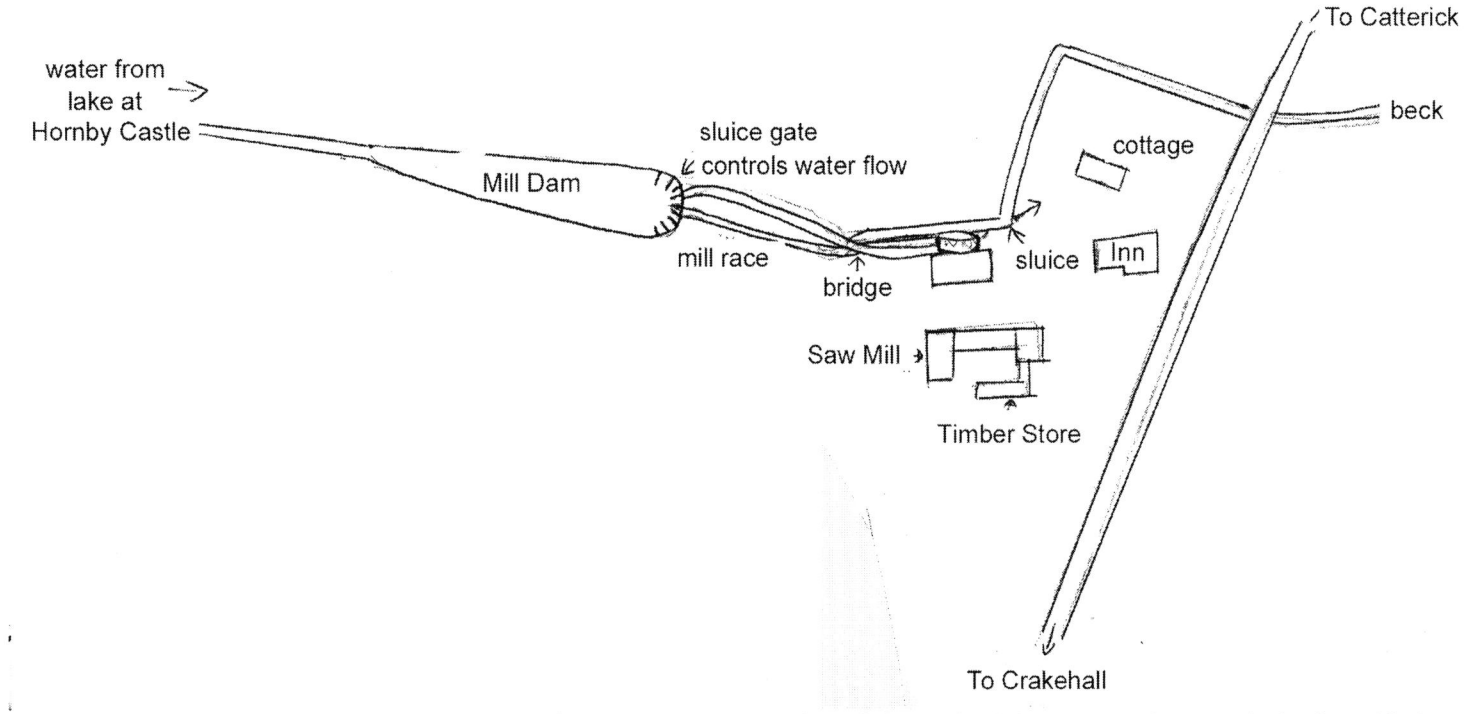

Diagram showing the layout of the Saw Mill: water from lake at Hornby Castle flows into the Mill Dam, through a sluice gate (controls water flow) into the mill race, over a bridge, past a sluice, with a cottage and Inn nearby. The Saw Mill and Timber Store are located below. A road runs from To Catterick (north) to To Crakehall (south), with a beck to the east.

The sawmill was situated behind the Greyhound Inn. Water was collected from the lake at Hornby Castle in the mill dam, controlled by the sluice gate, and channelled into the millrace to drive the water wheel and subsequently, the power saw.

Ainderby Miers

Ainderby Miers is also deemed historically important, once having had strong links with the Conyers and D'Arcy families. It is said to be the site of a medieval village, due to pottery found there and aerial photographic evidence. A 16-feet stone circle with large cobbles in the centre still remains, which may have been a kiln. A religious house has also been mentioned in association with Ainderby Miers. The 19th Century census, lists labourers from Norfolk, employed by the Duke of Leeds to help drain the land by Ainderby Miers and Langthorne.

Langthorne

Langthorne Hall, now a listed building, was built for Thomas Roper, a travelling magistrate in 1719. A spring runs under the Hall, so consequently the water table is high, and the cellars are packed with clay to make them watertight. The Duke of Leeds bought the property in 1802, but sold the Hall, along with Cobshaw Farm, Wassick Farm and East Appleton Farm at Auction in 1919.

(sketch-Cathleen Ashcroft for Hird's Annuls)

These cottages in Langthorne (right) date from the 18th century. They had access to a well, fed from an underground spring. The water closet tended to be a pit in the back garden, treated with ashes and emptied occasionally. Most were condemned in the 1950's and replaced by brick built houses.

The Crown Inn (left) dates from the 18th Century. There was no bar, and jugs of beer were run off from barrels stored on trestles. The Inn was knocked down in the 1950s and a bungalow built on the site in the 1970s.

The Primitive **Methodist Chapel** (above) was built in 1846 of local brick and enlarged in 1872 at a cost of £200.

St. Mary Magdalene Church (left) was built of stone in 1877 for £1,800 on a site donated by the Duke of Leeds. Designed by Mr Armfield, it had a chancery, a nave, a vestry, and a bell-cote with one bell.

Both the church and chapel have now been converted to residential use.

East Farmhouse in Langthorne was built in 1750. The front room was used as a village shop, selling paraffin, and groceries.

A brick and tile works were mentioned in the 1841 census, operating from Cobshaw Farm in Langthorne. Clay was taken from a pond nearby, cut into bricks by machine, put into the drying shed and then fired in a kiln. The brick works ceased working about the time of the First World War and were then sold.

After the Second World War a farm vehicle repair workshop was started up, in an old cow byre in Langthorne. Today the garage is a vehicle recovery business.

* * * * *

The Dukes of Leeds took good care of their tenants and workers, and when the estate were broken up in 1930, they ensured that each cottage in every village was sold with an allotment so that villagers could grow their own fruit and vegetables.

1900-1910

The Hornby Castle Kennels & Hounds

(Arthur Adamson)

The Duke of Leeds kept greyhounds, both for racing and hare coursing. Mr Adamson was employed to look after the greyhounds, which were kept four to a room in the purpose built kennels.

Ledger — from Arbour Hill Farm

(June Thompson)

Maize, bran and wheat, ordered from Arbour Hill Farm were cooked in the ventilated central tower. One of the end rooms was used to store the dog food and biscuits, while the other end room was a drying room for blankets.

1900 – 1910

Mr Adamson Senior with Jack Shaw and two greyhounds

(Arthur Adamson)

The Marquis of Carmarthen, who later became the 11th Duke of Leeds, with his sister in front of the kennels.

(Arthur Adamson)

Lonely Musing : Lonesome : Loadstar : Lottery : Lacerta : Lanthorn

(Martin Webster)

The greyhounds pictured with Mr Adamson, senior, all had names beginning with L (Was this for Leeds?) They were used for hare coursing, often at Winterfield. The Duke of Leeds also took the greyhounds to other country estates by horse and cart to the train station at Newton Le Willows. Links between the castle and the school were mentioned in the school logbook of February 24th 1904 when 'seven or eight older boys were absent, acting as drivers for the greyhound coursing in the village'.

1900 – 1910

The Duke of Leeds greyhounds at Hauxwell Vicarage (demolished 1953)

(Arthur Adamson)

The horses and hounds assemble at Hornby Castle ~ 1900

(Arthur Adamson)

The Duke of Leeds

The Duke of Leeds was the Master of the Bedale Hunt from 1898 to 1904. As a large landowner, and devoted to all field sports, he was considered a good man for the position. He hunted at least three days a week and kept a sufficient number of hounds to enable him to hunt for a fourth day. To improve the hunting, the Duke purchased 23 couples (of hounds) in 1902 and 16½ couples in 1903, calling them the Belvoir Draft.

The kennel buildings were not very healthy, so the Duke urged the Hunt Committee to build some new kennels on higher ground to the south west of the old kennels. The old kennels were then upgraded and put back into use. Fred Holland was employed as a huntsman to the Duke of Leeds, until he retired in 1902 when he was replaced by Harry Chandler. The Duke retired at the end of the 1904 season, due to several bad falls from his horse, an attack of scarlet fever and a decline in the hunting caused by a mange epidemic in the fox population.

From *The Bedale Hounds 1832-1908* by Frank H. Reynard

(Martin Webster)

1900 – 1910

Every year a shooting lunch was held at Holly House, (now Blairgowrie) with the food provided by the Castle. The Duke and the shooting party were served in the sitting room, the shooters in the living room, and the beaters in the kitchen (all with different food!). The Duke of Leeds always made a point of thanking everyone involved.

Below: John Baraugh Dawson the gamekeeper, who lived at Holly House, with his wife, Margaret Dawson (née Easby) and four children, Harold, Herbert, William and Mary. *(Mrs Nelson)*

Above: Lizzie Morley, the daughter of head gamekeeper with a greyhound ~ 1900.
(Arthur Adamson)

Granddaughter Margaret Cox remembers: Holly House had a kitchen with running water, but no taps! Lard and butter were stored on stone slabs. Every week a trip was made, on foot, across the fields to sell butter at Bedale Cross.

The Duck Decoy

Christmas Among the Wildfowl
Sport in a Yorkshire Decoy

Harwood Brierly

While Christmassing at Hornby and Hackforth, near Bedale, last year, I was so lucky as to get permission from the Duke of Leeds to see worked his decoy for wild fowl, the best of its kind in the kingdom. The stream issuing from the central pond within the decoy and flowed down some pastures past Roundhill Farm, giving effect to the mill-race, which turned the water wheel of his Grace's saw yard and joiner's shop, after which it flowed beneath the cellars of the Greyhound Inn at Hackforth, keeping the ales, spirits, and wines in first-class condition.

The Duke had recently acquired a new gamekeeper in the person of Mr. H. Morley, after weeping over the grave of his old and valued servant, Reuben Barrett, who was well known to many Yorkshire naturalists. Morley I found to be a splendid fellow who had done good work for the Earl of Harewood, and more recently for the Duke of Marlborough at Blenheim Park. In him I discovered not only a tower of strength, but a very engaging observer of Nature, and picturesque withal in his blue velveteen coat, his light blue figured tie, and well got up linen, his two-nebbed tweed cloth headpiece, with the brim turned down, and his snuff-coloured breeches and yellow leggings. I first met Morley ranging the ducal park on a large grey pony of great mettle.

Locked Up In A Decoy And Forbidden To Speak

From his hospitable dwelling in a corner of the park we started out with a quiet little terrier named Toby by way of the grim old castle towards the south-east corner of the park enclosure, where a natural stream of crystal-clear water flowed into what seemed like a fenced-in thicket of firs and other evergreen cone-bearing trees. Morley took careful notice of a weather vane erected on a staff on the hilly slope as we dropped down to the belt of trees. Here stood Dawson, the burly decoyman and underkeeper, waiting for us, and consultation took place as to which of the four "pipes" in the decoy it would be desirable to work in view of the rising wind. Dawson had heard – and heard – a wedge of wild duck come overhead towards the decoy on the previous night, flying under an acknowledged leadership. With the foxy-coated little terrier, Toby, walking demurely by our side we entered a secret gate in the wood fencing. Morley locked it on the inner side, then, calling for strict silence, we all behaved like poachers in this ducks' paradise of an un-frozen rushy pond secluded by fine, if sombre, trees and tall undergrowth. At different openings I caught glimpses of the early morning sun-rays as they slanted down upon the tops of the fir trees opposite, giving them the golden hues of balsam poplars in the spring-tide. In the tree-tops sounded the wind; down below the silence was broken only by the wild ducks. We recognised the querulous "quark" of the mallard, the "krik, krik" of the little teal, the "we-oh" of some wary old widgeon, and the chattering kitten-like note of the pintail or sea-pheasant. As yet the pond was invisible, being enclosed by a peculiar shutter-like screen of wood pales; and the ducks were unconscious of our presence, or they would certainly not have tarried on the mirror of that pond to risk the slightest suspicion of danger. Morley's warning finger at the outset was supported by a continual "sh-h-h-h!" as we three crept stealthily over the soft carpet of turf and fir needles, and little wood bridges spanning lesser runlets, these having been sawdusted as a precaution against anybody's too heavy footfall. We might not even whisper, for the decoy seemed to magnify sound; and above all, we had to take care that the wildfowl did not "wind" us.

A Stolen View Of The Wild Ducks' Paradise

In the screens fixed obliquely at the mouth of each "pipe" leading at so many points into the central pond there were any number of spy-holes. Stooping down a little, we could lift up the pear-shaped wood slide which stopped each hole, and look sideways through the mouth of a net tunnel as far as the reedy pond three acres in extent. To this secluded spot great numbers of wild fowl had come from the coast from frozen northern fjords and marshes to find rest, food, company, and entertainment. Nothing could they know of the fact that a parcel of tame ducks which could be hand-fed on the sly were living their midst for the purpose of giving them confidence and a feeling of security in their new-found paradise. Charming was the vision of so many kinds of beautiful wild ducks – sometimes males and females together, probably paired for life-not a few of which had travelled thousands of miles to this place. Of common wild ducks (females) there appeared to be hundreds. Their orange-coloured bills were dashed with black, and bodies and wings a lively buff toned with black, or merging oft into the hues of a partridge's plumage.

There were hundreds of mallard-male wild duck-mirroring their form in the enclosed pond as they floated about in companies, and dived or fed upside down, performing other Christmastide antics, and oft chattering one to another. I could see the greenish yellow bill of these fine birds, their rich velvety green head and neck, purple-blue, white-bordered spangles on their wings, and occasionally their orange-coloured webbed legs and was also a little knob of teal - the smallest of our indigenous ducks - saying "krik, krik," constantly as they followed each other around the edge of the pond. Plump little fowl are teal, with light chestnut head and neck, a peacock blue band which encloses the eye, pale buff throat ornamented with blackish spots, and a brilliant spangling of peacock green on each wing. Then there was a bunch of widgeon - the most sought after but the wariest and least accessible of all wildfowl - with their chestnut and cream-coloured polls and exquisite grey and white bodies. I could see them chivvying each other about playfully, and hear the male birds' occasional "we-oh," or "whewer," which is their distinctive call-note. There were also a few red-headed, red-eyed pochards, with bills blue in the centre and black at the sides, and solid black neck and bosom; but pochards, being remarkably good divers, like the little grebe and sea-parrot, we stood no chance of getting one into our netted pipe this morning. I saw the duck which some naturalists have called the golden-eye garret, and also the morillon (male and female) in that jostling crowd, this species being in some parts known as "rattlewings" from the noise it makes in getting up on being disturbed, beside which it has a loud sonorous voice. The morillon - a name sometimes used for the female - is most commonly seen. These duck can always be told at once by an irregular geometric snow-white patch near the bill – which is conspicuous as the bald patch of the better-known coot – and the mallard-like green neck of this golden-eye duck shows off the patch to advantage.

On terra firma, nearer the pond was blue-winged shoveller, noted for its long lead-coloured bill, which is out of all proportion with the size of its head; while from the centre to the tip it is flattened out and rounded into a shape not dissimilar to the end of a shovel. This duck cares less for water than any, and it never appears to dive, yet, even in spite of the white breast, which reminds one of a seabird, it is an excellent article of food. The shoveller's head is as green as a mallard's, the lower part of the neck, scapulars, and some of the tertials being white, and wing-point, lesser wing-coverts, and outer web of some of the tertials, pale blue. Then I had a vision of two or three pintail ducks, the most elegant of all lady-ducks, sometimes called the sea-pheasant from its extended tail, and recognised by its chattering note almost like a kitten. But like the widgeon, the pintail is particularly dangerous because of its extreme vigilance and unless we are careful it will wind us, and put all the different squads of ducks on the 'qui vive', and just possibly send them up. Finally, I may say that there is a record of that great rarity, the harlequin duck (which Linnæus calls 'cramonetta histrionica'), having been captured here is passably like a harlequin in its feathering, being decorated with not a few white bands and figures

Performing Toby, The Dog Decoy.

Some of these shy fowl would be ours in a few minutes, and submitting to have their necks wringed without making the least sign of pain or uttering a single cry. Yet if one of us laughed, or the little fox-terrier barked, or anybody stumbled against the screen, or the wind conveyed our scent towards them, nearly every fowl in the pond would get up and fly away.

The Duke's gamekeeper, plucking me by the sleeve, motioned me away from my stolen view of the ducks' winter paradise. Interest now centred on foxy-coated Master Toby, an important performer in the decoy – he himself the decoy, in fact; and in order that he shall do his work well he has come down here without his usual breakfast of bread and meat. The gamekeeper will provide his breakfast in so many pieces and the little terrier will be furthered in his training to the decoy work by being coaxed into the pond by a novel system of hand-feeding.

At a respectable height are four "pipes" of black-tarred netting, opening on to the pond at different points, each one spanning from the canal-like banks a tongue-shaped inlet of water about six yards wide at its mouth. Having long ere decided which of the four pipes we should work, we took up our position inside an outspread screen, or traverse, with low openings in each ford, which gave a view part way up the curving netted pipe. Morley despatching Dawson, his assistant, as near to the mouth of the pipe as possible, where he hides behind the trees, takes Toby's bread and meat, shows him a morsel, throws it through opening No. 1, and waves him off to the inner bank. Some of the ducks sailing about in the pond instantly see the dog, and begin to make a move for him. At first this movement may appear strange, since the wild duck is such a shy and wary fowl, having little in common with the nature of the domesticated duck. Toby hops through the low opening for more meat leaving the ducks to come along, and on receiving a second mouthful he is waved over opening No. 2 between the next set of shutters, so many yards higher up the netted pipe. Now the keeper opens a spy-hole to see how many ducks are following, and signals "all right" with a series of winks, for by the time Toby returns from the bank by the second passage crowds of ducks have begun to muster up into one body from all parts of the lake, each one anxious to know what the "row" is about, yet scenting no danger as yet. Another step higher up the pipe; another mouthful for old-fashioned Toby, and away he slips through the third opening, re-exposing his foxy coat on the bank. Once more he returns to his master eager for more meat.

THE DUCKS TRY TO MOB THE DOG.

But the effect on the ducks is magical. They begin quacking out "A fox! a fox !" in their own language. The nearest mallards amid female duck become very excited; they tell the little teal all about the intruder, and the teal inform the widgeon and pochard. All, without more discussion, decide to mob this mammal intruder and drive him away. Toby reappears several times, but always higher up the bank. "There he goes! There he goes!" cries every duck, and nothing remains to be done but to "bottom" this mystery at once, and mob the suspicious little animal. Toby decoys them forward by still another leap. By this time all the wildfowl within eyeshot are crowding into the mouth of the fatal pipe, and are practically lost souls! Morley must use his judgment as to how far they may come up the funnel before they are flushed by Dawson, now in the rear. If he waits too long they will scent him and dive or fly above the palisade revealing our presence; or, not liking the looks of the netting, they may coolly turn round and sail out of its compass.

At the proper moment Dawson is signalled. He immediately appears from behind the trees presenting himself to the ducks at traverse No.1. Startled by this apparition, which cuts off all hope of retreat in the event of the ducks having their heads turned up the pipe, they all get up in a panic, and away they go to their doom, only a few of the cool-headed divers - pochards, for instance making good their escape. One or two of the mallards, however, get clicked by their bills or necks in the mesh of the narrowing net, and hang there, or fall into the channel fatally hurt. The two keepers race the rest of the whirling mass along, condensing them as the tunnel closes down and releasing the first drop-net section as soon as they have passed it, which falls readily with the weight of its iron bow. Half a second more all the fowl are beyond the tongue of water, and the second iron bow is dropped. There they lie helplessly huddled together in a taper cul-de-sac on dry land, the tip of the pipe being a circular net supported by small hoops, and held back with a piece of twine attached to a stake. In this last section of the tunnel decoy we are in possession of a big bolster of ornamental living feathers tossing helplessly on terra firma. From a poulterer's point of view it is magnificent work. While one looks on with eyes of wonder Dawson takes the small end of the bolster between his knees, and proceeds to wring the necks of the unhappy victims. For a minute the ducks are fluttering about on the grass; but not the least noise of any sort had they made once they found themselves betrayed in the pipe. The first step is to tie them together by the neck, and make up two nice little bundles, which Dawson hangs over his shoulder; then they are carried up to the game-house at the castle, where, along with dry hares and rabbits, they are booked, packed in hampers, and conveyed to Bedale Station on their way to a contracting poulterer at Stockton-on-Tees.

THE REFLECTIVE GOURMAND

The reflective gourmand, picking the last bones of a mallard or pigeon, may have wondered why no wild duck in fifty of those which at one time or another had adorned his table seemed to bear any evidence of the sportsman's pellets. And he might contemplate on this subject in vain, for the decoys in England are most surely becoming institutions of the past, though they are common enough in the fens of Holland. I would point out that the Hornby Castle decoy is a great improvement on the old style of thing once so common in Lincolnshire and Norfolk, and even in Yorkshire, where a wedge of duck had to be called for or "fetched to the picnic" by tame ducks that home on the central pond. The Hornby decoy has never worked to death for the sake of big bags; it was entered only at intervals of a few days, so that there were always plenty of ducks on the pond throughout the winter: and a pipe is worked with such great care that hundreds of ducks who do not join in mobbing innocent little Toby are left behind, quite oblivious of the fate which befalls their luckless comrades. The Duke's decoy is not prostituted, as some places I wrote of are, the money-making use of over-stocking a contracting a poulterer's shop.

Gamekeepers on the Hornby Estate

(from Peter Knox)

There were three or four gamekeepers on the Hornby Estate, each competing with each other to rear as many pheasants as possible. An old clocher (a broody hen) was used to hatch pheasant eggs, often eight hens to a coop. Most gamekeepers kept Labrador dogs, and had to keep the wildcat population down in the woods.

No body of men does more than the gamekeepers to uphold the country way of life, even if some others do as much. Gamekeepers have always been considered friends by their employers and that confidence has seldom been abused. A gamekeeper's duties in the last 50 years have changed little, if at all. Wages, of course, bear no comparison: in 1908 the average headkeeper received about £2 to £2 10s.; a single-handed man £1 7s. to £1 15s.; and an underkeeper about 18s. to £1 2s. Today it is about seven to eight times as much, except in the case of a headkeeper, whose remuneration has increased only about four times.

In some cases accommodation has improved with modern conveniences—bath, electricity, and so on—but in others there has been but little progress because estate owners are finding it difficult, owing to the isolation of the property, to get the electricity authorities to connect up without the payment of an exorbitant sum. Slowly but surely the difficulties are being overcome; modern transport has brought the shopping centres, schools and other essential amenities almost to the keeper's door, whereas formerly, with his wife and family, he had perhaps to walk or cycle. Very large estates provided horse transport for shopping and other outings once or twice a week, and the headkeeper had his own horse and trap, but generally the keeper's life, and more especially that of his wife, was a rather lonely existence. That has all changed. With many of the well-known estates having been broken up into small "parcels," the keeper and his family take their place in the life of the village community, which, in the country today, centres around the village hall with its Women's Institute, youth organisations and other communal activities.

The life of a keeper in 1908, when the Master of Foxhounds and Hunt committees regularly entertained the gamekeepers of their country is illustrated by the remarks of Sir John Miller, of Heywood, Wiltshire, when he presided at a dinner at Manderston, Berwickshire. To the tenants on that estate and the adjoining tenantry and gamekeepers Sir John proposed the toast: "The tenantry on the Manderston estate," and spoke with great appreciation of the cordial relations between landlord and tenant. In proposing the toast of the neighbouring estates he thanked them for their efforts to help the gamekeepers on the Manderston estate.

Mr. T. A. Swan, in reply, said that "the neighbouring tenantry took as good care as they could of any Manderston game that came their way, and sent it back fat and strong." The chairman said there was one more most important toast which he desired to give 'the gamekeepers'. He expressed his thanks to the gamekeepers on neighbouring estates for "the help they were always so ready to give at the shoots at Manderston. If it had not been for this help his friends and himself could not have made such bags as they did on two days of that week."

The gamekeepers had a very difficult duty to perform: one proprietor wanted foxes and another pheasants, and some both. The gamekeepers present all knew how "my late brother, who was a Master of Foxhounds, kept both foxes and pheasants, and his gamekeepers were successful in doing so. He thought the gamekeepers in Berwickshire the very best gamekeepers he had ever come across."

A shooting parson of the same period said of the gamekeepers. "During his curacy days a parson is compelled by circumstances to be somewhat of a wanderer, to move from place to place as his services are required. Wherever I happened to be located fate and, I suppose, my love of sport were certain to throw the local gamekeepers into my way. Perhaps, too, my skill as a shot and the consequent invitations it procured me to various shots in the district where my tent happened to be pitched for the time being, had something to do with my popularity amongst the keepers."

Morley, the Duke of Leeds' head gamekeeper in 1908, beside the Duck Decoy at Hornby Castle

1900 – 1910

The Castle Estate was available for use by local farmers to graze their cattle.

Gaits in Hornby Park. — Cattle will be taken to graze in Hornby Park from the 12th day of May to the 11th day of October at sums varying according to age and size. The Gaits to be paid for before the animals are taken away. Attention will be paid to the Stock, but the Owner of the Park will not be answerable for Loss or Damage from whatever cause arising. It is requested that all applications should be made before the 1st day of May, 1900 — Apply to Mr S.T. Jones, Estate Office, Hornby Castle, Bedale. — March 19th, 1900.

Quote from D & S May 5th 1900

Hackforth School

The school had about 50 pupils in the 1900s. The school was closed in 1904 for about four months so a classroom for the infants could be added.

"Colonel Archer from Rudd Hall called today at 3.10. He checked the registers and also brought with him smoked glasses and showed the children the eclipse of the sun through them. He also explained what an eclipse was."

(School log book.)

William Richard Thompson with his parents at Roundhill, after winning a prize at Hackforth School about 1904.

(June Thomson)

Langthorne 1900-1910 ~ Horse and cart unattended

1900 – 1910

Top left: William & Christina Thompson at Roundhill ~ 1900

(June Thompson)

Top right: Thompson family at Roundhill ~1900

(June Thomson)

Far Left: Aggie Hurworth at the Lodge, Hackforth ~1900-1910

(Dennis Hurworth)

Left: Lillie Hurworth at the Lodge, Hackforth ~1900-1910

(Dennis Hurworth)

1900 – 1910

Street House Farm Tenancy Agreement

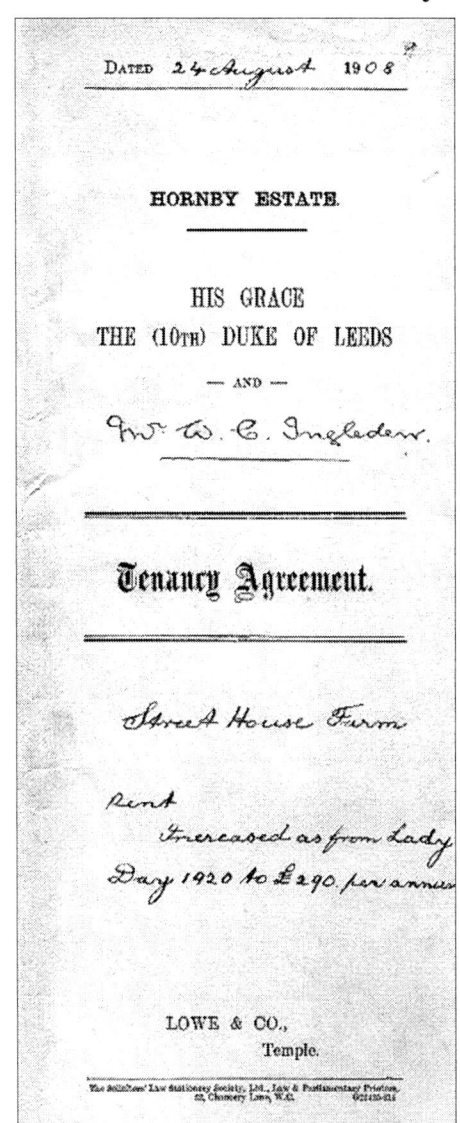

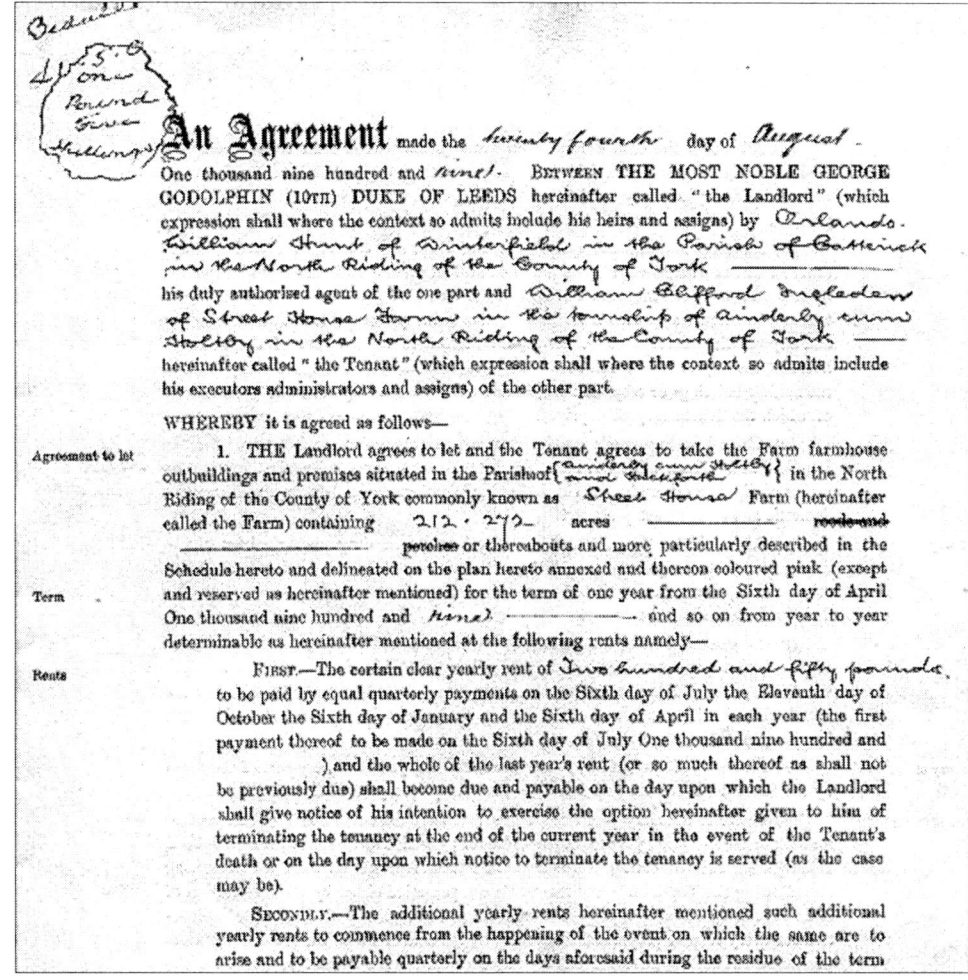

DATED 24 August 1908

HORNBY ESTATE.

HIS GRACE
THE (10TH) DUKE OF LEEDS
— AND —
Mr W. C. Ingledew.

Tenancy Agreement.

Street House Farm

Rent Increased as from Lady Day 1920 to £290 per annum

LOWE & CO.,
Temple.

An Agreement made the twenty fourth day of August One thousand nine hundred and nine. BETWEEN THE MOST NOBLE GEORGE GODOLPHIN (10TH) DUKE OF LEEDS hereinafter called "the Landlord" (which expression shall where the context so admits include his heirs and assigns) by Orlando William Hunt of Winterfield in the Parish of Catterick in the North Riding of the County of York his duly authorised agent of the one part and William Clifford Ingledew of Street House Farm in the township of Ainderby cum Holtby in the North Riding of the County of York hereinafter called "the Tenant" (which expression shall where the context so admits include his executors administrators and assigns) of the other part.

WHEREBY it is agreed as follows—

Agreement to let 1. THE Landlord agrees to let and the Tenant agrees to take the Farm farmhouse outbuildings and premises situated in the Parish of Ainderby cum Holtby in the North Riding of the County of York commonly known as Street House Farm (hereinafter called the Farm) containing 212.272 acres roods and perches or thereabouts and more particularly described in the Schedule hereto and delineated on the plan hereto annexed and thereon coloured pink (except and reserved as hereinafter mentioned) for the term of one year from the Sixth day of April One thousand nine hundred and nine and so on from year to year determinable as hereinafter mentioned at the following rents namely—

Rents FIRST.—The certain clear yearly rent of Two hundred and fifty pounds to be paid by equal quarterly payments on the Sixth day of July the Eleventh day of October the Sixth day of January and the Sixth day of April in each year (the first payment thereof to be made on the Sixth day of July One thousand nine hundred and) and the whole of the last year's rent (or so much thereof as shall not be previously due) shall become due and payable on the day upon which the Landlord shall give notice of his intention to exercise the option hereinafter given to him of terminating the tenancy at the end of the current year in the event of the Tenant's death or on the day upon which notice to terminate the tenancy is served (as the case may be).

SECONDLY.—The additional yearly rents hereinafter mentioned such additional yearly rents to commence from the happening of the event on which the same are to arise and to be payable quarterly on the days aforesaid during the residue of the term

Mr W Ingledew ~ 1908

The farm was owned by the Duke of Leeds and rented out to William Clifford Ingledew for £250 per year.

1900 – 1910

Old Street House

Topping out the stack at Old Street House

A horse and cart (left) and the workers with Mr Ingledew senior (above)
(Jenny Pybus)

1900 – 1910

New Street House built in the 1900s.
(from glass slides: Jenny Pybus)

Behind New Street House – rearing pheasants
(Jenny Pybus)

Lucy Thompson, born in 1851, moved to Langthorne after she was married. Although not trained, she acted as a nurse and midwife to Dr. Eddison. The photo shows from left: Lucy Thompson with Molly the dog, daughter-in-law, Sarah, and granddaughter, also called Lucy.

1910-1920

1910 – 1920

Frederick Thompson left school at the age of 13 to be a groom at Rudd Hall. He became an accomplished horseman, and was later to hunt with the Duke of Leeds.
He enlisted in the Royal Army Service Corps in 1914. After the war he returned to work at Hornby Castle as a butler, and his family moved into a tied cottage at 1 Church View Hornby. He was directly responsible to the Duke of Leeds for the running of the house and the working of the staff.

(Mr Frederick Holtby)

The castle had an indoor **Riding School**, which was used for training horses and soldiers for war. It dates back to the late 18th Century and was used by the Yeomanry to train soldiers for the Napoleonic Wars. The Duke of Leeds was probably Colonel of the Yeomanry Regiment. The riding school was also used in the 1914-18 Great War

Frederick Thompson (1887-1978) riding one of the Duke of Leeds hunting horses from Hornby Castle in 1910

The School

June 16th 1911 – The school was closed all day to celebrate the coronation of King George V.

November 27th 1913 – The school was closed in the afternoon for the funeral of Rev W. Drury.

Attendance at school was affected by a range of activities: -

June 13th 1913 – The Langthorne Sunday School has gone on a trip today. There are 18 children absent this morning and 26 this afternoon.

February 14th 1914 – Very poor attendance this morning owing to the coursing being held in the village. (14 absent).

February 27th 1914 – Several boys absent today, acting as caddies at Hornby Castle.

Children were often expected to help their parents when required – July 16th 1911 – The cottagers in Hackforth village are all busy haymaking. A good number of the children are assisting their parents in their allotments.

'July 11th 1913 – Owing to the haymaking operations in the cottagers' allotments, the attendance has been greatly affected.'

'June 7th 1915 – Several cattle belonging to the cottagers have been poisoned by eating grass that has been treated with weed killer near the edge of the road in the park. Three of the older girls are absent keeping the cattle from the road.'

Part of a painting by John Bacon of the Coronation of George V ~ 1911

1910 – 1920

During this decade, the Local Education Authority (LEA) began to play a more active role in the life of the school. In 1912, provision was made for the older girls to receive additional instruction in cookery. On August 9th 1912, the local authority Building Inspector came to school to make arrangements for the stand for the cookery van. When the stand arrived on September 5th, it was placed in the head teacher's allotment. On September 9th the 14 elder girls began a cookery course organised by Mrs E Day, based with the North Riding Cookery Van.

In 1913, several LEA advisors were visitors to the school. Mr Slater, organiser of rural subjects, inspected the garden on May 7th. Mrs Prince, the Physical Training instructor, watched the older children at drill. While June 25th saw a visit by Miss Robson, the organising sewing mistress.

In 1914, the LEA issued a new memorandum on Nature Study (January 20th). On November 2nd they asked the school to requisition continuous readers for the infants and suitable poetry books for the upper standards (as recommended by His Majesty's Inspectors). On November 23rd these inspectors, after a visit to the school, reported that 'the playground has an unsatisfactory surface, and after wet weather is quite useless for either recreational or physical exercise. The whole, or at least part of it, should be paved or treated with gravel and rolled to a smooth compact surface.'

The school was routinely closed down for certain illnesses. A Measles epidemic caused the closure from June 18th – July 7th 1915, and from May 17th until June 24th 1918. This latter epidemic was closely followed by an outbreak of Influenza 17th July 5th 1918 – 'Owing to the prevalence of Influenza, the Medical Officer of Health in Bedale District has ordered the school to be closed until the 12th of July'.

July 12th 1918 – Influenza is still prevalent, and the managers have decided to close the school for the midsummer holiday, until August 6th. With the school closed from 28th November until 20th December for another Influenza epidemic, the school was closed for at least 11 weeks in 1918 due to illness!

Exceptional weather conditions were noted in the school Logbook.

On May 25th 1914 – 'There was a very heavy frost during last night and a good deal of damage has been done, especially to the potatoes in the school garden.' The next day there was a 'frost again, during the night and both potatoes and French beans were destroyed in the garden.'

On March 16th 1916 – 'Rain fell incessantly all yesterday afternoon, last night and this morning. The roads and fields are flooded. The attendance (at school) is therefore affected.'

Arthur Adamson, aged 6, at Hornby Castle with his dog Bob ~ 1915

He remembers walking across the park to Hackforth School everyday, taking his packed lunch of sandwiches and cold tea.

(Arthur Adamson)

1910 – 1920

The Great War 1914 –1918

The war was not directly mentioned in the Hackforth School logbooks, but obviously had some impact on school life. The labour shortage meant that the older children were asked to help on the farms e.g.:

21st September 1914 – 'Mr Thompson of Roundhill, had been into school to enquire if he could have 6 of the older boys to gather potatoes.' Also that year, the Attendance Officer gave permission for the boys to work on several other farms.

12th May 1916 – Mr Ingledew of Street House Farm; employed Marcus Robinson, with approval from the LEA.

November 1917 – Some boys received permission from the LEA to work on local farms for specified periods.

21st October 1918 – A letter from the LEA gave permission for boys over 10 years of age to assist farmers in the potato harvest for not more than 10 working days.

The school register listed some Belgian refugees living in Hornby, who attended Hackforth School. They included Julia De Becker (June 8th 1915), Corrallin Yousseus (July 13th 1916), and Joseph Yousseus (August 19th 1937). On April 11th 1919 the logbook stated that Julia had left school, as her family had returned to Belgium.

February 14th 1916 – 'George H Gill, a former scholar at the school, on active service in France, paid a visit for a few minutes this afternoon.

August 21st 1918 – there was a holiday in the afternoon 'as Military sports are held in Hornby Park.'

On November 23rd 1918 – 'The children have collected about 14 stone of chestnuts, which have been sent today by goods train, from Bedale Station to Kings Lynn'.

Suggestions for their use have been – the manufacture of explosives

– as seeds?

To end the decade, on July 17th 1919 – 'the school closed today for a trip to Redcar'

Writing about it afterwards, 'the children to the number of 57, were taken to Redcar by train yesterday. This should be instructive to them, as only 2 children in the school have been to the seaside before.'

War Memorial

There is a Memorial tablet in St Mary's Church, to commemorate the soldiers who died in the First World War. Several men from the local area are mentioned:

Sergeant Alfred Brigham lived in East Appleton and was killed in action in Mozambique, Africa on 6th September 1918, whilst attached to King's African Rifles. He is buried in Lumbo.

Sergeant William Brigham from Catterick served in the Durham Light Infantry and died on 24th September 1916.

Private W.L.B. Brown from Ovington nr. Darlington was killed in action on 18th June 1916. (probable)

Private Frederick Crabtree was from Newton-le-Willows. He died from his wounds on 24th December 1918 and is buried at St Patrick's, Patrick Brompton – named in St Mary's though not of this Parish.

Private Harold Hodgson, from Rose Cottage Hackforth was killed in action on 3rd August 1916 – aged 22 years during the Battle of the Somme. His brother, Herbert, was killed in action on 27th April 1917; aged 24 (and was the husband of Edith Hodgson from Langthorne).

Major R.H.E. Hutton-Squires DSO, lived at Holtby Hall. He died of his wounds on 8th April 1917 at Arras, aged 39, after he and two other officers were hit by enemy shellfire. He was awarded the Distinguished Service Order in the New Years Honours List. He left behind a wife, Violet, and one son. His relatives still live at Holtby Hall.

Sergeant Charles Nicol was from Hornby Castle Gardens and was killed in action in Flanders on 10th April 1918, aged 26 years. He was awarded the Distinguished Conduct Medal and the Military Medal for Gallantry.

Private Frederick Robinson was killed in action on 27th May 1918, aged 18 and came from Hackforth.

Saddler George Terry from Arrathorne died from his wounds 23rd May 1915.

(Authority: Commonwealth War Graves Commission)
(compiled by Mike Deverill)

1910 – 1920

The eldest four Dawson children outside Hornby railings ~ approx. 1910 – Roland (eldest), Ivy, Kitty and Bobby (youngest)

(Colin Dawson)

The Hurworth Wedding Party at North Road, Hackforth ~ 1912

Front: Florrie and John, with Oswald and Fred

Back: Florrie, Lillie, Tom, Alison, Bob and two female relatives of Alison.

(D Hurworth)

1920 - 1930

Remembrance Day

Remembrance Day was first mentioned in the school logbook on the 11th November 1924 when the entry read 'Remembrance Day poppies distributed to children and two minutes silence observed.' The following year, the vicar, plus representatives of the school managers, participated in a much lengthier service; which included the two minutes silence. After the service, 'the children, under their team leaders, filed out into the yard, took up their positions in a semi-circle facing the flagstaff; and sang the National Anthem.'

By 1929 the Armistice Day service was obviously well established since 'owing to the rainstorm, the usual parade around the flagstaff was omitted, and the salute to the flag was carried out in school.' The address by the vicar and the headteacher emphasised 'the resolve to work for peace.'

School & Village Life

During August and September 1928, a range of small repairs were carried out in the school by local tradesmen, such as Mr Arthur North, the mason, Mr Forrest, the plumber, Mr Dobby, the joiner and Mr J Cook, the blacksmith. The following year, local public transport links ensured the delivery of school stock, when on 20th March the logbook entry read 'received word that the stock has arrived at Bedale Station.' A few days later they 'received stock from Bedale Station per Dennis bus.'

Illnesses that affected the local children at school in the 1920's were measles, mumps and influenza. The school was closed in January 1923 because of a measles epidemic, and again in March 1924, because of mumps. In February 1927, school attendance suffered during an outbreak of influenza.

After the war, the children were still helping on the farms but absences were now reported to the authorities. October 1921 'all children residing in Hackforth, with the exception of two are absent today. They are gathering potatoes for a local farmer. They have been reported.' On 27th August 1926, attendance was low, with 'boys away working in the harvest fields,' and in October 1927, 'a number of boys and girls are absent, potato picking.'

The weather affected attendance, as on March 12th 1928 'owing to the snowstorm which raged over the weekend, only 12 children at school as all the children present live close to the school, I have kept them at school.'

1920-1930

The School

Infant Class ~ 1929 *(Peter Knox)*

1920-1930

On June 19th 1922, 'Miss Ingledew visited school to make arrangements for the school excursion to Redcar by charabanc,' – which took place on Friday 30th June.

Also in 1922, the children were encouraged to save money when 'the School Transfer Branch of the Yorkshire Penny Bank', opened on 4th September.

School links with the local families meant that the closure of school for a day was still used as marks of respect. In September 1921, there was a 'holiday today to allow the staff and scholars to attend the funeral of the correspondent, Mr Hunt (of Winterfield)'. There was also a holiday for the 'Eclipse of the sun', when 29 children went to high ground on Mr Maidment's farm to see the sun rise, and to follow, at intervals, the progress of the Eclipse.

Royal occasions continued to be celebrated with holidays from school, such as the wedding of Princess Mary on 28th February 1922.

The traditional Christmas 'treat' for the children continued, as in 1924, the school logbook mentioned 'The Misses Ingledew called to give details of the school Children's Christmas Tea and Entertainment on the 23rd of December.'

No Sports Days at Hackforth School are mentioned in the 1920s, but an Inter-School Sports Day took place in Bedale on June 7th 1929; when the school was closed for the day. The next month the school was again closed, when one pupil represented the District in the long jump at the School Championship Sports Day at Redcar.

George Knox ploughing at Mill Close

(Mavis Heeley)

A view of Langthorne, with Langthorne Hall in view.

(June Thompson)

1920-1930

Sports Teams

Hornby Cricket Team *(Colin Dawson)*

Villages often had their own cricket team. The Hornby Cricket Team (pictured above) played at Hornby Park. Langthorne Cricket Team played at Langthorne Hall. Hackforth Cricket Team played at Manor Farm, Hackforth.

1920-1930

Their scorebooks, written in pencil, were often re-used.

Football Team

(Colin Dawson)

Roland Dawson, born 1905 in a cottage in Hornby, played for the local football team based in Catterick, before he joined the Air Force, aged 21.

The Castle and Dukes of Leeds

On 13th May 1927; the school logbook said: 'closed the school this afternoon as a token of respect to his Grace, the 10th Duke of Leeds, whose funeral was arranged for today.' The remains were brought by rail from London to Bedale Station, and then by motor hearse to St Mary's Church, Hornby. The coffin was carried by a party of estate workmen, and afterwards buried in Hornby churchyard. There was a memorial service held at St Margaret's Church in London.

The 11th Duke of Leeds, a 26-year-old bachelor, decided to sell Hornby Castle. It was the first time that the castle had been sold; previously, it had always been passed on by inheritance.

Frederick Thompson still worked for the Duke of Leeds and his knowledge of the house and its contents proved invaluable, as he prepared the house and contents for sale. His task was to check the Castle, lock the doors for the last time and hand the keys over to the Estate Agents.

The buyer in 1929 was Mr John Todd, who bought the Castle, 5,850 acres of land, 22 farms and many houses in Hackforth, Hornby and Arrathorne. The asking price was £140,000, but it is thought that Mr Todd only paid about £125,000 for the estate. Mr Todd was part of a group of businessmen, known locally as 'The Forty Thieves'. They were renowned for buying up country estates, then splitting them up, selling off the buildings, contents and land, and even demolishing buildings to capitalise on the fittings.

The 11th Duke of Leeds, born in 1901, went on to marry three times, but had no sons. When he died in 1963, the title was passed to his cousin Sir Francis D'Arcy Osbourne (12th Duke of Leeds) who was unmarried. When the 12th Duke died, a year later in 1964, the title ceased.

A family group of the period

(Mavis Heeley)

1930 - 1940

Hornby Castle Auction

(Mrs Bardon)

On April 3rd 1930, the Castle was auctioned off. There were 127 lots, which included most houses in Hackforth, Hornby and Arrathorne, the outlying farms, farmland and woodland. In many cases, the local tenants managed to buy their houses and farms.

1930 – 1940

Plan 1 (Original displayed in the Greyhound Inn)

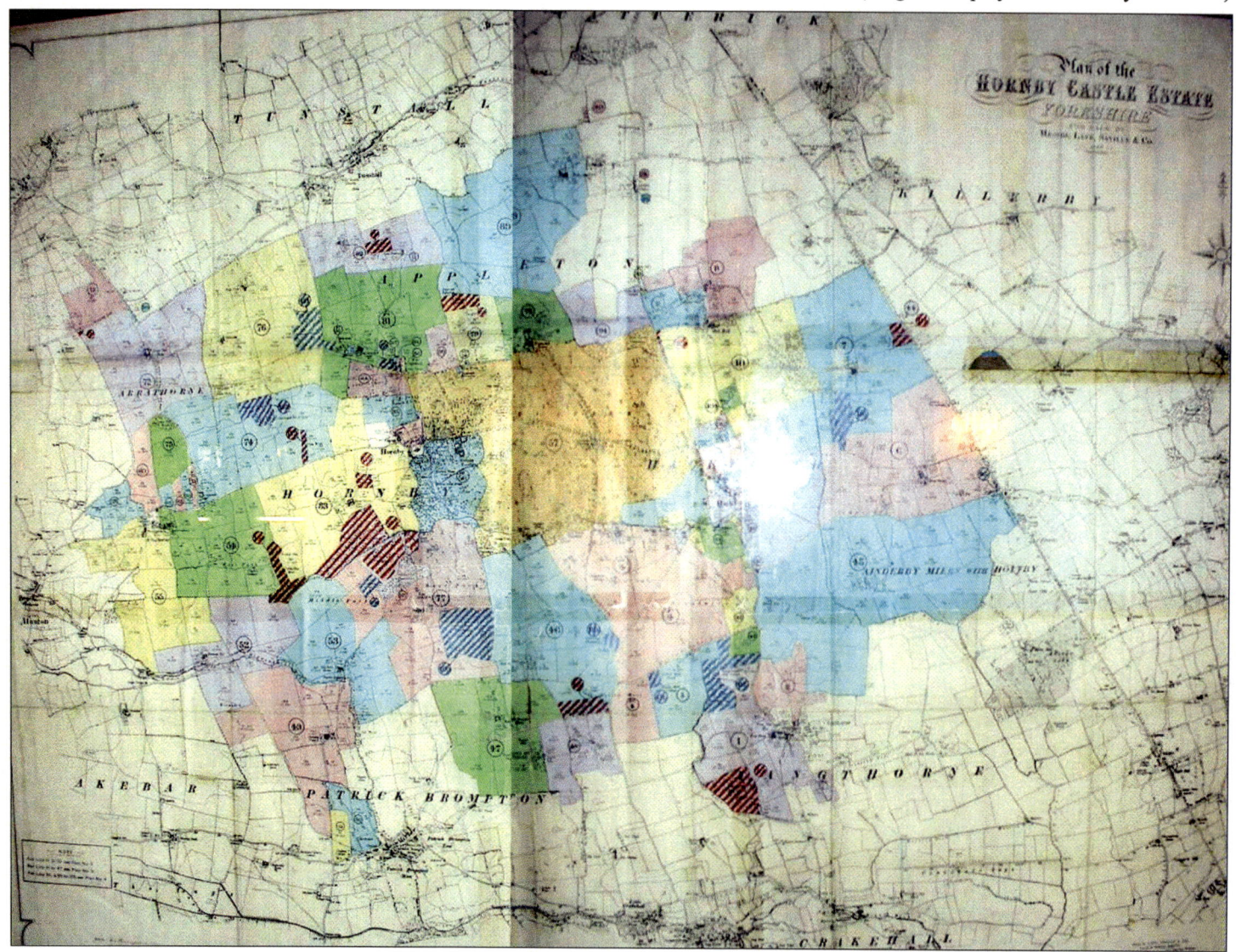

Lot No.	Description	Principal Tenant	Ordnance Area	Plan No.
1.	West Farm, Langthorne	J. Hobson & Son	178·377	1
2.	East Farm, Langthorne	J. Hobson & Son	41·600	1
3.	Manor Farm, Hackforth	Mr. A. Hodgson	182·496	1
4.	Round Hill Farm, Hackforth	Messrs. E. & C. Hawkswell	277·390	1
5.	Hollow Moor Smallholding	Do.	55·723	1
6.	Street House Farm, Hackforth	Mr. W. C. Ingledew	214·521	1
7.	Goskins Farm, Hackforth	Mr. E. E. Greenwell	220·593	1
8.	Rudd Hall	In Hand	27·866	1
9.	Rudd Hall Farm	Mr. John Smith	91·152	1
10.	Gyll Hall Farm	Mr. Sidney Smith	178·120	1
11.	South View Holding, Hackforth	Mr. J. North	3·242	1
12.	The Hackforth School	Mr. T. Lyall and Hackforth School Managers	6·108	1
35.	Accommodation Land, Hackforth	Mr. H. Leyburn	6·108	1
36.	Accommodation Land, Hackforth	Mr. J. North	5·067	1
37.	Accommodation Land, Hackforth	Various	16·721	1
38.	Accommodation Land, Hackforth	Various and E. & C. Hawkswell	30·938	1
39.	Accommodation Land, Hackforth	Various	19·973	1
40.	Accommodation Land, Hackforth	Mr. J. T. Hodgson	1·836	1
41.	Accommodation Land, Hackforth	Messrs. E. & C. Hawkswell	1·627	1
42.	Accommodation Land, Hackforth	Exors. Mrs. Thompson	15·472	1
43.	Accommodation Land, Hackforth	Mr. Alfred Hodgson	9·983	1
44.	Site on Great North Road	In Hand	4·505	1
45.	Ainderby Mires Farm, Ainderby	Messrs. D. & S. Sanderson	406·301	1
46.	Mill Close Farm, Hornby	Mr. T. E. Knox	212·973	1
47.	East Brompton Farm, Hornby	Mr. T. E. Knox	146·695	1
48.	Hunter's Hill Farm, Patrick Brompton	Mr. W. Maidment	68·400	1
49.	Carnaby Pasture Farm do.	Mr. J. Lamb	177·257	1
50.	Accommodation Land, do.	Mr. J. Lamb	80·253	1
51.	Accommodation Land, do.	Mr. J. Lamb	14·553	1
52.	Diamond Hill Farm, do.	Messrs. G. & R. Towler	139·130	1
53.	Old Park Farm, Hornby	Mr. Thomas Franklin	147·071	1
54.	East Arrathorne Farm, Arrathorne	Mr. R. Heeley	165·212	1
55.	West Arrathorne Farm do.	Mr. J. W. Simpson	159·478	1
56.	Hornby Castle	In Hand	76·483	1
57.	Hornby Park	In Hand	553·347	1
58.	Hornby Castle Gardens	Mr. T. F. Wilson	9·696	1
59.	The Manor House Holding, Arrathorne	Mr. J. Lambert	28·349	1
60.	Small Holding, Arrathorne	Mr. M. Plant	80·974	1

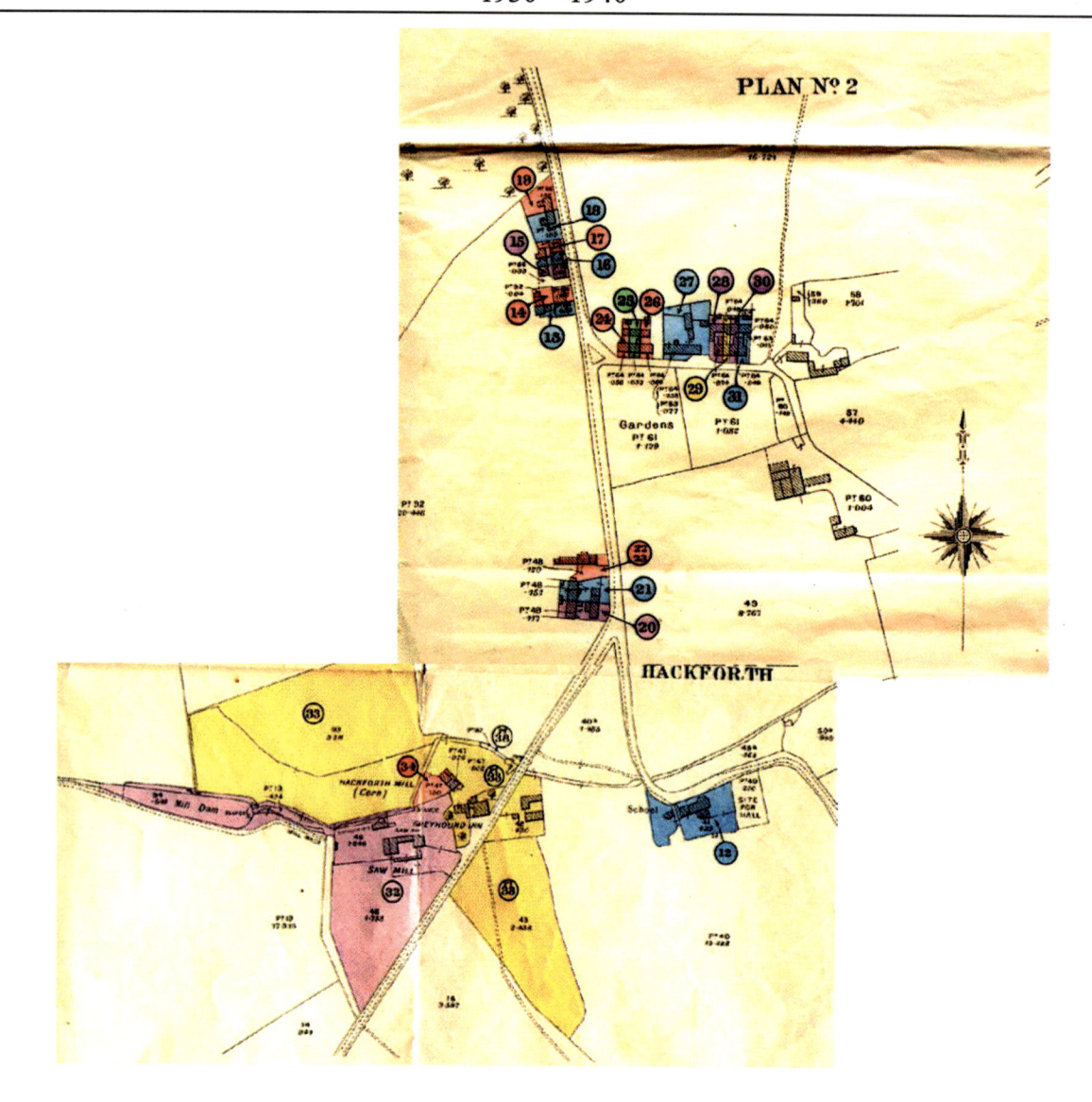

1930 – 1940

1930 – 1940

Lot No.	Description	Principal Tenant	Ordnance Area	Plan No.
13.	The Post Office, Hackforth	Mr. T. Bentley	·629	2
14.	No. 2, North Road, Hackforth	Mr. George Thompson	·058	2
15.	No. 3, North Road, Hackforth	Mr. E. E. Greenwell	·071	2
16.	No. 4, North Road, Hackforth	Mr. M. Johnson	·039	2
17.	No. 5, North Road, Hackforth	Mr. W. Hillary	·038	2
18.	No. 6, North Road, Hackforth	Mr. Fred Robinson	·047	2
19.	No. 7, North Road, Hackforth	Mr. R. Hillary	·105	2
20.	No. 1, Rose Cottage, Hackforth	Mr. J. T. Hodgson	·152	2
21.	No. 2, Rose Cottage, Hackforth	Mr. H. Gill	·117	2
22.	No. 3, Rose Cottage, Hackforth	Mr. F. Fullerton	·151	2
23.	No. 4, Rose Cottage, Hackforth	Mr. J. Pearson	·120	2
24.	No. 1, Silver Street, Hackforth	Mr. T. Balmer	·056	2
25.	No. 2, Silver Street, Hackforth	The Misses Ingledew	·052	2
26.	No. 3, Silver Street, Hackforth	Mr. R. Thompson	·056	2
27.	The Blacksmith's Shop, Hackforth	Mr. H. Leyburn	·815	2
28.	No. 5, Silver Street, Hackforth	Mr. Robert Hartley	·074	2
29.	No. 6, Silver Street, Hackforth	Mr. F. Hodgson	·049	2
30.	No. 7, Silver Street, Hackforth	Mr. T. Merrington	·049	2
31.	No. 8, Silver Street, Hackforth	Mr. H. Gill	·071	2
32.	The Estate Sawmills, Hackforth	In Hand	3·996	2
33.	The Greyhound Inn, Hackforth	The Exors of the late Mrs. Thompson	9·281	2
34.	Sawmill Cottage, Hackforth	Mr. A. Oselton	·150	2

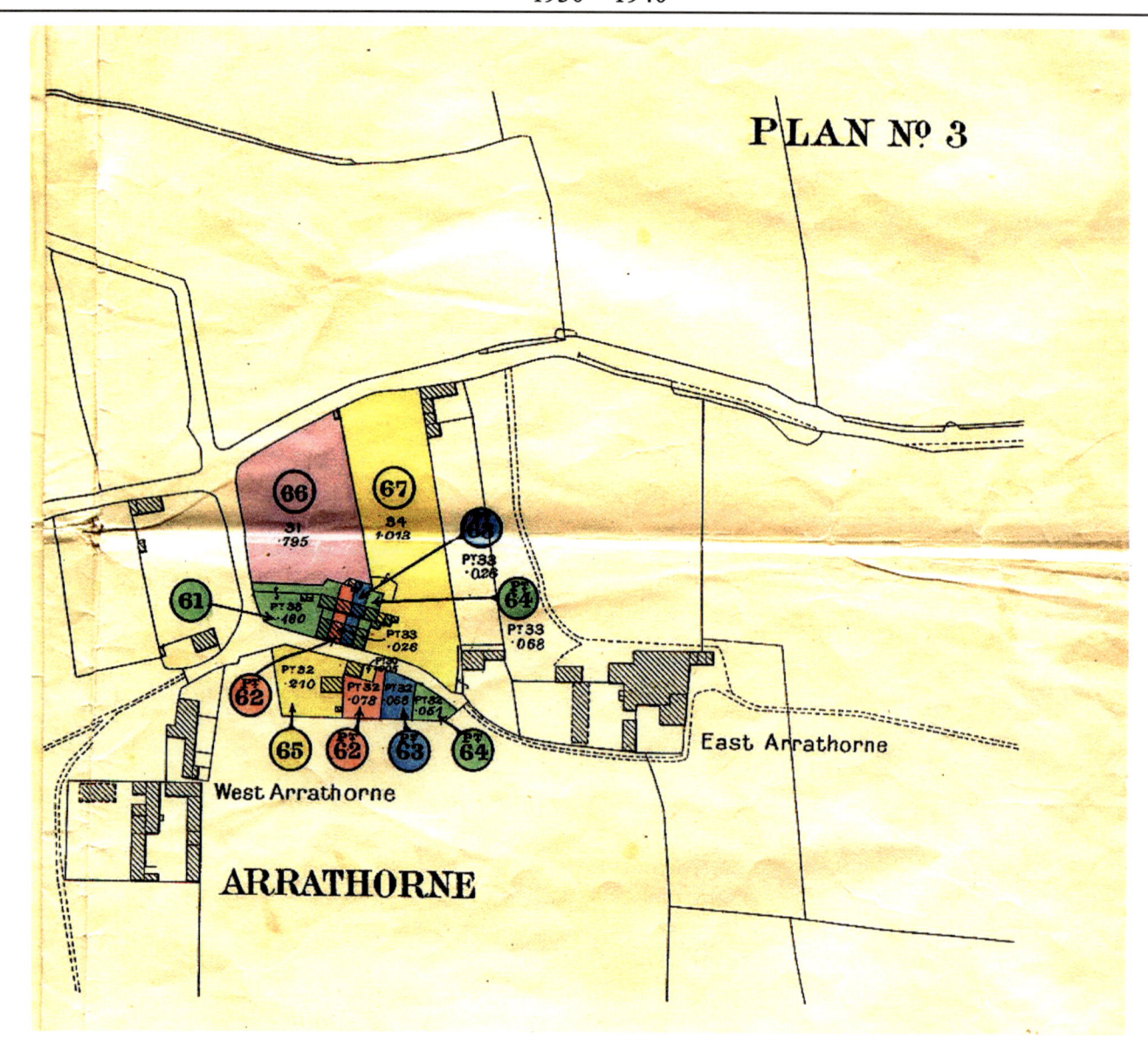

1930 – 1940

PLAN Nº 3

ARRATHORNE

West Arrathorne

East Arrathorne

1930 – 1940

61.	No. 1, Arrathorne	Mr. J. Muir	·180	3
62.	No. 2, Arrathorne	Mr. W. Burton	·104	3
68.	No. 3, Arrathorne	Mr. S. Greaves	·094	3
64.	No. 4, Arrathorne	Mr. E. Terry	·119	3
65.	The Bungalow, Arrathorne	Mr. W. Muir	·215	3
66.	Accommodation Land, Arrathorne	Mr. E. Terry	·795	3
67.	Accommodation Land, Arrathorne	Mr. W. Burton	1·013	3
68.	Accommodation Land, Arrathorne	Mr. M. Plant	4·860	1
69.	Accommodation Land, Arrathorne	Mr. E. Terry	5·108	1
70.	Accommodation Land, Arrathorne	Mr. J. Muir	4·912	1
71.	Accommodation Land, Arrathorne	Mr. E. Terry	4·303	1
72.	Craggs Lane Farm Arrathorne	Mr. G. Metcalfe	179·762	1
73.	Accommodation Land, Arrathorne	Mr. C. Metcalfe	41·521	1
74.	Langlands Farm, Arrathorne	Mr. E. Ellerton	194·945	1
75.	Accommodation Land, Arrathorne	Mr. R. Heeley	83·789	1
76.	Belmont and Highfield Farms, Arrathorne	Mr. J. Kay	248·054	1
77.	Arbour Hill Farm, Hornby	Mr. E. Smith	280·755	1
78	Winterfield House, Appleton	In Hand	44·657	1
79.	Accommodation Park Land, Hornby	In Hand	46·025	1
80.	Small Holding, Hornby	In Hand	17·197	1
81.	West Appleton Farm, Hornby	Mr. James Greaves	166·722	1
82.	Hollin Close Farm, Hornby	Mr. James Greaves	93·810	1
83.	The Home Farm, Hornby	Mr. T. Green	208·457	1
84.	Accommodation Park Land, Hornby	Mr. James Greaves	26·877	1
85.	Accommodation Park Land, Hornby	Mr. James Greaves	19·419	1
86.	No. 1, Kennel Cottages, Hornby	Mr. R. Morris	·755	1
87.	No. 2, Kennel Cottages, Hornby	Mr. E. Tweddle	·364	1
88.	Dairy Cottage, Hornby	Mr. A. W. Adamson	·723	1
89.	East Appleton Farm, Appleton	Mr. Isaac Slater	242·607	1
90.	Accommodation Land, do.	Mr. Isaac Slater	·998	1
91.	No. 1, East Appleton Cottages	Mr. E. Dobbie	·116	1
92.	No. 2, East Appleton Cottages	Mr. Isaac Slater	·116	1
93.	Rudd Hall Cottage	Mr. J. Smith	·225	1
94.	Accommodation Land	Mr. J. Smith	44·350	1

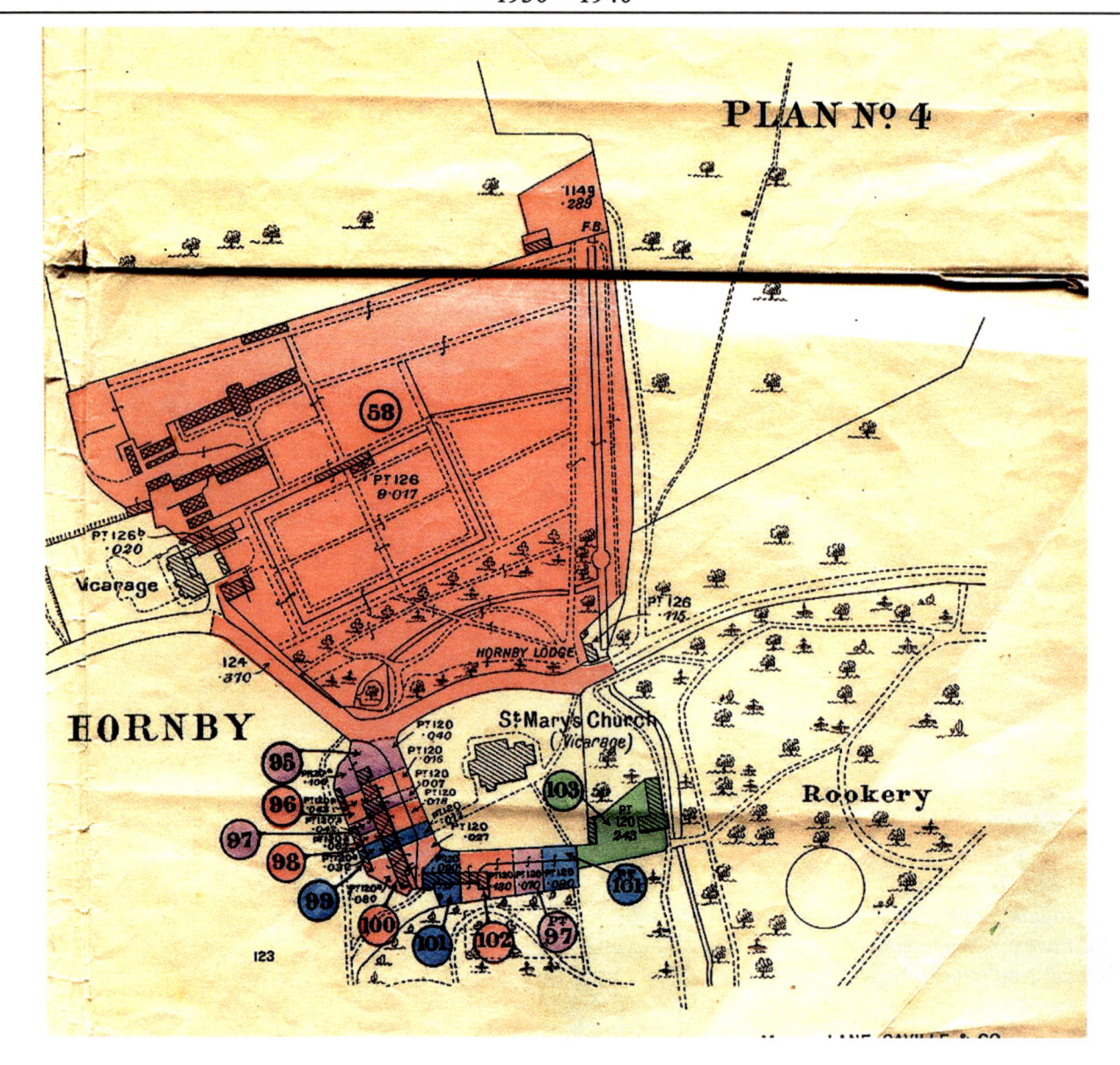

1930 – 1940

PLAN Nº 4

HORNBY

1930 – 1940

Lot No. Description	Principal Tenant	Area	Plan No.
58. Hornby Castle Gardens	Mr. T. F. Wilson	9·696	4
94. Accommodation Land	Mr. J. Smith	·146	4
95. No. 1, Church View, Hornby	Mr. F. Thompson (service)	·078	4
96. No. 2, Church View, Hornby	Mr. J. Thompson	·119	4
97. No. 3, Church View, Hornby	Mr. F. Stockill	·080	4
98. No. 4, Church View, Hornby	Mr. T. Green	·044	4
99. No. 5, Church View, Hornby	In Hand	·107	4
100. No. 6, Church View, Hornby	Mr. J. Scott	·170	4
101. No. 7, Church View, Hornby	Mr. J. Robinson	·180	4
102. No. 8, Church View, Hornby	Mrs. Alderson (in hand)	·243	4
103. The Laundry Cottage, Hornby	In Hand	5·626	1
104. The Gravel Pit, Hackforth	Mr. S. Smith		1
105. Standing Timber, High Clay Pits and Cocked Hat Belt			1
106. Do. Renforth Oak			1
107. Do. Birch Carr, Low Claypits and Middle Park			1
108. Do. Waste Wood			1
109. Do. Great Rush			1
110. Do. Pickering Plantation			1
111. Do. Hollow Moor Wood			1
112. Do. Langthorne Old Cover			1
113. Do. Langthorne New Cover			1
114. Do. High Goskins.			1
115. Do. Street House Belt			1
116. Do. Jackall Wood			1
117. Do. Gyll Hall Belt			1
118. Do. Milky Hill Plantation			1
119. Do. Dairy Wood			1
120. Do. Hutchinson's Whin			1
121. Do. Kennels Whin			1
122. Do. Oak Wood			1
128. Do. Sandhole Cover		·688	1
124. Do. and Land on Moor Lane			1
125. Do. Hawkswell Lane			1
126. Do. Briery Bush		68·177	1
127. Land, Middle Park			

Hornby Castle, Bedale, Yorkshire

CASTLE CATALOGUE

OF THE
RARE INTERIOR AND EXTERIOR
FIXTURES AND FITTINGS
INCLUDING
11 COMPLETE ROOMS
OF
RARE OAK AND PINE PANELLING
MANTELPIECES AND GRATES
ALSO
THE FABRIC OF THE CASTLE
TO BE SOLD FOR DEMOLITION BY AUCTION
ON THE SITE, ON
WEDNESDAY, THURSDAY AND FRIDAY
3rd, 4th, AND 5th SEPTEMBER 1930.
COMMENCING AT 11 O'CLOCK EACH DAY
AUCTIONEERS

PERRY & PHILLIPS LTD WALLIS & ARNETT (Mr Towler)
59, HIGH STREET 5, HUNDGATE
BRIDGNORTH DARLINGTON

Fixtures and Fittings including
    16,000 sq ft of Old Oak and Pine Flooring
    7,000 sq ft of Old Oak and Pine Panelling
    75 Rare and Carved Wood and Marble Mantelpieces
    Original XVIth Century Carved Stone Doorway
    Three XVth Century Oriel and Angle Windows
    A Rare Tower Clock
    Old lead water heads, Garden Ornaments
              also
    The Fabric of the Castle
    The Fabric of the Domestic Wing
    The Fabric of the Museum
will be sold for Demolition

Refreshments will be supplied on the premises by Miss Thompson, Greyhound Inn, Hackforth.

1930 – 1940

The Castle failed to sell, so the North, West and East sides of the building were demolished, and the architectural features were sold off on 3rd September 1930. It was only because "LEAVE" was written on the South side that it was not demolished as well.

Everything that could be sold, was, including windows, doorways, flooring, panelling, and fireplaces. Many items were sold to buyers from America. It is interesting to note that William Randolph Hearst, an American newspaper publisher, bought two stone portals, dating from the 14th or 15th Century. Sir William Burrell, a collector of historical and artistic objects bought them from him. He decided to give his collection to the City of Glasgow, and also gave them £450,000 towards displaying the collection in a special building. Mr Barry Glasson, the architect of the project, wanted to incorporate the portals in this new building. The visitors now actually pass through the portals when they visit the Burrell Collection in Glasgow.

The remaining South side of the Castle was bought by John Hammond who restored it and then sold it again to the Clutterbuck family in 1938.

Arches (Burrell Collection)

1930 – 1940

A copy of Redemption of Tithe Annuity, ref. John Hobson, Langthorne *(June Thompson)*

Receipt No. 253

Benefice V. Hornby

County York. Diocese Ripon.

QUEEN ANNE'S BOUNTY OFFICE,
3, DEAN'S YARD, WESTMINSTER, S.W.1.

REDEMPTION OF TITHE ANNUITY.

By an Order under his Official Seal dated the 2nd October, 1922 the Minister of Agriculture and Fisheries in pursuance of the powers vested in him by the Ministry of Agriculture and Fisheries Acts 1889 to 1919 and the Tithe Acts 1836 to 1918 directed that certain tithe rentcharges amounting together to £85:14:- apportioned upon fields numbered 213 etc. on the tithe map for the Parish of Hornby in the County of York should be redeemed and that the consideration money payable on such redemption should be discharged by an annuity of £101:8:4 payable half yearly on 25th June, and 25th December in every year for a period of forty years (the first payment thereof to be due on the 25th December, 1922) to the Governors of Queen Anne's Bounty.

By a further Order under his Official Seal dated the eleventh day of June, 1931 the said Minister in pursuance of the powers vested in him by the Tithe Annuities Apportionment Act 1921 apportioned the said annuity in the manner appearing in the said Order, an apportioned annuity of £-:5s:7d. being charged upon certain lands belonging to Messrs. John Hobson & Son.

As Treasurer for the time being of the said Governors of Queen Anne's Bounty I acknowledge to have received from Messrs. John Hobson & Son the sum of four pounds 19/6d. which sum is accepted by the Governors in full discharge of the said apportioned annuity of £-:5s:7d.

Dated the second day of July, 1931.

Treasurer

All farmers, by law, had to pay tithes to the church. These payments continued until about 1985.

Mr Prime's Memories

"I was a twelve year old boy playing with friends round the Castle Lake. I remember being chased by a Copper. We were playing on a punt! It was the day of the sale.

It was 1930, I think. The Hornby Castle sale was on the same day as James Ramsey McDonald, first Labour Prime Minister, visited Catterick Aerodrome.

There were terrific storms. The heavens opened, it was cold and wet. My two friends and I rode home on our bicycles through the floods.

Mr Brigham went to all the big sales to buy books and pictures. He lived in a large Georgian house in Darlington and did not like selling anything. He had to move house to accommodate it all. He bought books and pictures at the sale.

When he died I cycled to Darlington to the sale and bought, with my pocket money, some books with the Duke of Leeds Coat of Arms printed in them.

A builder from Bedale bought the Castle and gave me permission to look round the Castle and grounds when I wanted, which I did. A lot of the Castle was knocked down."

THIS TESTIMONIAL

together with a Cheque

was presented to

MR. FRED M. HILL

as a slight token of appreciation for the kindness and consideration shown during

the Nine years as

Estate Agent to His Grace The Duke of Leeds, Hornby Castle.

Your dealings have always been carried out in a genial and straightforward manner, winning for yourself the highest respect of every one with whom you have come in contact.

The Tenant Farmers assure you of their sincere good wishes for your future success, health and happiness.

J. KAY	N. HAWKSWELL & SONS	T. E. KNOX
J. HOBSON & SON	A. HODGSON	J. SANDERSON
W. C. INGLEDEW	W. W. MAIDMENT	M. PLANT
I. W. SLATER	G. METCALFE	G. TOWLER
T. W. GREEN	E. ELLERTON	T. FRANKLIN
S. SMITH	J. W. SIMPSON	E. GREENWELL
E. SMITH	R. HEELEY	EXORS. MRS. THOMPSON
J. GREAVES	J. W. LAMB	

Tenants on the Hornby Castle Estate.

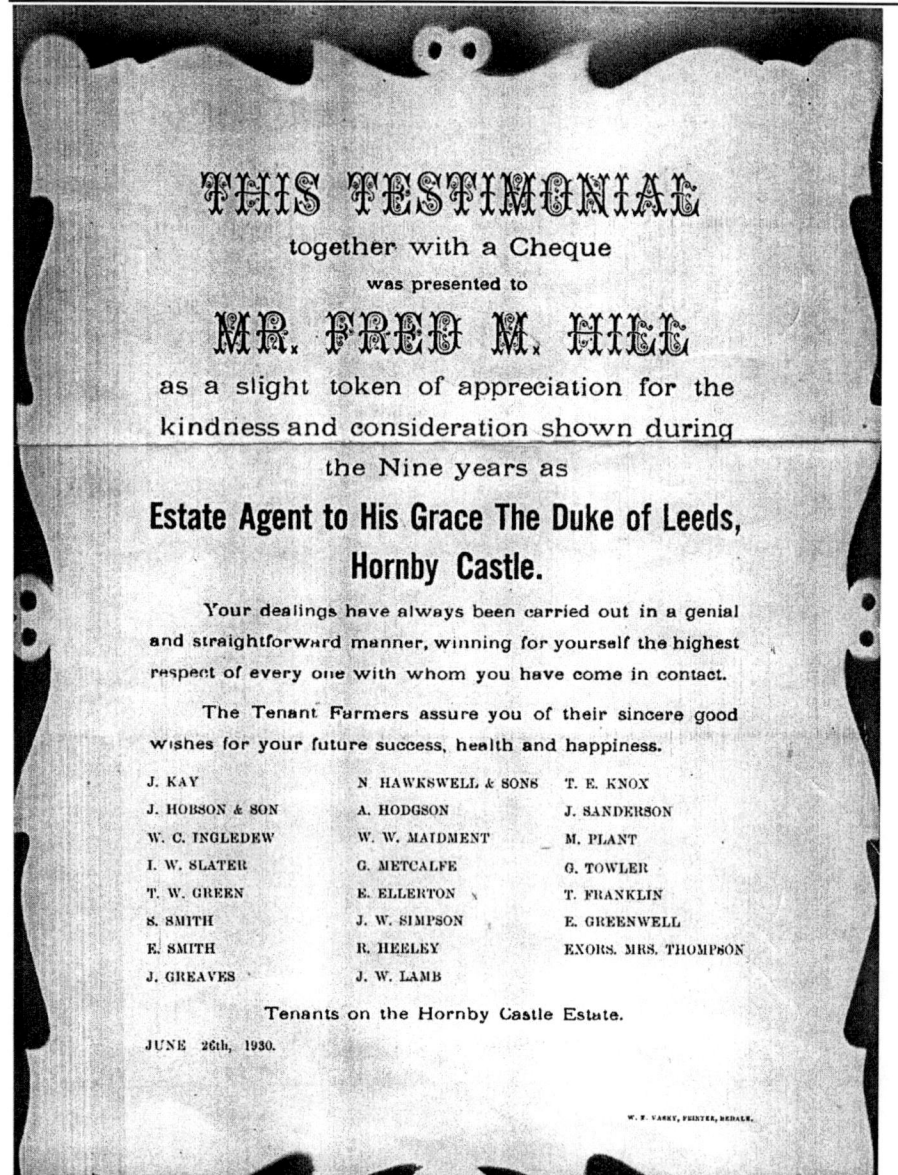

JUNE 26th, 1930.

This testimonial illustrated how the workers from Hornby Estate respected the estate agent Fred Hill.

Original: Mr P. Knox

Hackforth School

The school logbook refers to the sale of the Hornby Castle Estate to Mr John Todd. The head teacher received information from the school correspondent that "the school will be carried on and that the way is open to transfer the property to some definite local body." The Diocesan Board took over responsibility of the school premises and a range of repairs was carried out.

The involvement of local people in the school was revealed at the end of 1930 when the school managers were listed as:

Mrs Clifford Ingledew	Street House
Capt Tyson	Rudd Hall
Mr Sidney Smith	Ghyll Hall
Mr James Greaves	Butterwell
Mr John Richard Hobson	Langthorne

Further involvement, of a very practical nature, was illustrated in the entry for June 1934 which reads: 'This afternoon, at playtime, Daisy Anderson, aged 7, fell in the yard and hurt her right forearm. Have applied splints and slings and, through the kindness of Mr Wesley Johnson, who took her home in his car, she is, I learn, quite comfortable.'

1930 – 1940

1931

The school role in the 1930 was approximately 30. Attendance at school was not affected much by the demands of agriculture except for the occasional potato picking. However, the attendance was affected by several health problems. There was a measles epidemic in 1931, while scarlet fever caused the closure and fumigation of the school in 1935. There was a mumps epidemic in 1936 followed by a flu epidemic in 1937. Sadly, two deaths of pupils were recorded, one from hay fever and one from pneumonia.

The children were involved in the caring for the health of others, as in 1932, an appeal for eggs for Morris Grange Sanatorium was made.

1930 – 1940

North Riding of Yorkshire County Council.

EDUCATION COMMITTEE

++++++++++

Hackforth and Hornby C.E. School.

March 31st 1934

To. *Peter Knox*

(Name of Child)

On your leaving school to enter upon the more serious business of life, the Education Committee and your Head Teacher wish you every success in the future, and hope that you will always keep in your mind the honour and good name of your old school.

Always remember that Cheerful obedience to duty, Consideration and respect for others, and Truthfulness in word and act are the foundations of Good Citizenship.

WORK HARD, PLAY HARD, AND NEVER TELL A LIE

William H. T Worsley
Chairman of Education Committee
J.C. Wrigley
Secretary of the Education Committee
J. Emmerson - Lyall
Head Teacher

A copy of the School Leaving Certificate issued when children leave school at 14.

1930 – 1940

School photograph – 15 September 1933

THE NORTHERN ECHO, FRIDAY, 15 SEP[TEMBER]

WHEN THE SUN SHINES. Boys of Hackforth School, near Ca[tte]rick, who come from outlying farms, take their dinner to school. A Northern Echo photographer came upon them yesterday picnicking by the brook at Hackforth.

1930 – 1940

Farming

Diamond Hill Farm about 1930

(photos: Mr Towler)

Cloud burst removed bridge and wall

Mary Evelyn Towler and Horses

The Sheep Wash

95

VALE OF MOWBRAY
Annual PLOUGHING & HEDGE-CUTTING
COMPETITIONS
ROOT AND CORN SHOW

WILL BE HELD

ON SATURDAY, NOVEMBER 20TH, 1937,

(Weather permitting), or the first Saturday following which may be favourable,

On land kindly lent by G. A. PENTY, Esq., Oak Tree Farm, Burneston, Bedale.

President—MAJOR ALAN HILL-WALKER V.C.   Vice-President—CAPT. LEYLAND

Patrons

J. M. BARWICK, M.F.H.   MAJOR W. W. BURDON   MR. BROOKS   R. DAND, ESQ.   MRS. DOXFORD   CAPT. DUGDALE   MAJOR GROTRIAN   CAPT. A. W. MALLINSON
H. MARSHALL, ESQ.   J. MAUGHAN, ESQ.   A. McINTYRE, ESQ.   MISS M. MOUBRAY   MISS M. C. MOUBRAY   SIR T. W. NUSSEY, BART.   F. SAMUELSON, ESQ.
P. SLINGSBY, ESQ.   MAJOR TYSON   MAJOR WRIGHT   CAPT. F. C. R. PRIOR-WANDESFORDE, D.S.O.   MR. RIDLEY

Class 1. For best work done by a Chill or Digging Plough. Open to all. 1st, £2 10s. 2nd, £1 10s. 3rd, 15s.
Class 2. For best work done by a Chill or Digging Plough for those who have never won a first prize. 1st, £2 10s. 2nd, £1 10s. 3rd, 15s.
Class 3. For the best Ploughing by a Youth under 21 years of age and Men who have never won a prize. (3ft. 6ins. Mouldboard). 1st, £2 10s. 2nd, £1 10s. 3rd, 15s. 4th, 10s.
Class 4. Champion Hedge Cutting (Open Class). 1st, £2. 2nd, £1. 3rd, 10s.
Class 5. Hedge Cutting. For the best Hedge Cutter who has not won more than two firsts on any occasion. 1st, £1 10s. 2nd, £1. 3rd, 10s.
Class 6. Hedge Cutting. For the best Hedge Cutter who has not won a first prize on any previous occasion. 1st, £1 10s. 2nd, £1. 3rd, 10s.
Class 7. Hedge Trimming. For the best Hedge Trimmer. 1st, £1. 2nd, 10s. 3rd, 5s.

Set of Hames for best pair of Horses.

1930 – 1940

ROOTS.

	1st	2nd	3rd			1st	2nd	3rd
Class 1. Best 6 Yellow Mangolds	7s. 6d.	5s.	2s. 6d.	Class 6. Best 14lbs. Barley		7s. 6d.	5s.	2s. 6d.
Class 2. Best 6 Swede Turnips	7s. 6d.	5s.	2s. 6d.	Class 7 Best 14lbs. Wheat		7s. 6d.	5s.	2s. 6d.
Class 3. Best 4 Stones Potatoes for Table use	7s. 6d.	5s.	2s. 6d.	Class 8. Best 14lbs. Oats		7s. 6d.	5s.	2s. 6d.
Class 4. Best 4 Stones Chipping Potatoes	7s. 6d.	5s.	2s. 6d.					
Class 5. Best Collection of 3 Swedes, 3 Mangolds and 1 stone Potatoes	7s. 6d.	5s.	2s. 6d.					

All Roots and Corn to be on the Ground by 12 noon.
Entries taken on the Field.

SPECIAL PRIZES.

Messrs. Clibrans, Altrincham, give 10s. for 1st an...
Messrs. Finneys, Newcastle, give 10s. for 1st and...
Messrs. Finneys, Newcastle, give 10s. for 1st and...
Mr. J. Smith, Aiskew, Bedale, gives 10s. for 1st a...
The Langdale Chemical Manure Co. give 10s. for...
The Langdale Chemical Manure Co. give 10s. for...
The Langdale Chemical Manure Co. give 10s. for...
Mr. R. Pease gives a Piece of Plate value 20s. for...
and 14lbs. Potatoes grown by users of...

General

1—Each Competitor in Classes 1, 2 and 3 to plough about half an acre, not more than 5¼ inches deep.

2—All Competitors must be on the ground by Nine o'clock in the morning, to finish their portions by 3 o'clock prompt, or their work will not be judged.

3—That every Ploughman makes two clear furrows in the first three rounds.

4—Any Competitor in the last-mentioned Classes allowing anyone to assist him either in the setting of the plough, or the management of his team will be disqualified, except for the last two whole furrows. No boats allowed, no foot marking, or any hand packing in any of the Classes.

5—Any of the premiums may be withheld if the Judges decide

Entrance Fees :—1s. in the £ o...

Entries close Tuesday, Nov. 16th.   Entries (wh...

Chairman :—E. E. GREENWELL.   Hon T...

DINNER at the ROYAL OAK HOTEL, BEDALE, at 6-30 o'clock.   Tickets 3s. each.
BUS SERVICE FROM RIPON AND BEDALE PASSES THE GROUND.

OPEN TRACTOR DEMONSTRATION.

W. F. VASEY, PRINTER, BEDALE.

Mr Knox taking part in a ploughing competition

1930 – 1940

Horses at work on the farm at East Arrathorne ~ 1933

(Mavis Heeley)

The children enjoy a pony and trap ride at the farm ~ 1930

(Mavis Heeley)

Everyone helps with the harvesting

Harvesting at Arrathorne ~ 1935
(Mavis Heeley)

A binder at Diamond Hill
(Mr Towler)

1930 – 1940

Horses with G. Scarf making a haystack ~ 1939
(Mavis Heeley)

A stationary Saw Bench
(Mavis Heeley)

A steam engine sawing stakes and logs at Arrathorne ~ 1939

(Mavis Heeley)

Loading timber onto a lorry at the Clay Pits ~ 1937

(Mavis Heeley)

1930 – 1940

Potato picking

(Mr Towler)

The rear of the car is converted to a grass cutter

(Mr Towler)

1930 – 1940

Robert Hurworth ploughing at Rudd Hall Farm ~ 1933

Tom Ingledew with two 'baby beef' cattle – taken in Front Paddock ~ 1936

[Left – Strawberry Roan Shorthorn; Right – Red & White]

1930 – 1940

St Mary's Church

Times — www.thisisthenortheast.co.uk — LOCAL NEWS — FRIDAY, OCTOBER 8, 1999

63 years of musical service ends

BY BRIAN REDHEAD

THE forthcoming retirement of Mr Alex Forrest, of Romanby, will signal the end of 63 years' service to music and churches in North Yorkshire, New Zealand and Scotland.

His first appointment in 1936 was as organist at Hornby Castle, near Bedale, on condition that he took lessons, his chosen teacher being Dr C H Moody, the doyen organist at Ripon cathedral.

As a pupil, then articled, he became assistant organist and began a long association with Ripon, riding his bicycle from Hornby in all weathers.

While living in Bedale he sang with the choral society and played violin for Northallerton orchestra, both being conducted by Sir Claude Dodsworth.

While at Ripon cathedral, he held other posts at Bishop Monkton, Aldborough and Holy Trinity, Ripon.

He said: "I can recall many wonderful days at the cathedral, one being the military parade services, playing to a packed building of men."

With the precentor, Mr Forrest – pictured left – began the 9.15 sung communion, which became a popular service. He was associated with Toc H and, for the YMCA, he arranged many concerts and a music club attended by German prisoners of war. He ran singing classes at the grammar school and St Olave's preparatory school, Ripon.

To broaden his musical experience he attended courses run by Sir Sydney Nicholson for the school of church music at Chislehurst, Kent. He became a regular visitor to the Three Choirs festival, Leeds festival and the Edinburgh festival.

He left Ripon in 1953 to become organist at the Episcopal church in Dunfermline and taught music at the Carnegie Institute. He became well known as a recitalist and adjudicator and, for his fellow organists in the area, he formed the West Fife organists' association.

In 1958 he was chosen by the bishop of Dunedin, New Zealand, to become organist and choirmaster at Dunedin. He was also music master at McGlashen college for boys, where numerous private pupils came from all ethnic groups including Maori and Chinese. He also formed the Otago organists' association for the area.

Moving to Napier, in the North Island, he played at various churches, formed the Hawkes Bay organists' association and edited a countrywide publication called *Organ News*. As a city organist, he formed the Napier boys' choir, taught music at the girls' high school and was organist at St Andrew's church in nearby Hastings.

He returned to England in 1981 and began teaching organ, piano, violin, guitar and singing in Romanby, where he now lives at Kirk House.

For several years he managed the choir at St James's church, Romanby, and took junior choristers to sing at other churches in the area, promoting activities to encourage church and music interest.

The annual St Cecelia festival was another of his achievements. Over the past 11 years in Romanby he has taught more than 10 pupils who have passed more than 270 music examinations.

Mr Forrest, aged 83, said: "Having played and taught music for the past 63 years I feel it is time to retire, although I will continue my interest in music."

"Alex Forrest was appointed to be trained as the organist at Hornby Castle (Church) in 1936. He lived in Bedale and cycled to Hornby. He also played the violin and sang with the Choral Society in Bedale."

D & S Times

The Choir boys from Hornby Church

(Mavis Heeley)

(Mrs M Smith)

A Sunday School trip to Walmersley
Kenneth Smith far right back row.

(Mrs M Smith)

A church outing to Whitby
(Mrs M Smith)

1930 – 1940

The new Burial Ground is consecrated at Hornby Church ~ June 1938

Group 1:
Walter Berriman carrying the Cross. V. Morris, Jim Muir, George Heeley and Ken Smith

Group 2:
Mr Robinson, Herbert Smith, Wally Smith, A. Hillary, Ralph Mackenzie

Group 3:
Edith Ellerton, Annie Plant, G. Williams, Peggy Smith, Muriel Smith, Bessie Knox, Biddy Smith, Dora Metcalfe

Church Wardens: R. Heeley & Harry Knox
Vicar: Rev Moss Blundel, Bishop & his Curate

A Wedding Group at Ghyll Hall after the ceremony ~ 16th June 1938

Mr & Mrs Miles Ward, Miss Peggy Smith, Rev. Crawford, Mr & Mrs Thomas Ward (Biddy Smith), Mr & Mrs S. Smith, Miss Muriel Smith, Mr Francis Smith

1930 – 1940

Extracts from 'Hipswell-with-Tunstall and Hornby Parish Magazine

No.7 dated July 1932 – price 3½d

Vicar - The Rev J Forster Beamish
Licensed Lay Reader in charge of Hornby-Mr FR Battensby
Wardens at Hornby - Messrs. R Heeley and G Metcalfe

1. Hornby Altar Flowers

Mrs G Metcalfe of West Appleton has kindly arranged for the altar flowers in Hornby Church to the end of this year. The following persons have been made responsible for each month: June-Mrs Valks; July-Mrs Ellerton; August-Miss M Knox; September-Mrs Ingledew; October- Mrs G Metcalfe; November-Mrs Smith; December-Mrs Tyson. Mrs Marshall and Miss Henderson have signified their willingness to assist If anyone is willing to take a month will they kindly communicate with Mrs G Metcalfe, who will no doubt arrange for 1933.

2. Hornby Vicarage.

The Vicar has now succeeded in letting the Vicarage to Capt. E.B Pope, who is coming from Gravesend in Kent and expects to arrive in September. Captain Pope will be stationed at Catterick Camp for four years. Both he and Mrs Pope are church people and regular communicants.

Hornby people we are sure will extend to them a hearty welcome and trust that they will be very happy at the Vicarage. They are both keen gardeners and they were delighted with the Vicarage Garden.

3. Ancient Font.

The old Font, which stood in the Vicarage garden for many years, has now been removed to Hornby Church and looks quite imposing. We hope to be able to find out something about its history soon and intend to get expert opinion from some well-known Archaeologist.

4. Organist's Holiday.

Miss Brown, organist at Hornby is going down to Lursby to see her parents. Her place is being very kindly filled by Mr Bateson and Mr Henson, the organists of Hipswell and Tunstall.

5. Collections taken at St Mary's Hornby

	£	s.	d.	
June 5th		10	7	Church Expenses
June 12th		13	3	S.P.G.
June 19th		12	10	Church Expenses
June 26th			4	Church Expenses
At Early Service		2	6	S.P.G.
	£2	8	6	

It is with deepest regret and heartfelt sympathy with the bereaved parents and family that we record the sudden death of David Knox, of Mill Close, in the Parish of Hornby, which took place early on Saturday morning.

7. Funeral at Hornby Church – Tuesday July 5th 1932.

A large congregation, which nearly filled the Nave of the Church, assembled at the funeral of little David Knox, when his body was laid to rest in the beautiful God's Acre of the ancient Church. The children of Hackforth Day School and his own Class of boys, in charge of the Headmaster Mr Lyle, were present with the Church Choir, and sang a Special Hymn and the 23rd Psalm. The Vicar conducted the Service attended by Mr FR Battensby, Licensed Lay Reader in charge of Hornby. The Choir sang *Nunc Dimmitis* as the cortege left the Church. Mr Bateson, organist of Tunstall presided at the organ.

The Service was most impressive, and there was hardly a dry eye amongst the congregation.

"May he rest in peace"

The coffin was smothered in beautiful wreaths of flowers.

8. Advert inside back cover.

J. F. WILSON

Market Gardener & Florist

Bedding, Herbaceous and
Rockery Plants a speciality
Wreaths and Crosses made to order.
Fresh Fruit and Vegetables in Season

HORNBY CASTLE, BEDALE.

Attends Richmond & Bedale Markets.

1930 – 1940

Dated November 1937 – price 3½d

Vicar - The Rev J Forster Beamish.

Licensed lay heads in charge of Hornby - Mr Walter Berriman
Wardens - Mr R Heeley and Mr H Knox
Sunday School in the Church – 2.30pm

Jumble and Auction Sale and Tea at Hackforth on October 23rd 1937

Well done, Hornby, you have indeed exceeded our highest hopes and cheered the hearts of a pessimistic Vicar, who asked for £50 but never thought his request would be granted. We do not know what the actual grand total will be, but we are informed it will be about £53, a truly wonderful achievement. We will not soon forget the scene of activity, both at the Jumble Sale and the Auction. Our warm thanks are offered to Mr C. W. Tindall, Auctioneer and Valuer, Catterick Camp, who came and gave his services and worked hard for more than two hours, and got every penny that could possibly be got for the articles to be sold. And what a collection of articles they were! Every conceivable thing, from a cock of hay to a thimble, and every rag was sold!

Our thanks are due to all the stall holders and workers, and the farmers who gave of their bounty and also came to buy, and we must not forget to warmly thank all those who came to support us by buying, they did it manfully and womanfully.

Gift to Hornby Church

Many, many thanks on behalf of the Church Council and Churchwardens of Hornby to the Hackforth and Hornby Needlecraft and Social Guild for their gift of £6-14-0 to the Church Funds.

Burial "Until the day breaks and the shadows flee away"
October 28th JANE GILL aged 73 years

Church Offertories "Freely ye have received freely give"
Two Services on Sunday – Acts of Communion - 34

Monthly Notes

A former parishioner has presented to us a Pulpit Fall, Book Marker and two Alms Bags, all worked by hand in a beautiful shade of green, for which we are very grateful. Thank you.

Harvest Thanksgiving October 15th and 17th.

We tender our grateful thanks to all who laboured to make the Church look so beautiful as it did for our Thanksgiving Services, and as we joined in singing the well known hymns, the whole atmosphere was one of thankfulness. The inspiring address by the Bishop will long live in our hearts and minds, and give us encouragement to strive for better and higher things.

The services were continued on the Sunday following, when in the morning the Vicar preached to a good congregation, and afterwards 34 of us joined in offering the greatest of all thanksgivings - The Holy Communion, and together we received "The Bread of Life"

In the evening Mr Walter Berriman preached, and once more our Harvest Thanksgiving Services were over, leaving us full to overflowing with thanks to Him "who givest all"

Walter Berriman

Advert in 1937 Parish Magazine

Come to

**J. POCKLINGTON
LANGTHORNE, BEDALE.
JOINER, UNDERTAKER AND WHEELWRIGHT
FOR
POULTRY HOUSES, COOPS, GATES
WHEELBARROWS, SHEEP RACKS
AND TROUGHS etc**

The Village Hall

On March 17th, 1921, a declaration of trust was made between Rev. George Sulivan Edgecome, (the Vicar of St. Mary's Hornby). Nicholas Hawkswell (Roundhill) and William Ingledew (Street House). An account was set up with the aim of building a Village Institute at Hackforth, on land given by the Duke of Leeds.

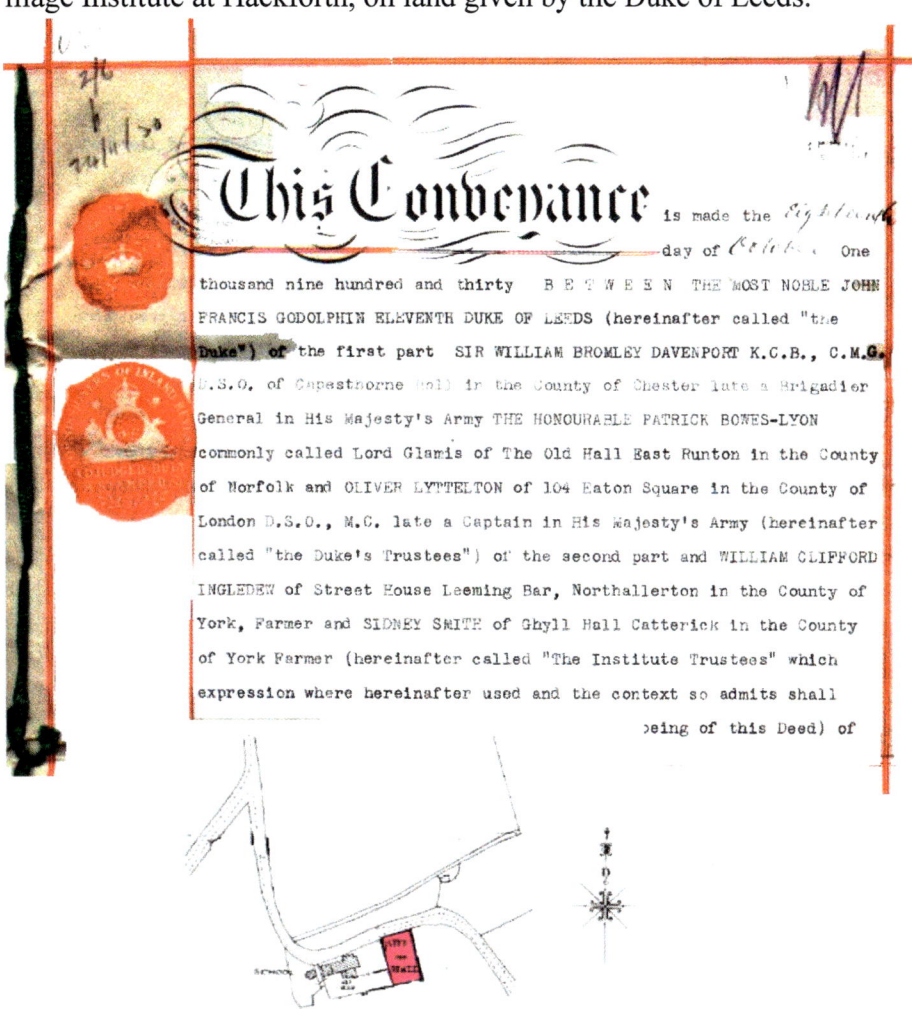

> **This Conveyance** is made the *Eighteenth* day of *October* One thousand nine hundred and thirty BETWEEN THE MOST NOBLE JOHN FRANCIS GODOLPHIN ELEVENTH DUKE OF LEEDS (hereinafter called "the Duke") of the first part SIR WILLIAM BROMLEY DAVENPORT K.C.B., C.M.G., D.S.O. of Capesthorne Hall in the County of Chester late a Brigadier General in His Majesty's Army THE HONOURABLE PATRICK BOWES-LYON commonly called Lord Glamis of The Old Hall East Runton in the County of Norfolk and OLIVER LYTTELTON of 104 Eaton Square in the County of London D.S.O., M.C. late a Captain in His Majesty's Army (hereinafter called "the Duke's Trustees") of the second part and WILLIAM CLIFFORD INGLEDEW of Street House Leeming Bar, Northallerton in the County of York, Farmer and SIDNEY SMITH of Ghyll Hall Catterick in the County of York Farmer (hereinafter called "The Institute Trustees" which expression where hereinafter used and the context so admits shall ... being of this Deed) of

THIS CONVEYANCE is made this *Eighteenth* day of October One thousand nine hundred and thirty BETWEEN THE MOST NOBLE JOHN FRANCIS GODOLPHIN ELEVENTH DUKE OF LEEDS (hereinafter called "the Duke") of the first part SIR WILLIAM BROMLEY DAVENPORT K.C.B., C.M.G., D.S.O. of Capesthorne Hall in the County of Chester late a Brigadier General in His Majesty's Army, THE HONOURABLE PATRICK BOWES-LYON commonly called Lord Glamis of The Old Hall East Runton in the County of Norfolk and OLIVER LYTTELTON of 104 Eaton Square in the County of London D.S.O., M.C. late a Captain in His Majesty's Army (hereinafter called "the Duke's Trustees") of the second part and WILLIAM CLIFFORD INGLEDEW of Street House Leeming Bar, Northallerton in the County of York, Farmer and SIDNEY SMITH of Ghyll Hall Catterick in the County of York Farmer (hereinafter called "The Institute Trustees" which expression where hereinafter used and the context so admits shall include the trustees or trustee for the time being of this Deed) of the third part.

WHEREAS : -

(1) By a Vesting Assent dated the Twentieth day of November One thousand nine hundred and twenty nine and made between the Duke's Trustees of the one part and the Duke of the other part the Duke's Trustees as the Personal Representatives of the late George Godolphin Tenth Duke of Leeds assented to the vesting in the Duke of (amongst other property) the freehold property hereinafter described and conveyed Upon the trusts subsisting or capable of taking effect concerning the same under the Will therein mentioned of the said George Godolphin Tenth Duke of Leeds or other the trusts on which the same ought from time to time to be held. And it was thereby declared that the Duke's Trustees were the trustees of the Settlement made by the said Will for the purposes of the Settled Land Act 1925.

(2) The Duke is desirous of conveying the said freehold property hereinafter described and conveyed to the Institute Trustees upon with and subject to the trusts powers and provisions hereinafter declared.

NOW THIS DEED WITNESSETH as follows: -

1. IN pursuance of such desire the Duke as Settlor in exercise of the power for this purpose conferred on him by Section 55 of the Settled Land. Act 1925 and of every other power enabling him hereby freely and gratuitously conveys unto the Institute Trustees ALL THAT piece of freehold land situate adjoining the School Playground at Hackforth in the County of York more particularly delineated on the plan hereto annexed and thereon coloured pink to hold unto the Institute Trustee in fee simple discharged as provided by Section 72 of the Settled Land Act 1925 but nevertheless Upon the trusts and with and subject to the powers and provisions following (that is to say) : -

2. THE Institute Trustees shall hold the said property as a site for the erection of an Institute to be used in perpetuity as a non-sectarian and non-political place of recreation and social intercourse under the name of the Hackforth Village Institute for the advantage or benefit of the inhabitants of Hackforth and the surrounding district and either gratuitously or in consideration of any money payment or on such terms generally as the Institute Trustees may think fit.

3. THE Institute Trustees shall permit any buildings suitable for the purposes aforesaid to be erected on the said site and as and when need shall require shall permit all or any of the buildings for the time being standing on the said hereditaments to be pulled down altered or rebuilt.

4. THE Institute Trustees shall not be liable for the maintenance or repair or insurance of the said premises or for the payment of any charges thereon.

5. THE management and control of the property and affairs of the trust aforesaid shall be vested in the Institute Trustees with full power and authority at their discretion at any time to appoint or make provision for the appointment of any persons (including all or any of the Institute Trustees) as Committee-men or otherwise for the purpose of the administration of the trust aforesaid in such manner and subject to such rules and regulations (including regulations admitting to the benefits of the trust any person or persons on payment) as the Institute Trustees may prescribe.

6. THE following provisions as to the appointment of new trustees and the discharge and retirement of a trustee shall apply to this Deed by way of extension and variation of the statutory powers:

    (a) The number of trustees shall not exceed five and. shall not be less than two who shall be residents in the Ecclesiastical Parish of Hornby near Bedale in the County of York.

    (b) Any one of the trustees may when there are more than three retire from the trusts of this Deed on giving two month's notice in writing of his intention so to do to each of the other trustees for the time being and upon the expiration of such two months the trustee giving the notice shall ipso facto cease to be a trustee.

    (c) If any trustee becomes bankrupt or remains out of the United Kingdom for more than twelve months he shall *ipso facto* cease to be a trustee.

7. THE parties hereto hereby certify that the transaction hereby effected does not form part of a larger transaction or of a series of transactions in respect of which the value or the aggregate value the property conveyed or transferred exceeds Five hundred pounds.

    IN WITNESS whereof the said parties to these present have hereunto set their hands and seals the day and year first above written.

SIGNED SEALED AND DELIVERED by the
above named The Most Noble John
Francis Godolphin Eleventh Duke of
Leeds in the presence of (various signatories)

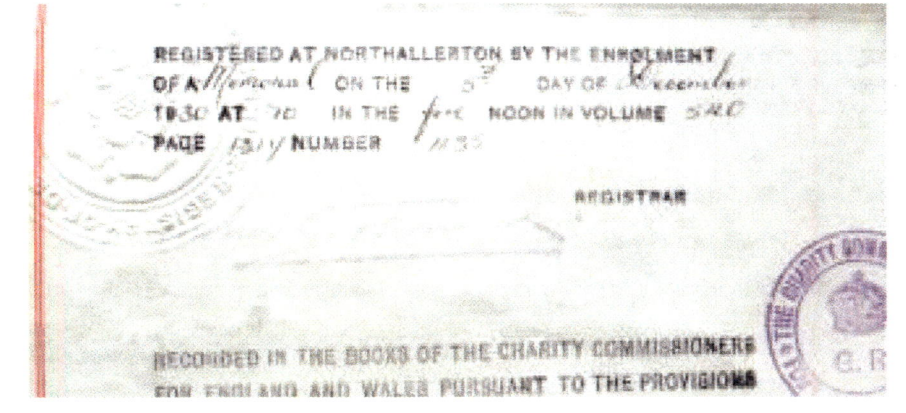

1930 – 1940

An example from the Hackforth Institute Building Fund Note book 1923. For fundraising carried out:-

Sports — June 2nd 1923 (Cont.)

Sundries acc.

	£	s	d
By Jumper Raffle	4	5	-
Cake Raffle (Mrs Dawson)	2	14	-
Hearthrug (Miss Warriner)	1	15	-
Jumbles etc on Stall	8	16	9
Tea receipts	4	2	10
Collection (Miss Hawkswell)		12	9
Entry fees. Foot Races		14	2
Ditto. Pony Races	2	14	-
Mrs J. Greaves. donation	-	10	-
Mr G.A. Metcalfe do.		10	-
Mrs Courage do.	1	-	-
Mrs Pocklington do.	-	5	-
Amount subscribed by farmers towards Pony Races	12	12	6
Carr'd fwd £	46	15	0

	£	s	d
To Prize Winners. foot races	3	1	-
Ditto. pony races	14	10	-
Advertising	1	5	-
Printing raffle books and posters	1	3	9
Rubber Stamps & pads	-	11	-
Police Charges		13	4
Mrs Merrington		10	-
Mrs Robinson	-	14	-
Postages	-	3	6
Carr'd fwd £	22	1	4

After a public meeting in Hackforth School, a Hackforth Village Institute Building Committee was formed and had its first meeting at the Greyhound Inn, Hackforth on Monday, March 3rd 1933.

The committee comprised of Capt Tyson, Mrs. Ingledew, Mrs. Tyson, Mr. Smith, Mr. Ingledew, Mr. Marshall, Mr. Johnson, Mr. Green, Mr. Murfin and Mr. Valks. Capt. Tyson was elected Chairman, and Mr. Valks elected Secretary.

The committee asked three architects to tender their charges for drawing plans for the Institute, taking into account the position of the car park. It was decided not to build a billiards room, as there was insufficient money, and "its maintenance would necessitate the employment of a full-time caretaker, whose wages would be too great a strain on the finances of the hall."

Committee Meetings throughout 1935 discussed the application for grants, borrowing money from National Council funds, and the design of the building. The committee chose the Architect, Mr. Wetherall. The building contractors, Messrs Willoughly and Co. of Northallerton, agreed to build the institute for the sum of £1,397. Fundraising over the years totalled £640, and was to continue. Also members of the committee agreed to be guarantors to a limit of £45 each, "and should be refunded according to the surplus in hand."

It is interesting to note that on 6th April 1937 the builders were given an extra £75 because of "the rise in building materials." On 20th September 1937, when the committee met, they decided to change the stone with 'Village Institute' on to 'Village Hall', because this would affect how the building could be used.

August 1937

(Muriel Dodd)

1930 – 1940

As the building neared completion, the committee organised the insurance, (for £1500) the Calor Gas lighting, the interior decoration, and the installation of the clock. The opening ceremony and concert were planned, with Mr. Smith and Mr. Knox to be doorkeepers, Mr. Heeley to officiate as M.C, and Mr. Johnson and Mr. Murfin to show people to their seats. The school playground was to be used as a car park, and the police were asked to send representatives. Finally, a caretaker was to be paid £6 p.a. to keep the hall clean, including the windows, floors, fireplaces, stoves and cloakrooms. Fees to hire the hall were 3/6d for a concert or whist drive, 5/- for a dance, 2/6d for W.I meetings, 1/- for committee meetings and 5/- for wedding receptions.

When the village hall was completed, the stones by the main entrance had names, engraved on them. These refer to the people who gave generously to help finance the building of the Hall.

The opening concert on Wednesday 12th January 1938 raised £25.15.10d.

The Hall ~ present day
(Sandra Webb)

Women's Institute (W.I.)

The Inauguration of Hackforth W.I was in 1931, with Mrs. Tyson as President. By 1937, they had established themselves as a large active group.

1937 W.I.

Back row:

Vivien Ingledew, Miss Hulse, Miss Morley, Bessie Knox

Front row:

Biddy Smith, Edith Ellerton, Mrs Hutchinson, Sylvia Smith

(E. Blenkiron)

(and from 1937 newspaper article)

"Hackforth Women's Institute dancing at the Yorkshire County Federation of Women's Institutes folk dance Festival at Azerley Chase, Ripon, on Saturday. This team scored highest points (92) in the advanced class."

(E. Blenkiron)

1930 – 1940

Life in Hackforth Village in the 1930s

(Memory sketches by Joan Atkinson)

The Shop

"Visits to the shop (the Post Office) with the 'Saturday penny' were the highlight of the weekend. We asked for a penny worth of comfits (or aniseed balls) and were given a large packet full – plenty to keep us chewing for a day or two!"

"Often families went for picnics on the moors, and up the dales (before petrol rationing!)"

"Every year there was a Sunday School Trip. Two or three buses were hired, and everyone piled in, with buckets and spades ready to build sand castles, at Redcar or Scarborough"

"After school, on warm evenings, we would paddle in the stream or catch 'bully heads' in the nearby pond, which we had made by blocking up the stream so that the water flooded part of a low-lying field."

Some of the villagers of Hackforth worked at the saw yard. In the joiners shop there were 5 joiners. About 10-15 other men were employed to saw the wood, or make and repair gates. Adjacent to the joiner's shop, was a room with 2 big fireplaces. In this room glue was heated for repair work, and iron bars were heated until white-hot, to bore holes into the wood. An upstairs room was used for painting or tarring of gates, stakes and doors.

The Saw Yard also had a saw bench, where trees were made into stakes and logs. The large, jagged edge saw was powered by a water wheel built over the water flowing from the mill race.

The Old Mill

Situated near the Greyhound Inn, was another water wheel, grinding flour from corn. Local farmers brought the corn to the miller, and went away with flour. The miller lived in a small house adjoining the mill.

1930 – 1940

The Black Smith (Silver St.)

Originally, there were two large furnaces and an anvil. The fires were used for heating the iron bars and the hoops of cartwheels. Big benches were used for some of the work, such as making chains.

The house adjoining the Blacksmith was used as a public house (or meeting place?) where the men used to gather and talk over their work or gossip. Some of the men would take their tankards of ale and sit over the large fires at the Blacksmith at the end of the day.

Before the war, Joan remembers all the nice things they had to eat. Every Sunday, "we had a tin of peaches, pears, cherries or tangerines."

Visiting Vans

"The fruit van came around with apples, oranges, bananas, cherries and tomatoes. We used to go and eat them, either hiding inside the laurel bushes, or climb to the top of the haystack.

"On Thursday nights, a horn would sound, heralding the fish and chip van, as it stopped outside the Greyhound Inn. A small crowd of people holding hot tureens and dishes, would be waiting. The fish and chip man was relied upon to provide Thursday night's supper in all the surrounding villages.

1930 – 1940

... sat on the wall waiting for the ice cream man ...

The ice cream we waited for

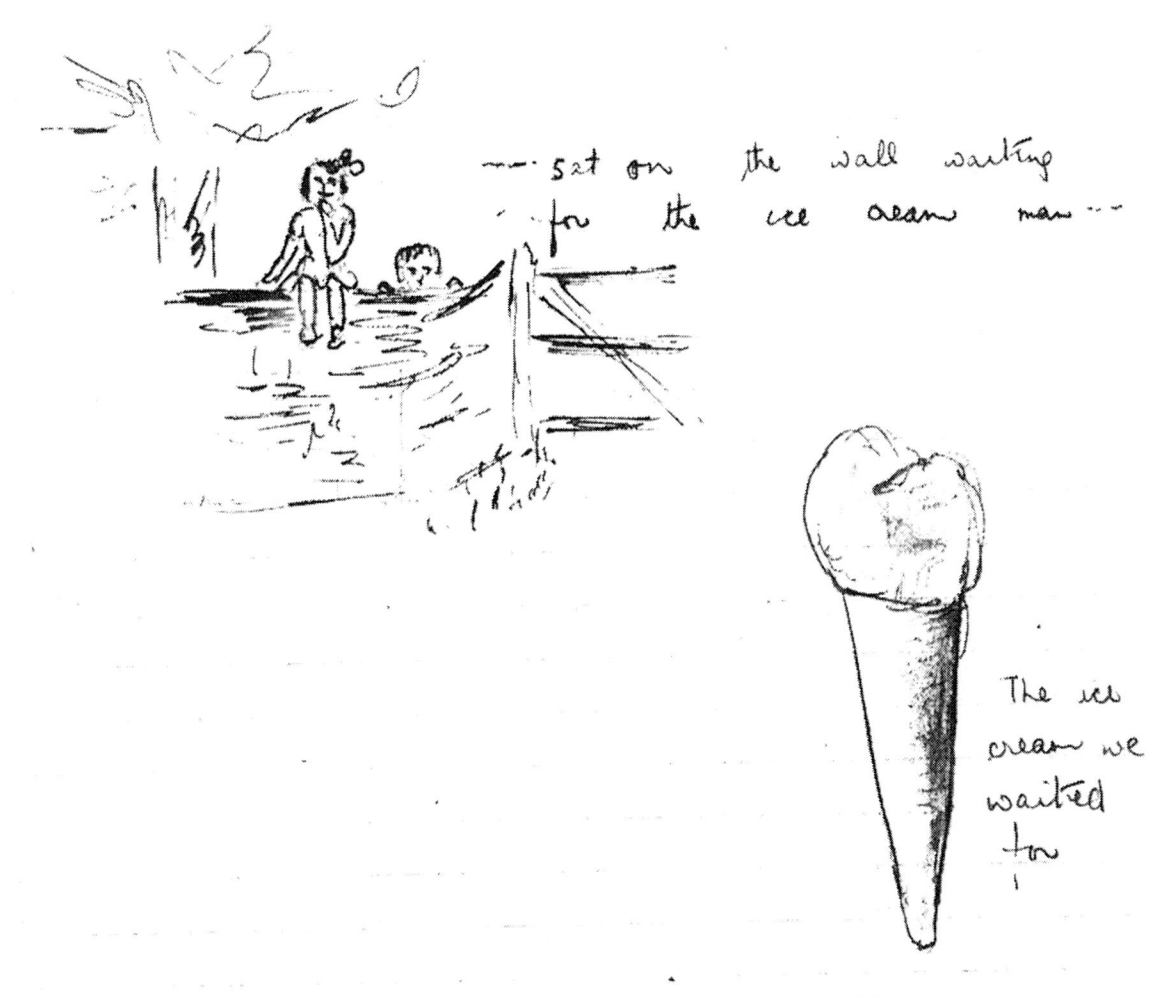

"Sundays we sat on the wall waiting for the ice-cream man from Bishop Auckland to arrive"

Royal Occasions

Royal occasions continued to be marked by special holidays:

29/11/34	School closed for the wedding of Prince George to Princess Marina of Greece
6-7/5/35	School closed for the 'King's Silver Jubilee Holidays' (George V)
06/11/35	School closed for the wedding of the Duke of Gloucester and Lady Alice Scott
28/1/36	School closed for the funeral of King George V (The entry for 21/01/36 reads "Death of the King. The portrait draped and references made during prayers.")
12/5/37	School closed for Coronation Holiday

The Coronation picture of King George VI with Queen Elizabeth and the Princesses, Elizabeth and Margaret

1930 – 1940

Christmas Memories of School before the War by Joan Atkinson

Before the end of term, the school was decorated and a large Christmas tree smuggled into school, always seeming to nearly touch the roof! The party was held at the school, with food provided by Mrs. Tyson (and her cook) from Rudd Hall. Every child received a present, which was rumoured to have come all the way from Santa at the North Pole. When the Village Hall was completed, the party was held there, which the children preferred as "the floor was like glass, and one could slide from one end of the room to the other!"

Friday afternoon was the favourite day for the infants, as for good behaviour, they were dismissed from school ¼ hour before the Juniors. However, Friday was also Library day, when both children and parents changed their library books, and then often didn't get home until 4 o'clock.

"When I was eight years old, war was declared – most of the nice things I mentioned were forgotten."

Girl guide and Scout 1937-1940
(Mavis Heeley)

1940 – 1950

The War Years (1939 – 1945)

The School log book gave an indication of impending war, as on 27th October 1938 the head teacher 'received and read out the circular regarding the Air Raid Precautions Care of Gas Masks' and in September 1939 he was preparing for, and admitting evacuees to the School.

The war had an increasingly noticeable impact on the area. Although initially, as Joan Atkinson in her diary reported, "Nothing much happened in the village, that was directly concerned with the war."

Then a few of the village men were called up, although many involved in essential services stayed. As food and commodities became scarcer, ration books, identity cards and gas masks were issued.

Talk in the villages centred on the German occupation of Poland, Holland, France and other European countries; and the heroism of the soldiers at Dunkirk. With the threat of invasion to Britain looming, everyone began to take the war very seriously indeed.

Silver Street in the black out

In the first six months of 1940, Hackforth School attempted to maintain some degree of normality with the children's education. Children, from Gateshead, who were evacuated to Hackforth, brought the number on the school role to over 60, and so extra staff was needed. A Gateshead teacher accompanied the children, and the 'Gateshead Party Leader', made many visits to ensure the well being of the evacuees. Seven children from East Appleton also joined Hackforth School about the same time, as the school they were attending closed.

School days were disturbed by war-related official visits. Inspector Smithson came to inspect the blackout curtains, while Mr Harold Webster, the local A.R.P. warden called to examine, test and readjust the gas masks of all the children. The children had already been issued with gas masks that had to be taken everywhere they went; if you forgot to bring your gas mask to school, you had to go back home for it! At school, if there was an air raid in the area, a whistle would blow, and the children immediately ran across the fields to the air raid shelter situated under the water wheel at the saw yard.

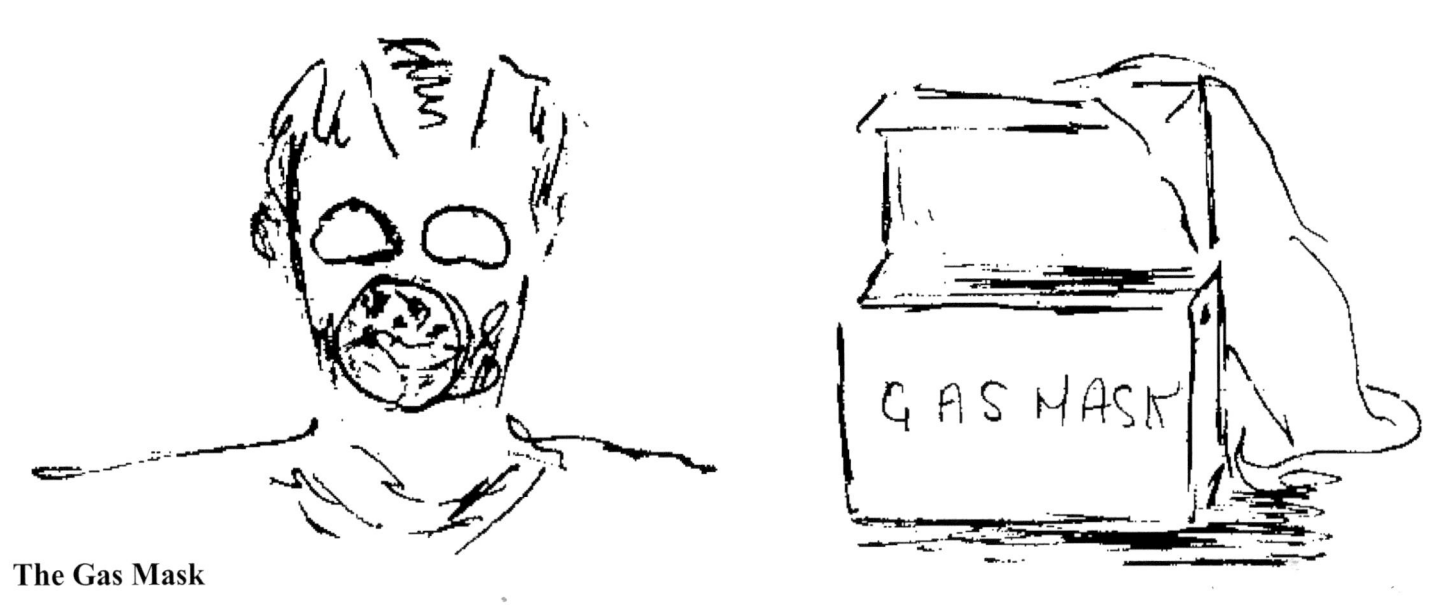

The Gas Mask

A pig, or someone in a gas mask? Yes, it was a gas mask!

The Vicar also took some interest in the safety of the school children. Over several visits he discussed the procedure for air raids and advised the children how to 'take cover'. He advised on making the windows splinter proof and the children assisted by pasting brown strips of paper on to the windows. The Vicar, together with Jeff Pocklington, the local glazier and joiner, discussed taking out and storing the glass from the fixed partition in the centre of the school. Five senior boys were sent over to the air raid shelter to help in its final construction.

The Air Raid Shelter

These precautions were all necessary, as air raid warnings were mentioned from July 11th 1940 onwards. There was a poor attendance at school on that day, as there had been two air raid warnings at 12.15 am and 6.15 am and school officially opened at 10.00 am. On August 14th, there was a daytime air raid warning just after the afternoon session opened. The Hackforth children were sent home while the remaining infant and junior children, with teachers Mrs Ross and Miss Bolton went to the Mill House shelter. The elder boys stayed at school with the head teacher, and took cover under the desks. After the all clear was sounded at 2.20 pm, the children reassembled at 2.30 for the remainder of the session.

By March 1941, the school timetable was changed to help in the country's need for food production. Gardening replaced handwork, drawing, history, geography and nature study. In fine weather essential digging replaced some lessons. On June 11th extra time was given to gardening, as more ground was required for potato planting. In September the school children were needed to help lift and dry the onions, and plant out a second batch of winter greens.

The school also became an Emergency Rest Centre at the end of 1941. The head teacher had to attend a meeting of Emergency Rest Centre Officers in Leyburn, and later '15 mugs, 1 dozen safety pins and a hose pipe were delivered to add to the equipment'. The ladies of the Rest Centre Volunteers had a rehearsal, organised by the head teacher, in which they had to assemble at the school as quickly as possible. Some got to the school fifteen minutes after the call.

Apart from education, 'there was a desire that the social amenities of the school should be a major concern.' So deliveries of 2 gallons of *Jeyes Fluid, Hygenol* and *Jeyes Corporation Powder* were recorded. The children and teaching staff 'attended a demonstration staged by the local military authorities. A bomb was exploded in the gravel quarry to demonstrate the danger of picking up strange articles that may be laying about.' (School log book) The demonstration arose from the fact that some of the children had found a live phosphorous bomb, which had to be removed by the Ordnance Squad.

Against this war background, low school attendance was also caused by a measles epidemic, and locally blocked roads due to severe winter snowstorms. However, school life continued as normally as possible. Various academic examinations were taken, and a Christmas party, arranged by Colonel and Mrs. Tyson, was held for the children in the Village Hall. Although it was mentioned that bomb damage to the ceiling was repaired on March 2nd 1945 there is no indication in the log book as to the extent or date of the damage.

There were at least four plane crashes locally that may have been linked to the fact that there were several aerodromes around this area. One fighter plane from R.A.F. Catterick crashed at East Appleton, killing the pilot, leaving the remains of the plane buried 2 feet deep in the ground. On the 8th November 1940, a Spitfire from 54 Squadron, again based at R.A.F. Catterick, was on a training flight. After take off, the plane gained height, but then went into a dive and crashed near Street House Farm. The plane caught fire, and the ammunition started to explode. Jimmy Ingledew, who was ploughing nearby, was able to pull the pilot, Sgt N R Miller from the flames, but he died later. Jimmy Ingledew was awarded the M.B.E. at the end of the war. The relatives of the dead airman returned every year to visit the Ingledews, and attend Hornby Church in his memory. In 1986 the site was excavated, and parts of the cockpit, canopy frame and a compass were recovered.

Another Spitfire crashed near to a barn at Roundhill, but the pilot was able to bail out and parachute to the ground.

1940 – 1950

After Dunkirk, a home defence force was formed, meeting in the Courtyard of Hornby Castle. Initially, the L.D.V. (Local Defence Volunteers) had no uniforms, and no guns, only hay forks or their own personal weapons. Later they received gas masks, a few rifles between them and an armband printed with L.D.V. Eventually, they all got uniforms and a rifle, and used to have shooting matches with other teams from the Home Guard.

They usually met on a Sunday morning for training at Hackforth School Yard or in the Castle grounds. One of their jobs was to take turns in watching all night from a tent near Street House Farm. They also got called out each time there was an air raid warning.

Home Guard at Hackforth School 1942 *(Mavis Heeley)*

Colin Dawson ~ aged 17 as a Home Guard

Hackforth Home Guard ~ 1943   *(Mrs Bardon)*

B. Scott K. Smith R. Pearson H. Robinson S. Hudson H. Blenkiron L. Robinson R. Ramsay A. Smith
H. Smith J. Rowntree G. Smith H. Ellerton F. Robinson T.K. Smith V. Morris J. Atkinson P. Ellerton
J. Pearson T. Carruthers P. Knox E.B. Johnson H.M. Webster R. Heeley E. Potts J. Ingledew H. Petch C. Dawson
J. Philips G Scurr J. Metcalfe O. Pearson C. Hart G Bardon C.G. Kilding

Home Guard Memories

by Peter Knox

The Home Guard was formed on the evening of the 14th May 1940 with a broadcast by Anthony Eden the Secretary of State for War. I am told that 40,000 men answered the call. We were given the title L.D.V. – Local Defence Volunteers. Comedians nicknamed us Look, Duck and Vanish. Later the name was changed to Home Guard and by the 31 July 1940, 1,600,000 had enrolled.

A local platoon was called the Hackforth and Hornby Platoon, of which I was a member. Any person with a gun, rifle or shotgun was encouraged to become a member. Those who had not a gun were encouraged to carry pitchforks or poles. I was issued with ball cartridges along with other members. Unfortunately the lead ball would not go down the choke barrel and later we were issued with buckshot.

Our first meetings were held at Round Hill Farm, Hackforth, our Headquarters. Our Commanding Officer was Mr Harold Webster who owned a car and a telephone, which was a great asset as he could soon be in touch with our HQ, the 12th North Riding Battalion with its Headquarters at Gilling. The Colonel was Lt Colonel Sir Richard Pease BT.

We were delegated watch duty. We went out in the early hours of the morning in pairs. A rota was formed and that meant we went out every 10 to 12 days, to keep a sharp eye on any intruders that were lurking around. We had no uniforms for six months and a bright bunch we looked, doing drill in the schoolyard at Hackforth in our wellingtons or hobnail boots. We were eventually issued with uniform and army rifles and a small amount of ammunition. We wore the cap badge of the Green Howards. We were given military tuition from the regulars from the local Garrison at Catterick Camp - Drill and, in particular, handling of guns and hand grenades. We had a very strict Sergeant in the name of EBD Johnson of Arbour Hill, a local farmer. We took part in rifle shooting competitions with other platoons and on an odd occasion against the regular army. We became quite expert at it. No drinking or smoking at least 5 days before a competition. Eventually we were issued with a Sten gun, which was a small automatic, not particularly good. Later on we were issued with the Lewis sub-machine gun, for which I was Corporal in charge. Ammunition was in short supply, but for target shooting we were issued 22 small-bore rifles.

The summer of 1941 – there was a danger of enemy dropping incendiaries, and as harvest was near, we had to go on duty all night long, from the top of Hornby Castle and another point was Street House Farm, the home of Corporal James Ingledew. There were four of us on duty at one time – 2 resting and 2 on watch. When not on duty we would rest, or sleep in a hen hut which had been prepared for us, but when we got the oil heater going we found that we had other company coming out of the woodwork.

1940 – 1950

One Sunday morning when we were on drill duty at Hornby Castle, a message came through that there was a farm fire at Mr Ingledew's farm, Street House, and help was needed. A number of us dashed off at full speed. My duty was being in charge of a horse and cart, leading sheaves of corn out into the field after the fire brigade had sprayed water on it to stop it burning. The horse was very nervous and could not be left.

Another instance was when one of our planes crashed on Street House Farm land. Corporal James Ingledew was very courageous in trying to save the pilot but unfortunately he was dead. Corporal Ingledew was awarded the MBE.

We were fortunate that we saw very little of the enemy. On one occasion an enemy plane passed over our farm, Mill Close, and dropped his unexploded bombs. It was my duty to report it to our Officer in Command. He notified the authorities, who 2 days later came and put up signs 'Unexploded Bombs - Keep Out." A considerable time passed before they were dug up and rumours had it that they were filled with sawdust!

We had many happy times in the Home Guard, however, it was hard work doing our work on the farm and doing our guard duty. The Home Guard was disbanded in December 1945 and I am told that 1,206 were killed and 557 injured. They received many decorations, 2 George Crosses and 13 George Medals.

This is how I remembered my time in the Home Guard. My memory is not improving and unfortunately there are very few of our members still alive to help me out with this report.

Some of the elders in the Parish should remember some details of a very large Ammunition Dump in the grounds of Hornby Castle during WW II.

Hackforth Camp

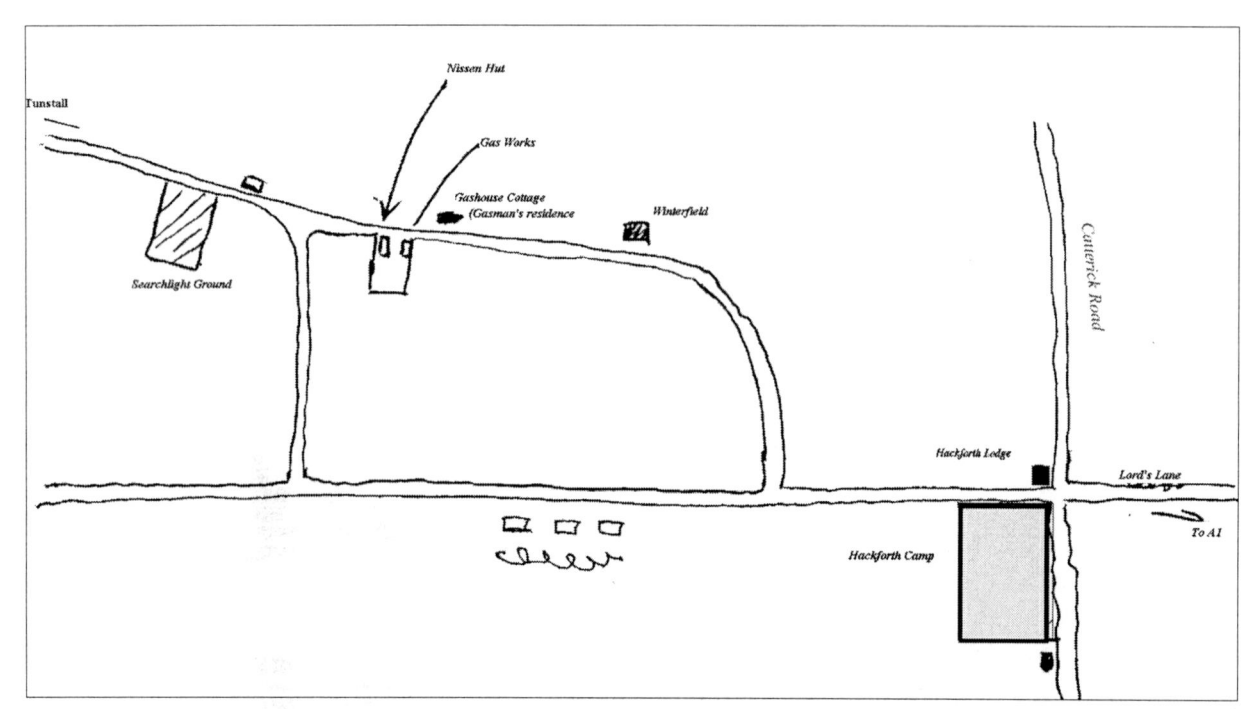

(Dennis Smith)

Hackforth Camp was built at the cross roads by the Park gates on the Hackforth/Hornby Road. The hutted camp was used by about 200 Pioneer Corps, who were responsible for bombs and ammunition in the area. They used a Nissan hut for cleaning, and repacking the bombs and ammunition. A lot of ammunition was stored at Winterfield, along the road from the crossroads on the Hackforth/Hornby road to the Castle, and in Langthorne at Cobshaw Lane, the Brickyard, and the fields, beyond. The Brickyard was also used as a gas cemetery – the gas was kept cool in the pond there but sometimes forgotten and found years later! On one occasion there was a gas leak, and the men involved had to wear their gas masks and return home.

Soldiers in tanks and Army lorries went on convoys through the villages. The Searchlight team used a hutted camp built a quarter of mile from Hornby Castle at Stripe Lane. They manned a light and a gun on the top of the Castle tower. The Army needed access to the A1, so laid tarmac on Winterfield Road, Stripe Road and Lords Lane.

1940 – 1950

The Castle had an indoor riding School that was used for training horses and men during the 1914-18 War. The Army had various effects on the local community. Initially, they used the Castle water supply, but it could not cope with the extra demand, so a new pump house was built near Hornby Gardens.

Four soldiers from the camp were killed in an explosion on an ammunition train near Brompton-on-Swale and are buried in Hornby Churchyard.

Funeral Procession

Casualties during the War: (Buried in Hornby Church Cemetery)

1941	Arthur Hillary	Aged 35	RAF Volunteer Reserve
1944	George Stares	Aged 34	Killed at Catterick Bridge Station in ammunition explosion
1944	David Reece Hopkins	Aged 23	Killed at Catterick Bridge Station in ammunition explosion
1944	William Thomas	Aged 18	Killed at Catterick Bridge Station in ammunition explosion
1944	Norman Day	Aged 17	Killed at Catterick Bridge Station in ammunition explosion

The Army used to go to the E.N.S.A. Dances and Concerts and the local pubs. Quite a lot of soldiers used to attend the Chapel services at Langthorne. They were then invited to Langthorne Hall for supper by Mr and Mrs Thompson.

E.N.S.A. Concert and dance (Entertainment Services)
(Sketch by Joan Atkinson)

The Military Police patrolled the area during the War. One of their jobs was to guard the entrance to the ammunition stores at Cobshaw Lane. They used Alsatian dogs that were kept in Kennels along the lane.

(Dennis Hurworth)

The Village Hall

The Military took possession of the Village Hall on the 6th September 1940, and paid £10 per quarter to use the Hall for office work and social events. The Wartime Dances were very popular and every month there was dancing to a live band such as 'Johnny Johnston'. It cost 6d to get in (8-12pm) and served tea, coffee, cakes & soft drinks. On the 9th September 1941, it was proposed that the Gents cloakroom should be closed at Dances, and a temporary structure erected in the yard!

On the 27th May 1942 it was agreed that the Military would pay for the Caretaker and the Electricity when they used the Hall. The School Managers had to discuss, on July 22nd 1943, the nuisances caused on Saturdays from the dances held in the Village Hall. The Head teacher had earlier written, "I myself requested 2 Airmen and 2 girls to leave the school garden where they were drinking beer close to the School House."

The visiting School Dentist used the Village Hall twice a year as his Surgery. During the War, extractions were "all by gas because of the War time conditions"

— more pictures —

1940 – 1950

Left - Land Army Girls
(Mavis Heeley)

Right - Land Army Girl assisting the farm workers
(Jenny Pybus)

With so many men called up for War Service the country was short of farm workers. So women, known as the Land Army Girls were given jobs on farms. Some lived on farms, while others lived in a hostel at Leeming or Scorton, and were transported to and from the farms every day.

Prisoners of War, particularly Russians, Germans and Italians were used as farm labourers and usually housed at Catterick Garrison. They were dropped off every day at the farm and collected later and generally regarded as good workers. German Prisoners of War worked at Hornby Castle.

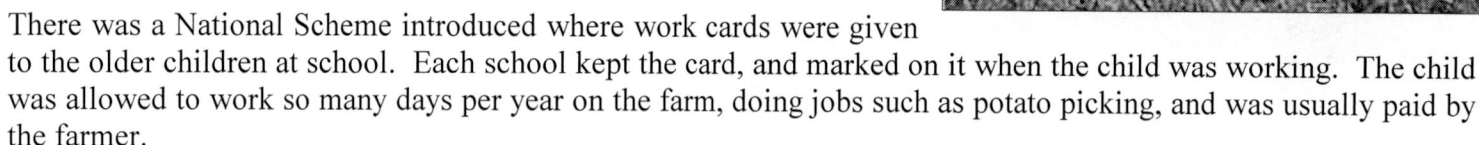

There was a National Scheme introduced where work cards were given to the older children at school. Each school kept the card, and marked on it when the child was working. The child was allowed to work so many days per year on the farm, doing jobs such as potato picking, and was usually paid by the farmer.

The Government wanted to increase farm mechanisation, so the Council set up Agriculture Executive Committees whose aim was for 99% of Agricultural land to be ploughed up for food production. The local one was called the North Riding of Yorkshire Agricultural Executive Committee, or WAR – AG for short! A Central Depot, near the railway station in Northallerton, would lease out equipment to undertake most mechanical farming operations of the time, e g Fordson Tractors. There were also local depots in Bedale, Leyburn and Richmond. The Council was also involved in local drainage contract work.

1940 – 1950

Everyone was issued with a ration card. Meat, eggs, butter, cheese, sugar, clothing and petrol were rationed. However, the country areas had advantages over the cities and towns, as they could provide extra eggs, lard, chickens, milk, rabbits, pigeons, and even eels from the Mill Race. The villagers grew their own vegetables and pig farmers were allowed to kill two pigs per year for food, although inspectors could come at any time to check this!

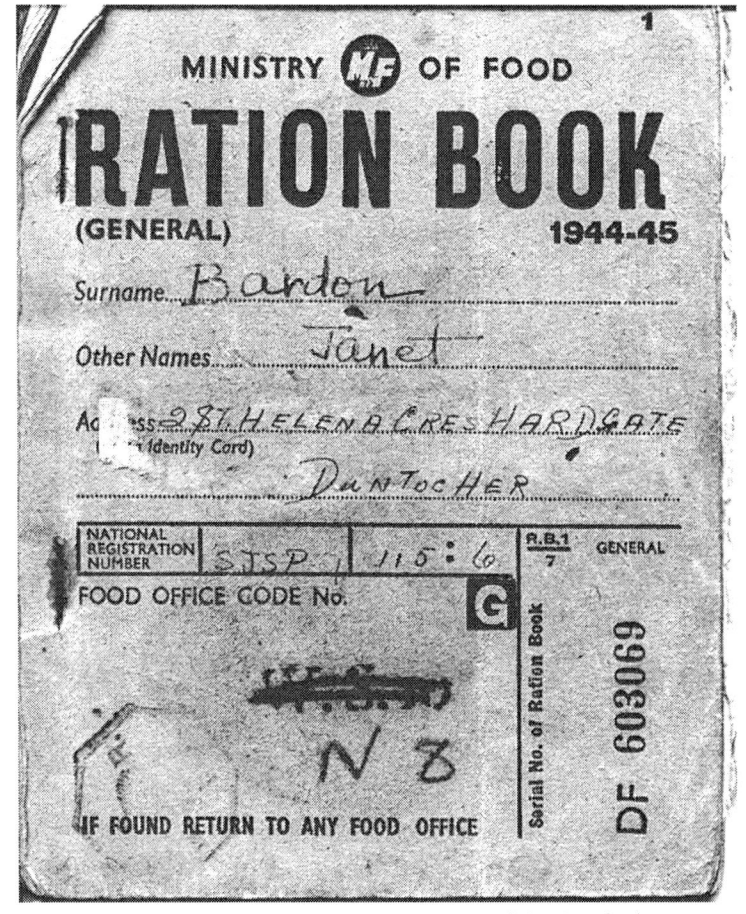

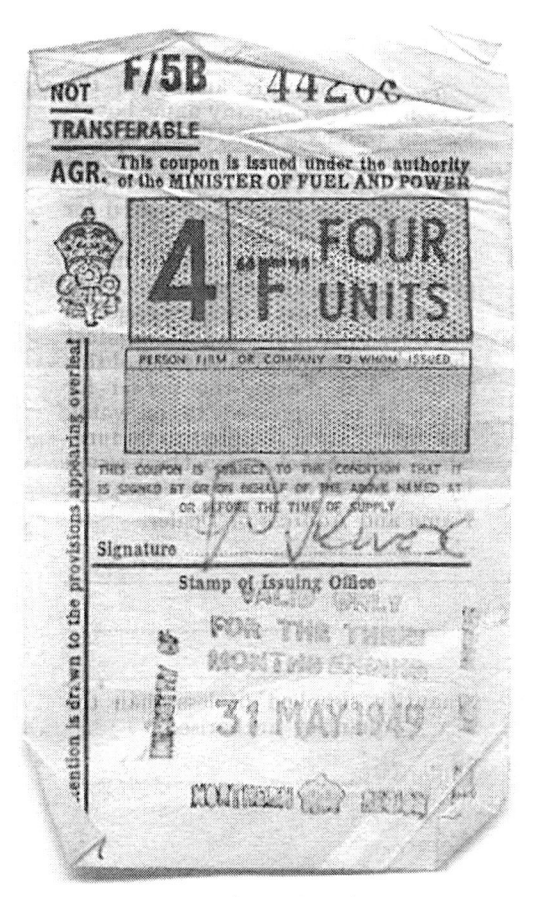

(Mrs Bardon)   *(Peter Knox)*

To supplement the clothing allowance, old clothes were recycled, and sweaters unravelled and re-knitted. Remnants of material could be bought from stalls at Bedale Market, and made into skirts, blouses and even coats.

1940 – 1950

Petrol was mainly reserved for essential services, so people did not go out very much. Instead, they sat at home by the fire, listening to the wireless, making sure there were no chinks in the black-out curtains! B.B.C. Radio broadcasts were easily received in the 1940s. The Home Service provided the local news, light entertainment and comedy were on the Light Programme, while the Third Programme was a restricted evening service of serious music. Farmers were given a special petrol allowance, and again random checks were made. 'The Black Market' operated especially at Christmas time, when certain goods and luxury items could be acquired.

The Pig Farm was started at the Saw Mill in Hackforth because of the waste food from the Army Camp. The swill was collected from the Camp cook house every day, put into barrels, cooked and then fed to the pigs. It took about an hour to feed the pigs every day, except on a Sunday. By the end of the War some 2,000 pigs were kept both at the Saw Mill and then at the Blacksmiths Farm in Silver Street, Hackforth, as well.

Aerial view of Pig Farm – Saw-yard at Mill House

The pigs were free to roam outside and used huts that were heated in winter. Litters of 14 – 16 were not uncommon, even then. However just after the War, swine fever affected the pigs and they all had to be destroyed.

The Corn Mill was brought back into operation during the War. Local farmers brought in their grain to be ground into flour.

End of War Celebrations

During 1944, dances, whist drives, and raffles were held in the Village Hall, to raise money for a Welcome Home Fund. Enough money was raised to give £10.0.0. to each of the returning soldiers, some of whom had been in Japanese Prison Camps, or in India for 4 or 5 years.

The W.I continued to meet every month, during the war years. Usually there was a talk, and a competition, which for example, may have asked members to bake a sponge cake, or to make a present for 6d. There was always a buffet, and all the members brought in a plate of food. The President, Mrs Tyson, had evacuees living in her home at Rudd Hall, and land army girls lived for a time at the Ingledews' home, Street House Farm.

1945 saw the end of the war in Europe, and Hackforth School was given 2 days holiday – May 8th & 9th. The School held a Victory Sports and Tea Party commencing at 2 pm on the 17th September 1945. On the 8th October, the school closed for the holidays to help the farmers.

In Hackforth, when the news of Victory in Europe (V.E. Day) came through, the children built a bonfire by borrowing a horse and cart and piling five loads of hedge cuttings on top. As soon as it was dark, the bonfire was lit. About 9 p.m., Captain Leach and his men started erecting some stands in a nearby field. A big pile of rockets, really for use as distress rockets on board ships, was let off, making a tremendous noise. The children were roasting apples and potatoes in the fire and having a singsong. Thunder flashes that were left over from when the Home Guard disbanded were let off.

Meanwhile the majority of parents were listening to the Kings speech at 9 p.m. before they came outside. Later, rockets were going up from all the villages around.

The Greyhound pub closed at midnight after free drinks all round, and the soldiers had gone back to camp. When they passed the dying bonfire, they had found two barrels of tar left by the road workers, and put them on the smouldering ashes, causing a big explosion!

V.J. Day (Victory in Japan) was another school holiday, and another bonfire was lit; this time a stuffed image of Hitler was carried on a stretcher and cremated. The Village was decorated with flags, and fireworks were let off. The children did not go to bed until 3 a.m.!

1940 – 1950

"England was so exhausted financially after the war, that doom and gloom, and rationing went on for years and years. Life was difficult because meat, bacon, butter, and sometimes even bread was scarce for a long time."

— Joan Atkinson's Diary.

Points had to be used to buy sweets and tinned food. Each district had an allocation of bananas, generally given to the children under 18, and oranges were becoming more plentiful. Rationing cards were needed for clothes, and petrol was still in short supply. However, people living in the country had the advantage of being able to obtain locally produced meat, vegetables and dairy produce. By killing a pig, a family could have plenty of bacon, ham and lard. Fruit, such as pears, apples, plums and vegetables from the gardens, could be stored or preserved. Eggs and milk were usually more readily available.

Hackforth School soon settled back into a peacetime existence with (over 50) pupils on the role. A return to the normal timetable was made, helped and advised by the regular visits of Education and Health Officials.

A school canteen opened on the 31st October 1945, and hot dinners were served to 45 children that day. This meant that children who travelled some distance to school could then have a cooked meal at lunchtime. Catering Officials now had to visit the school, and deliveries of orange juice and jelly were mentioned!

The weather had quite an impact on the attendance at school. In the winter of 1947, there was heavy snow, and on a particularly bad day, only 11 out of 53 children managed to get to school. The teaching assistant was also "absent from duty, owing to road conditions" (School Log Book)

School attendance figures were also affected by a variety of other causes; chicken pox was prevalent in the late 1940's. The older children, who possessed a working card, were allowed so many days off school each year to help on the farms. On a typical day, at these times, 28 pupils were present out of a total of 59 on the school role.

As the war ended, some of the traditional activities were resumed.

"Langthorne Methodist Church Sunday School Anniversary in 1948." *(June Thompson)*

Every year, as part of the Anniversary Service, the Sunday School children performed songs and poems. Afterwards a tea was provided by Mrs. Jenny Thompson at Langthorne Hall.

William Thompson, William, Robert, John, Richard and David Johnson.
Mrs Brown, Mrs Johnson, May Chapman, Mary Thompson and Jean Lumley.
Ivy Hall, Winnie Holland, Dora Johnson, Margaret Robinson, E. Starling, Margaret Holland, Dereck Brown – Colin Brown and Janette Hall (front).

Margaret Holland.
Ivy Hall, Winnie Holland, Dora Johnson, Dereck Brown, Margaret Robinson, Elizabeth Starling.
Colin Brown and Janette Hall

The Wedding of Miss Joan Heeley and Mr. Donald Chapman

(Mavis Heeley)

Miss Joan Heeley of East Arrathorne and Mr. Donald Chapman of Catterick were married at St Mary's Church, Hornby. The Reverend B.W. Crawford officiated, and Mr F. Bowe played the organ. The bride wore a heavy satin crêpe dress, and carried a sheaf of arum lilies. The reception was held at the Bridge House Hotel in Catterick Bridge, and the honeymoon was spent in London.

The two fathers had met 30 years before the wedding, while ploughing adjacent fields in Wensleydale.

"Little did either of us think that many years later, we would be related by marriage, although we have always been good friends."

Old Wedding Custom at Hornby

The wedding of members of two well-known farming families at Hornby, between Catterick and Bedale, on Wednesday, brought out a homely incident. At the reception the bride's father, Mr. Reginald Heeley, of East Arrathorne, recalled how, nearly 30 years ago, he was ploughing in a field in Wensleydale and had a chat with his neighbour, Mr. Tom S. Chapman, who was ploughing on the other side of the fence. "Little did either of us think that many years later we would be related by marriage, although we have always been good friends," he added.

When the bridal couple were held "to ransom" at the lychgate the bridegroom "paid up" and then threw a handful of silver and copper on to the road, but, strangely enough there was no rush to pick up the money. The elder children were at school and the "under-fives" who were present did not realise that the coins were there for their benefit. Eventually several mothers initiated their children into the mystery of the old custom.

During the wedding toasts, there was an apt description of Mr. Harry Marshall, the trainer, whom Mr. Johnson, of Arbour Hill described as "one who always looks happy, always is happy and always transmits happiness."

STARS OF THE PLOUGH GO "ON THE AIR"

IT TAKES THREE to plough furrows like these — two good horses and a good man to guide them. Picture was taken by Daily Express cameraman at the Skelton ploughing contest — biggest ploughing event in the north of England — at Calthwaite, Cumberland, yesterday. Moving here and there among competitors and spectators were (right) — B.B.C. men, recording the contest for tonight's broadcast (7.30 Northern). This one, his microphone attached to a long lead, is following a competitor as he ploughs. Snow at times spoiled visibility — and frost - hardened earth made things difficult for ploughmen.

Jim Knox ploughing and George Knox following in 1941, at the Skelton Ploughing Contest, in Cumberland.

"It takes 3 to plough furrows like these - two good horses, and a good man to guide them."

The contest was recorded for the BBC, with the interviewer following the competitor as he ploughed. Snow spoiled the visibility at times, and the frost hardened earth made things difficult for the ploughmen.

FAMOUS PLOUGH AT HORNBY

USED IN TRADITIONAL SERVICE

A "Speed the Plough" service was held in St Mary's Church, Hornby, on Sunday, when Divine Blessing was asked on the labours of the agriculturists of the combined parishes Crakehall, Langthorne and Hornby.

The service was conducted by the vicar (the Rev. B. W. Crawford) assisted by the members of the Bedale Young Farmers Club and Crakehall Agricultural Discussion Group, and was attended by a large congregation. Mr. Peter Knox, for the occasion, lent the famous plough with which his father, Mr. T.E. Knox, won numerous prizes all over the British Isles including the United Kingdom Open Championship at Nottingham in 1909. The plough was used by his sons also, in gaining their many successes.

The lessons were read by Messrs E B. D. Johnson (chairman, Crakehall and District Discussion Group), and Wm. Thompson (Jnr) and the plough team consisted of Messrs. P. Knox, G.T. Heeley, Wm. Thompson Jnr, W. Heeley and J. Downie.

The Vicar thanked all who had taken part in the service and in his address mentioned that the agriculturist's work was a labour of love and faith. In his opinion, he said, the request for a 'blessing' on seedling operations was a worthy prelude to a harvest festival.

1940s Farming

Grass was grown until it was long enough to cut for hay, usually towards the end of June.

The grass was turned once or twice after it was cut and then swept up into the stacks.

(Mavis Heeley)

Some farmers used an elevator to lift up the hay. One man put hay onto the elevator, while the man at the top passed the hay to the man who was stacking.

1940 – 1950

Willis Heeley, aged 16, forking the hay.
(Mavis Heeley)

If the haystack was not to be used until the spring, the stack was thatched with wheat straw, to prevent the rain getting in.

"All hands getting hay in using hand rake, horse rake and hay elevator, making a base for the stack with straw..." quote from farmer's diary June 21st 1949. *(Jim Ingledew)*

Oats, wheat and barley were all grown in this area. At harvest time, the fields were 'opened out' by a man using a scythe, followed by another man, who tied up the corn into sheaves with straw bands. This allowed the horse drawn binder to go round cutting and tying the sheaves of corn.

1944 ~ Stooking Rye at Langthorne

Left to Right: -
William Thompson, John Thompson, Oswald Hurworth and Mr. Thompson Senior.
(June Thompson)

The sheaves were stooked, about 8 sheaves to one stook, to complete the ripening and drying of the grain. Later, they were brought into sheds, or stacked outside. "One man scything oats, followed by another man tying up, then stooking up after the binder: from Jim Ingledew's farmer's diary, 3rd August 1949.

Father and son cutting the corn.
(Mavis Heeley)

More tractors were to be seen on local farms in the 1940s. They had cast iron wheels with road bands made of rolled steel at the rear, to allow them to go onto the roads.

After the harvest, came the potato picking, and the snagging of mangolds and turnips. They were piled up in the fields covered by straw and hedge cuttings, then soil, to protect them through the winter. They were used to feed the animals kept indoors, during the winter months.

1940 – 1950

1947 ~ Milk was put into churns in the farm dairy, then taken by horse and cart to the end of the road, to be collected by the Express Dairy Wagon.

(Mr Towler)

Miss Hutton-Squires taking part in the Point to Point, which took place every year at Hornby Castle.

(Mavis Heeley)

1940 – 1950

Extracts from Jim Ingledew's Farm Diary — 1949

Monday 3 January

Fine after hard frost

All riddling potatoes in L.B. after foddering except Mr Hunt who slashed fence down drive. Hunt took Leadbeatter's place riddling. Leadbeatter led homewares etc. then foddered. Oats - 51 grs loaded onto lorry from Collingham (NA. Leeds) to the order of Kenneth Wilson Std. Put up the 5 tons majestics.

Wednesday 9 February

Snow until 9.30, showers of sleet otherwise wind and sun

Sturdy here. Hunt got hay for lambs and ewes and turnips for ewes. He and self got 1 trailer load stones from W.P. heap. Hunt ploughing in B.H. until 1.45pm. Then loading manure from 2nd loose box to F.F. with cart. Leadbeatter and Clarkson took Mile's Roan heifer to bull after breaking. Sturdy and they cleaned out calf pens and 2nd loose box and helped to fill cart and tractor. Leadbeatter and Clarkson pulped. Self ploughed in F.F. until too wet in afternoon. Then led 2 loads manure.

Tuesday 8 March

Dull with bright intervals after more sun.

Hunt took hay out to ewes, all foddering. Hunt and self put new cogwheels onto corn drill. Clarkson changed engine oil in blue tractor. Leadbeatter grinding, Sturdy helping to bag meal and griping manure away from doorways. Lime spreaders here. Finished the 7½ acres in C.K. field, which did not get done in 1947. All clearing up after the spreaders except Leadbeatter who finished grinding and took and hung up the bacon in salt.

Saturday 16 April

Fine and very warm. Rain for 2 hrs at night

Bedale Point Races at Hornby Park

Wages		Insurance
5/-	Hunt	£5.00 + 15/- OT
5/-	Leadbeatter	£5.00 + 3/10d OT
5/-	Sturdy	£4.14.0

PAYE

5/-	Clarkson	£4.8.0
		£19.12.0 + 18/10d OT

Hunt scruffling early potatoes in O.F. Clarkson harrowing the rows down. Sturdy foddering and grinding. Leadbeatter ditto and put up 3 sheep nets in S.S. Thompson and self 2 trailer loads mangolds; 1 to ewes, 1 for cattle; also 1 load straw for pigs from mangold pie.

Thursday 26 May

Dull then bright periods.

Watch for Masham cow breaking. A Thompson not here. Clarkson away 2½ hrs at doctors. Hunt, Leadbeatter and self moved 9 Irish Bullocks and 1 English to High Balks. Dressed feet of 4 ewes and top and cut 2 lambs tails. Clarkson and Leadbeatter cleaned out pig box /carthorse stable fodder house and led it onto midden in B.H. Hunt dismantled damaged wooden draw-bar of low tractor trailer. Self helped vet's assistant who washed out Masham cow, inoculated Metcalfe's calf v. scour, and checked out Irish bullock. Hunt earthing up potatoes in B.H Self push-hoeing in peas in M.F. Leadbeatter and Clarkson finished luking thistles in O.F. Buck-rake delivered from Young's Motors Ltd

Monday 6 June

Fine and windy

Lost 1 ewe (died) when being clipped. R Pearson and J Rontree finished clipping sheep. Shot 10 wood pigeons

Paid R Pearson for clipping 50 ewes and 1 top at 10d each and 1/- top

Monday 25 July

Fine and very warm

A Thompson here. Started to pick Home Guard potatoes. All picking; estimated yield 3 tons to 1 acre. Hunt used potato digger. Received cheque from V.O.M. Bacon Factory for 6 pigs.

Monday 29 August

Fine, close/slight shower

1940 – 1950

A. Thompson here. Received cheque from Ministry of Food for potato and wheat subsidy (10 acres potatoes @ £12.0.0, 8 acres potatoes @ £8, 10 acres wheat @ £3.0.0) Hunt cut the 2" crop clover in 11 acre and finished it at 7.30pm. All others led B.H. Gartons seed barley and finished it. FINISHED HARVEST. Self tractor rake JL field after tea

Blue and white gilted pig had 8- total 3 gilts, 28 pigs, 2 still born

Tuesday 20 September

Fair and dull

A. Thompson here. Thompson and self cleaned out all pigs. Thompson and Sturdy led muck all day. Others also leading to IL with tractor and trailer. Sent 3 fat cattle to N/A (2 Irish and 1 heifer.) Pd N Hoddart cash for transport.

Friday 7 October

Fine, dull, warm

A Thompson here. All hands picked potatoes in BR except Leadbeatter and self who foddered and brought up 15 calves for subsidy. One calf was rejected. Weighed up and delivered all peas to Leeming Bar Station — 42 cwts 6½ stones (6½ st in own sack; 42 cwts in 21 BR sacks)

Tuesday 1 November

Fine, sun and mist

A Thompson not here. Hunt and Clarkson ploughed in B.R and finished it including headlands and ploughing in furrows at 3.45pm. Leadbeatter and self drew out 40 fat lambs, which were taken to N/A by N Hoddart. Paid cash. 1 lamb suffocated and had to be taken to the abattoir. Leadbeatter dodded the 11 gimmer lamb and put them to the top in S.S. Put up scarecrows in O.F. wheat, Clarkson disc-harrowed newly ploughed grassland in B.H. wheat land. Hunt and self-loaded trailer with 2 ton potassic supers and 9 cwt wheat and set it up. Small trailer load straw put in fold yard ex wheat rack heap.

Monday 19 December

Fair pm, heavy showers, windy, cold

GOOSE KILLING DAY

A Thompson not here. Clarkson and self killing and plucking poultry. Hunt, Sturdy and Leadbeatter forked out sheaves, left at bottom of bag, onto top of unthreshed bag. They then riddled pig potatoes. Hunt cleaned out pigs when Sturdy and Leadbeatter pulped.

The Farmer's Year – A 14-year-old's view of farming in the 1940s *(Joan Atkinson's book)*

January
Lambs begin to arrive in late January. When the snow melts ploughing can be done but there are still severe frosts, which hinder work. Hedges can be slashed or laid in spare time.

February
February is the month of lambing and the farmer is kept busy looking after the flocks. Ploughing is continued.

March
Corn is sown after the ground has been harrowed.

April
By April the weather has improved greatly and stock spend their nights outside. The lambs are quite big and their tails have been cut. Potatoes, turnips and mangolds have been planted.

1940 – 1950

May

The corn is about six inches high. All root crops are now planted and everyone is kept out of the fields where soon the hay cutter will work. In late May sheep are sheared ready for the warmer weather.

June

Sheep shearing continues. It must be finished in time for haytime, which begins in June.

July

The farmer makes hay while the sun shines, if not his crop will probably be spoilt by rain or wind. As summer has really come the sheep are dipped in disinfectant, which is used to keep flies and all the insects away.

August

The farmer is continually looking to see if his corn is ready to cut. By late August harvest has usually begun and everyone helps to gather it in. Sometimes haytime is not entirely finished by the time the harvest is ready and then the farmer becomes very worried.

September

September is the busiest time for the farmer. He 'rises with the lark' and 'works till dark'. All meals are taken to the fields because work cannot stop. The farmer's wife then is worried when there are eight or nine extra workers to feed.

October

October is usually potato picking month. Schoolchildren have two weeks holiday from school to help the farmer. They earn two or three pounds nowadays if they stick to their work for that fortnight. After the potatoes are safely gathered in, turnips and mangolds are 'snagged' – that means their roots and leaves are chopped off. Then they are put into 'pies' like the potatoes and are well covered with soil and straw as protection from the cold winter blasts. Threshing days are also busy days for the farmer and the farmer's wife: Feeding the workers – breakfast at 8 a.m.; tea break 10 a.m.; Lunch 12 noon; Tea 3 p.m. and Tea, etc, at 6 p.m. before returning home.

November and December

Odd jobs are done. Stock is inside for the winter, fed on hay and corn.

1940 – 1950

Transport

RIPON · BURRILL — Service 154

Thursday only

RIPON, Bus Station	0935	1318
North Stainley, Cross Keys	0947	1330
Mickley	......	1339
West Tanfield	0950	1349
Nosterfield	......	1354
Well	0956	1359
Snape	......	1403
Thornton Watlass	1006	1409
BURRILL	1012	1415

BURRILL	1015	1415
Thornton Watlass	1021	1420
Snape	1028	......
Well	1034	1431
Nosterfield	1039	......
West Tanfield	1044	1437
Mickley	1054	......
North Stainley, Cross Keys	1103	1440
RIPON, Bus Station	1115	1453

RICHMOND · BEDALE — Service 158

Tuesday only

RICHMOND, Market Place	0927	1227
Brompton, Crown Inn	0937	......
Catterick Bridge, Hotel	0939	......
Catterick Village, County Hotel	0943	......
Catterick Aerodrome	0945	......
Catterick Village, County Hotel	0947	......
Catterick Garrison, Post Office	......	1236
Catterick Garrison, Kemmel	......	1241
Scotton Village	......	1243
Tunstall	0951	......
Arrathorne Lane Ends	0959	1248
Hornby	1002	......
Hackforth	1007	......
Patrick Brompton, Post Office	......	1255
Crakehall, Green	1015	1300
BEDALE, Market Place	1020	1305

BEDALE, Market Place	1025	1310
Crakehall, Green	1030	1315
Patrick Brompton, Post Office	1035	......
Hackforth	......	1323
Hornby	......	1328
Arrathorne Lane Ends	1042	1331
Tunstall	......	1339
Scotton Village	1047	......
Catterick Garrison, Kemmel	1049	......
Catterick Garrison, Post Office	1064	......
Catterick Village, County Hotel	......	1343
Catterick Aerodrome	......	1345
Catterick Village, County Hotel	......	1347
Catterick Bridge, Hotel	......	1351
Brompton, Crown Inn	......	1353
RICHMOND Market Place	1103	1403

Tuesday was market day in Bedale, so a bus service was started in 1949 to link up some of the villages.

Service 158 ~ The bus service was only on a Tuesday, and continued until 1981. Langthorne also had a bus service on Tuesday. The bus from Richmond was always full, sometimes as many as 87 passengers, going into buy fish, cakes, bread and groceries from Bedale.

Every Monday, a bus went from Richmond, via Hackforth, to Darlington, returning later in the day, for the market there.

The service ceased in the early 70s.

1940 – 1950

Bedale Market Place

Marriage of H.R.H. Princess Elizabeth to Prince Philip of Greece ~ 20th November 1947

The school was closed for 2 days holiday on the occasion of the Royal Wedding.

After the war, school holidays changed, and resembled more closely, those of today. The end of the summer term was marked by a Sports Day. The children crossed the road and the beck to use the fields at Manor House Farm. Mr W. Johnson, a school manager presented the prizes to the successful competitors.

"A very enjoyable time was spent by all" (School Log book)

East Appleton 1920s – 1940s

Childhood memories of East Appleton – Jim Pearson

Late 1920 - 30s

"To the Manor Born."

Yes, we were born at Manor House Farm, East Appleton, delivered by Dr. Woodsend, who cycled many miles, in all weathers, looking after his patients, assisted by Nurse Coates, the District Nurse.

I have early memories of helping in the fields in springtime, haytime and harvest, potato picking and snagging mangolds and turnips. Farming in the 1930s was hard, manual work, with horses doing the ploughing, sowing and harvesting, receiving low returns for the produce. We went to Bedale market on Tuesdays, first by pony and trap, then by Fred Dennis's bus from Tunstall, or the Ashmans' bus from Scorton, both of which passed the lane end to the farm. Later, we went by motorbike and sidecar, then a *Morris Minor* car! The Jewish traders from Leeds would meet us coming into Bedale and haggle over the price they would give for the hens, rabbits, eggs and butter we had to sell. Then mother would pay the weekly shopping bill and collect groceries from Ernest Petch's shop, going onto Reg Hustwaite's shop for shoes, boots etc., and then maybe across to Natrass' or Hewson's for clothes etc. Always something was needed from Thompson's hardware shop, and an occasional haircut at Barber Shaw's. The accumulator for the wireless was taken into Gunner Watson's shop for re-charging about once a month, and where we also got replacement parts for our bicycles, brake blocks, pedals, tyres and tubes.

We lived mainly on home produced food, milk, butter and cheese, killing one and sometimes two pigs, nothing being wasted, even the bladder was blown up to make a football! The blood was used in black puddings. Rabbit, hare, chicken and ducks were also available with plenty of home grown vegetables and fruit.

Memories of East Appleton 1920s – 1940s

We walked to Catterick school, occasionally being taken by horse and cart during the heavy snow in winter. We took sandwiches for lunch, except when the mobile cooking van came for a week so that the senior girls could learn the art of cooking, for which they had to take ingredients from home. The boys ate what the girls had produced – and we survived! Joining us on the journey to school were Greta and Mabel Stockdale, Henry and Gordon Cartright, Pauline Peirson, Dorothy Salter, Alan and Stanley Thompson and Greta and Jessie Coates from Limekiln Farm.

We had plenty of jobs to do on the farm, before and after school, feeding calves and pigs, milking cows and taking the milk into the dairy, which was in the house, to be cooled by water pumped up from a well in the backyard. We hoed turnips and mangolds in the evenings after tea for about a penny for every hundred yards! Haytime and harvest were busy times, most of the work being carried out by horses, such as cutting, tuning, dashing, rowing up and sweeping it to a stack in the middle of the field. Sometimes making hay cocks and pikes, which were later led home into the shed. Again with corn, wheat, oats and barley, bindering (after having "opened out" around the outside with a scythe and fastening the sheaves with straw bands) stooking was next and then leading them home to be stacked in the Dutch barn. 'Thrashing' took place in springtime, and these were long, hard days. The thrashing machine (Ned Whitfield's from Tunstall) came between six and seven in the evening and was set up ready for an 8 o'clock start the following morning. They arrived early to fill up with coal and water and then get 'steam up' followed by a breakfast in the farmhouse. There was a prompt start at 8 o'clock, with men coming from neighbouring farms to help and often Bob Hurworth from Hackforth. As youngsters, our first job was in the Chaff Hole, so covered with barley corns and dust that we ended up as black as the Ace of Spades by night! As years went by, we graduated into 'cutting bands', giving the sheaves to 'Tony' who fed them into the machine, and who after a few pints the night before, would throw them back at us if they were the wrong way round! Later, we worked at the corn end of the machine, taking the sacks of corn round to the granary by horse and cart. Our three horses were *Maisie*, *Jet* and *Captain*, who remained on the farm until the mid forties.

Our mail was delivered by Postman Coates from Catterick and arrived mid morning. He would whistle all the time, no particular tune, just whistling! He came again in the evenings to collect letters from the post boxes at East Appleton and Rudd Hall. There was talk of war against Germany in 1938/1939, and we were issued with gas masks, identity cards and ration books. An army camp was built in the field next to the road, with pillboxes appearing in most fields, and an anti-aircraft gun on the hilltop manned by men from the Staffordshire Regiment. We dug out and built an air raid shelter in the garden with food and water in it, although we never had to use it.

Home from the Fields
– Jim Pearson

East Appleton in the 1940s

September 3rd 1939 saw things alter for us all, when war was declared with Germany. Also in September came a change of schools for me – to Richmond Grammar School until 1944. A girls' school was evacuated in to the area, St Bede's, and they shared our school premises and various other buildings in the town.

We had already been issued with gas masks and Identity Cards, which we had to carry with us all the time and show when asked for.

Each morning we milked four cows, then washed and had breakfast before cycling to Catterick Village, 1¼ miles, to catch the No.48 United Bus to Richmond. Later on, we cycled to Catterick Bridge Station, 3 miles, to catch the 8.40 train to Richmond. If we missed that, we had to cycle all the way up to Richmond and school.

We had numerous R.A.F. wives staying at the farm to be near their husbands who were serving at RAF Catterick. Special Constable (Full time) Gordon Brown lived at Holomoor (Hackforth) and was a frequent caller on his way home from Catterick. On occasions he brought bad news for some of the RAF wives who were staying with us, that their husbands had been killed in action, or were missing. Our nearest "Evacuee" was Henry Elliott, from the Tyneside area, who was billeted with Col. and Mrs. Tyson at Rudd Hall. I played cricket and rugby (no football at the Grammar School in those days) for the school, joined the Army Cadet Force under Major Joe Pattern, our Chemistry Master, and even gained a couple of stripes!

We still continued our work on the farm in the evenings and were allowed days off from school to help with haytime, harvest and potato picking. Locals and the occasional Italian prisoner of war who were billeted at Catterick Camp also gave a hand.

Whilst travelling back from school in Richmond on the 4 o'clock train on Friday 4th February 1944, we were between Broken Brea and Catterick Bridge Stations, when an ammunition explosion occurred in the goods sidings, where troops were loading ammunition, to support the D-Day landings. The train came to a sudden halt and all we could see and hear were massive flames and explosions. The train eventually moved on again, dropping us off to collect our bicycles and ride on home. Eight civilians and four soldiers were killed; the soldiers from the Army Camp at Hackforth are buried in Hornby Church Yard. No doubt there could have been many more casualties if a train had been in the station! (See page 135)
"There but for the Grace of God go I."

Leaving school in 1944, I went to work in the South of England for a firm called Pest Control Ltd set up by an Austrian Dr Ripper! Living and working in Kent from dawn till dusk, I saw RAF Typhoons chasing and sometimes shooting down 'doodle bugs'. Lying in bed at night, I wondered where the 'doodle bugs' were going to drop when the engines stopped! Then came the V2 rockets, which gave no warning! I remember coming home on holiday and sheltering in the tube stations waiting for the "All Clear" before catching a train from Kings Cross to Darlington and then on to Catterick Bridge. I moved to the Worcestershire and Hereford areas spraying fruit trees and hops, being based in Evesham.

In October 1945, an O.H.M.S. letter from His Majesty King George VI arrived, requesting my pleasure in the Royal Navy, and the rest is, as they say, history.

Jim, m'lad!!

1950-1960

St Mary's Church, Hornby

1950 Aerial View Showing the graveyard, but few trees compared to present day.

(Mrs Bardon)

The Marriage between Miss Joan Pierson (the Saw Mill, Hackforth) and Mr Frank Atkinson at Hornby Church

14th February 1953

1950 – 1960

Left & below:
Decorated for Easter and Christmas 1953
(Peter Knox)

Bottom left:
Decorated for Harvest ~ 1954   *(Mrs M Heeley)*

1950 – 1960

Television was first available in the area about 1951. The "BBC" was broadcast from Holme Moss transmitter, near Huddersfield, ABC Broadcasts were from mid-afternoon until 11.30pm approximately, with the first all day broadcast being the Coronation.

ITV was available from the transmitter at Emiley Moor, near Huddersfield, and later from Burnhope. Originally Granada T.V. operated during the week, and ABC T.V. at weekends, before Yorkshire and Tyne Tees took over. Both stations were more easily available once the Bilsdale transmitter opened.

Royal Occasions

Death of King George VI

On 6th June 1951, "Rev. Crawford visited the school again this afternoon at 2 p.m., and announced the sad news of the death of King George VI to all children present. Rev. Crawford granted the closure of the school for the rest of the afternoon session as a mark of respect to the memory of our beloved King." (School logbook)

Coronation of Queen Elizabeth II

The following year, the children "decorated the exterior of the school in honour of Her Majesty Queen Elizabeth II's Coronation." Their efforts were well received since on June 4th 1953, Mr. W. Johnson, a school manager, called on behalf of the Village Coronation Committee, and brought in a large bag of sweets for each child as a tribute to the way in which they had decorated the school for the Queen's Coronation."

A committee was formed to oversee the local celebrations in Hackforth.

Coronation Leaflet

Elizabeth R

Coronation 1953

HACKFORTH CELEBRATIONS

LONG MAY SHE REIGN

1953
CORONATION
HACKFORTH CELEBRATIONS
PROGRAMME OF EVENTS

1. Best Decorated House (Exterior) — Houses to be judged
2. Best Flower Garden
3. Best Vegetable Garden — Both to be judged end of May

Prizes: 1st £2, 2nd £1, 3rd £10/-

Entries to Hon Secretary, Mill Close, Bedale

---

2 p.m. FANCY DRESS PARADE and CHILDREN'S SPORT

Girls' Original Costume   Girls' Comic Costume
Boys' Original Costume   Boys' Comic Costume

Prizes: 1st 5/-, 2nd 3/-, 3rd 2/-

Age		1st	2nd	
Under 5	25 yards flat	2/-	1/-	3d others
5-7	40 yards flat	2/-	1/-	3d others
7-9	60 yards flat	2/-	1/-	3d others
9-11	80 yards flat	2/-	1/-	3d others
11-14	100 yards flat	2/-	1/-	3d others
14-15	100 yards flat	2/-	1/-	3d others
Wheelbarrow race boys		2/-	1/-	3d others
Potato race boys and girls		2/-	1/-	3d others
Three legged race boys and girls		2/-	1/-	3d others
Sack race boys and girls		2/-	1/-	3d others
Skipping race girls		2/-	1/-	3d others

It is hoped to give these prizes in Coronation souvenirs

Age		1st	2nd	3rd
15-17	100 yards flat ladies and gents	5/-	3/-	2/-
17-25	100 yards flat ladies	5/-	3/-	2/-
17-25	100 yards flat men	5/-	3/-	2/-
26-40	100 yards flat men	5/-	3/-	2/-
26-40	100 yards flat ladies	5/-	3/-	2/-
Over 40	men walking backwards	5/-	3/-	2/-
Egg and spoon race ladies (real eggs)		5/-	3/-	2/-
Three-legged race ladies and gents		5/-	3/-	2/-
Sack race ladies		5/-	3/-	2/-
Sack race men		5/-	3/-	2/-

Tug of war teams of six from areas if possible – Hackforth, Hornby, Appleton, Langthorne and Ainderby Miers.

WHIST DRIVE in the Schoolroom – good prizes

SOCIAL and DANCING in the Village Hall – 9-1 a.m.

JOHNNY JOHNSON'S BAND – Spot dances, etc.

TEA in the Village Hall 4-6 p.m. for all.
Presentation of souvenir mugs to the children

GOD SAVE THE QUEEN

1950 – 1960

Her Majesty Queen Elizabeth II

1950 – 1960

A summer fête was organised regularly at Hornby Castle.

The Children country dancing
(Mrs Bardon)

Visiting the Stalls
(Mrs Bardon)

The children perform
(Mrs Bardon)

Farming ~ 1950s

Above: A Ferguson tractor and binder cutting beans ~ 1958

(R Towler)

Top right:
Using an elevator to stack straw (a round straw stack) ~ 1954

(Mavis Heeley)

Right:
A bailer attached to a threshing machine ~ 1950s
(Taken in 1980s - Peter Knox).

1950 – 1960

Left:
Langthorne

(Mrs. June Thompson)

Below:
Saw Yard, Hackforth

(Mrs Joan Atkinson)

Left:
Silver Street, Hackforth

(Mrs. Joan Atkinson).

1950 – 1960

Jeff Pocklington, originally from Langthorne, off to the Festival of Britain Pageant held in Bedale in 1951. (He was an undertaker based in Crakehall.)

(Mrs. J. Thompson)

Point to Point at Hornby Castle ~ 1954

The horses get ready for the race, watched by a good crowd.
(Mavis Heeley)

Jumping a fence
(Mavis Heeley)

1950 – 1960

The Women's Institute

At Christmas time, the W.I parties were a great social occasion – dancing and party games. Mrs. Tyson was succeeded as President in 1957 by Mrs. Anne Clutterbuck

1950 – 1960

Mrs. C. Ingledew (oldest member) cutting the cake at the 25th birthday party of the Hackforth Women's Institute on Thursday. On her left is Mrs. C. E. Tyson, who has been president for the 25 years. Others in the group are members of the committee.

Hackforth W.I

Mrs. C. E. Tyson, of Rudd Hall, Hackforth, who has been president of the Hackforth Women's Institute for 25 years, receiving a bouquet presented by the treasurer, Mrs. J. Darling (right), at the Institute's garden party held at Rudd Hall on Thursday.

1950 – 1960

HACKFORTH W.I.

CORONATION 1953

PROGRAMME

FOR HOME AND COUNTRY

Committee

President: Mrs. Tyson

Vice-Presidents: Mrs. Clutterbuck
Mrs. Ingledew
Mrs. Murfin

Secretary: Mrs. Don Chapman

Asst. Secretary: Mrs. Douglas Chapman

Treasurer: Mrs. Darling

Press Correspondent: Mrs. Kitching

Magazine Secretary: Mrs. Johnson

Mrs. Gill, Miss V. Ingledew, Miss Metcalfe, Mrs. Piggins, Mrs. Ramshay

Meetings are held on the second Thursday in the month, unless otherwise stated at 7.15 p.m.

Annual Subscription 3/6.   Visitors 6d.

January 8th.
Talk "My Flight to New Zealand" by Mrs. Clutterbuck
Competition An addressed envelope to:—
The Reverend B. W. Crawford,
The Vicarage,
Crakehall,
Bedale,
Yorkshire
Social Half-hour Miss S. Rudd
Hostesses Mrs. W. Scott, Mrs. T. Scott, Mrs. H. Smith, Mrs. J. F. Robinson

February 12th.
Demonstration Knitting by Mrs. Dick
Competition Darn approx. 1" square with matching wool
Social Half-hour Mrs. Garget
Hostesses Miss S. Smith, Mrs Atkinson, Miss Atkinson, Mrs. Blenkiron

March 12th.
Demonstration Cooking by Mr. Mawer
Competition Bowl of bulbs
Social Half-hour Mrs. F. Robinson
Hostesses Mrs. Bardon, Mrs. J. D. Chapman, Mrs. Clutterbuck, Mrs. Darling

April 9th.
Demonstration Barbola work
Competition Decorated Easter Egg
Social Half-hour Mrs. R. Murfin
Hostesses Miss Darling, Mrs. Dodds, Mrs. Poteb, Mrs. Garget
EGG COLLECTION FOR HOSPITALS

May 14th.
Demonstration Smocking
Competition Tea Cosy
Social Half-hour Mrs. Piggins
Hostesses Mrs. Gill, Miss D. Hutchinson, Mrs. Hobson, Miss Ingledew

July 2nd
GROUP RALLY at BROUGH HALL

July 9th
Demonstration Flower Decoration by Miss Frank
Competition 7 blooms of any kind in a kitchen utensil any foliage—arranged for effect
Social Half-hour Mrs. Anderson
Hostesses Mrs. Johnson, Miss Johnson, Mrs. Kitching, Miss Metcalfe

August 13th
Demonstration Tatting by Mrs. Rogers
Competition Articles in a matchbox beginning with 'B'
Social Half-hour Miss S. Smith
Hostesses Mrs. Murfin, Mrs. R. Murfin, Mrs. Marley, Mrs. Peacock

September 10th
22nd BIRTHDAY PARTY
Competition Butter Iced Cake
Hostesses Mrs. Peirson, Mrs. Piggins and other helpers

October 8th
Talk "Denman College" by Mrs. Anderson
BRING & BUY STALL
Competition Knitting from Mrs. Dick's demonstration
Social Half-hour Miss E. Smith
Hostesses Mrs. Ramshay, Miss S. Rudd, Mrs. Weighell

November 12th
Talk by The Hon. Mrs. Schofield, V.C.O.
Competition Christmas Present
Hostesses Mrs. Player, Mrs. Wilson and other helpers

DECEMBER
SOCIAL EVENING

Hackforth School

Visitors see Hackforth Village School at work

Mr. Hayutu, in charge of Province of Misauna Education Department, and Mr. Ilyasu, Development Secretary in the same province, two of the Northern Nigeria officials on a fortnight's visit to Richmond, seen yesterday during a visit to the village school at Hackforth. The two children are Diane Dawson, of Hornby, and Graham Farnaby, of Hackforth, both aged five. The teacher is Mrs. D. F. Pontefract. Other officials visited Hunton School where they watched a PT display and took part in a cricket match.—[N.E.]

"Visitors See Hackforth Village School at work"

In the 1950's Hackforth School developed closer links with the Commonwealth.

The school received a gift of apples, sent as part of the Commonwealth Gift Scheme.

(Northern Echo)

1950 – 1960

School Timetable

The timetable from the 1950s shows similarities to our present timetable. Mornings were generally spent doing Mathematics and English. It is interesting to note that the infants always had 15 minutes of Physical Training at 11a.m. every morning, while the juniors had theirs from 10.25-10.45 every morning, except Friday. Afternoons were more practical. The infant boys had handwork and drawing, while the girls had needlework. In the junior class, the boys were expected to do gardening or craft, while the girls again did needlework.

Day	Morning 9.25–9.40	9.40–10.25	10.25–10.45	10.45–11.0	11.0–11.15	11.15–12.0	Afternoon 1.0–1.30	1.30–2.0	2.0–2.20	2.20–2.30	2.30–2.45	2.45–3.5	3.5–3.30
Monday	Assembly & Act of Worship	Group work in Reading Writing and Number		Music	Physical Training	Group work in Reading Writing and Number	Boys Handwork and Drawing / Girls Needlework				Games	Poetry History	Story
Tuesday	Assembly & Act of Worship	Do	Do	Recreation	Do	Do	English and Word Building	Handwork		Recreation	Do	Do Geography	Story
Wednesday	Assembly & Act of Worship	Do	Do		Do	Do	Boys Handwork and Drawing / Girls Needlework				Do Speech Training	Nature Study	
Thursday	Assembly & Act of Worship	Do	Do		Do	Do	History Story	English Word Building	Poetry		Do	Story Drawing	
Friday	Assembly & Act of Worship	Do	Do		Do	Do	Geography Story	Drawing			Do	Poetry Dancing	

DUPLICATE — INFANTS' TIME TABLE — Date 1st February 1951

The classes should be entered in descending order of age.

1950 – 1960

HACKFORTH and HORNBY C.E. School.   JUNIOR and SENIOR Department.

TIME TABLE for the Educational Year commencing 1st of 19.

MORNING / AFTERNOON

Day	Class	9.35–10.25	10.25–10.45	10.45–11	11.0–11.30	11.30–12.0	1.0–1.40	1.40–2.20	2.20–2.30	2.30–3.0	3.0–3.30
MONDAY	Senior	Arithmetic Oral and Written Training	Recreation	Physical Training	Music	English	Boys Gardening or Craft		Art and Craft	English	
	Junior				Music	English	Girls Needlework			English	
TUESDAY	Senior				Geography	English	Science and English		Art and Craft		
	Junior				English	Geography	English and Nature St.				
WEDNESDAY	Senior				History	English	Boys Gardening or Craft		English		
	Junior				English	History	Girls Needlework		English		
THURSDAY	Senior				Geography	English	Handwork	English	Music	English	
	Junior				English	Geography	Handwork	English	Music	English	
FRIDAY	Senior	English	History	English	Science	English	English	Games			
	Junior	English	English	History	English	Nature St.	English	Games			

ANALYSIS
Number of Minutes devoted to each subject per week.

	SENIOR	JNR
RELIGIOUS INSTRUCTION	175	175
ENGLISH — (a) Reading	170	150
(b) Recitation	30	30
(c) Composition and Grammar	180	170
(d) Literature	60	60
(e) Writing	30	30
ARITHMETIC (including Mental)	250	250
HISTORY	60	60
GEOGRAPHY	60	60
MUSIC	60	60
ARTS & CRAFTS (a) Art (Drawing, etc.)		
(b) Craft	100	100
(c) Needlework or Needlecraft GIRLS	160	160
SCIENCE (including Hygiene) Gardening BOYS	80 / 60	80 / 60
PHYSICAL TRAINING Games	80 / 30	80 / 30
DOMESTIC SCIENCE Cookery, etc. HANDICRAFT (Woodwork)		
RECREATION Any other subjects	125	125
Total No. of Minutes	1650	1650

NOTES

Registers are marked 9-0 a.m. and closed 9.15 a.m.
Registers are marked 1.0 p.m. and closed 1.20 p.m.

1950 – 1960

By the 1950s, the children were no longer expected to walk to school from Hornby, but snowy conditions still affected school attendance. "The school taxi did not run today," as "there is very deep snow and icy roads."

Opportunities for P.E. lessons improved when Mr. Johnson, a school manager, said the children could use his field opposite the school for games from May 7^h 1957.

The School Log Book mentioned on 13th January 1954, "It was a very dark, rainy morning, and the light was very poor." So in March, a request was made for "electric light throughout." This request was granted, but unfortunately, there was a delay in the installation of "the Electric light" It was noted on 8th November, 1954, that "There is still no light, in school, this afternoon was so dark we used candles," and three days later "my room is so dark, we cannot see to read at 9.30am." Some temporary lights were fitted in the school on 12th November 1954, and the permanent wiring was completed early in 1955.

Many residents in Hackforth, Hornby and Langthorne remember electricity being installed from the 1950s onwards. This replaced candles, gas and paraffin lamps, although some people still used candles until much later.

The Lodge 1955

(Mavis Heeley)

1960-1970

Hackforth School

1962

1965

1960 – 1970

The number of children on the school roll was 25 in 1960, and by 1965 had declined to 20. This meant that after Easter 1965, the school had only one teacher — Mrs. Dean.

Dec 13th 1963

This photo taken from the school log book shows the junior class with Mrs. Dean standing in the school playground.

Graham Farnaby, Terry Joblin, Brian Hunt, Ann Brunskill, John Murfin, Mrs Dean, Doreen Metcalfe, ?? , ?? , ?? , Linda Wilson, David Rudd, Barbara Hillary, Jacqueline Metcalfe.

The children used the field opposite school for games.

Back: John Reynolds, Terry Joblin, Jacqueline Metcalfe, Stephen Reynolds

Front: Robin Johnson, Philip Fullerton, Brian Hunt, David Errington

1960 – 1970

In 1961 Bedale Rural District Council requested that the Education Committee install flush toilets at Hackforth School. As there was no mains sewage in the village, this eventually took place in 1965, using a septic tank.

Road Safety instruction was considered increasingly important for school children, and was now becoming part of school life, with a cycle safety check being carried out on July 5th 1961.

North Road, Hackforth, with the Post Office

1960 – 1970

The Post Office

It was situated at 1, North Road, Hackforth in the 1960s. Mr. and Mrs. Metcalfe took over the business in December 1969, after being interviewed by the Head Postmaster at Darlington Post Office.

Quote from Jean Metcalfe's Memories:

"We arrived in Hackforth in December 1969. Before we were able to proceed with the purchase of the property and business we had to attend an interview with the Head Postmaster at Darlington Post Office. This was to make sure that we were suitable candidates to run a local Post Office.

As soon as we took over the Post Office an Officer from Head Office spent considerable time showing us the ropes. Certainly for the first week he was in attendance from opening to closing of the Post Office. Although much of the business was quite complicated, Head Office were always very helpful. Head Office of course had the right to call at any time, unannounced to check that all the stock and money was present and correct. This was not as worrying as it sounds, as they didn't expect us to balance to the nearest penny. We received a monthly salary from the Post Office. This was really essential to keep the village shop viable. The Post Office business consisted of selling stamps, TV licences, Postal Orders and even game licences — about one per year! We dealt with Giro Bank, Post Office Savings Bank and Premium Bonds (when you could buy one Bond for £1). Friday evening we did a Cash Account for Head Office — a long job if we didn't balance first time.

In conjunction with the Post Office we ran a General Store, stocking a large range of goods. We had daily papers but did not deliver. They were collected mainly from the shop. The Hornby papers were usually taken up by the Post van — completely off the record of course! The bread came in each morning at first but less regularly latterly. The milkman used the shop as a drop off point for collection by some of the more out of the way properties. The stock for the shop was mostly collected from trade markets in Darlington each week. We did however have regular deliveries of frozen foods, bacon, pork pies, sausage etc. We delivered groceries each week to Hornby and the surrounding area. Many of the farmers and owners of the larger properties were very loyal to the village shop and without them many village shops would not have traded for so long.

There were inevitably customers we will always remember. One Gentleman used to call each week to collect his pension on horseback, not expecting to dismount but knocking on the shop door with his crop. We used to know what time to expect him, so were ready for his summons! One other of whom I was very fond, used to call just before closing time on my half day, insisting on standing talking when I was probably ready to dash off on a shopping trip. He later admitted to doing this to see how long I would remain unruffled. Another I am reminded of each time we have a power cut and I get out the candles, which we kept when we finished with the shop. We used to deliver these to an elderly Lady who still lived without the benefit of electricity. We enjoyed our ten years at the shop and have many fond memories. We particularly enjoyed the fact that we knew every inhabitant of the village and many in the surrounding area. We also felt very much involved with every aspect of village life."

Bus Service

The United Automobile Services Ltd introduced a new bus service (No. 158) from 1st July 1969. This service left Catterick Aerodrome at 9.45 a.m. every Tuesday, via East Appleton, Hackforth and Crakehall, arriving in Bedale at 10.20 a.m. The bus left Bedale again at 13.10, for the return journey, allowing time to be spent in Bedale on Market Day. Two months later, the 158 Bus Services was re-routed for a trial period, and passed through Tunstall and Arrathorne Lane End as well.

UNITED AUTOMOBILE SERVICES LIMITED

21st August 1969

NOTICE TO PUBLIC

SERVICE 158 CATTERICK (AERODROME) - BEDALE

TUESDAY ONLY

Commencing Tuesday 26th August 1969 the above service will be re-routed for a trial period operating via Catterick Village, Tunstall, Arrathorne Lane End, Hornby, Hackforth and Crakehall to Bedale.

Catterick, Aerodrome	0945	Bedale Market Place	1310
Tunstall	0951	Crakehall	1315
Arrathorne Lane End	0959	Hackforth	1323
Hornby	1002	Hornby	1328
Hackforth	1007	Arrathorne Lane End	1331
Crakehall	1015	Tunstall	1339
Bedale Market Place	1020	Catterick Aerodrome	1345

The Bus Service provided by the United Automobile Services Ltd, continued until the 1970s.

1960 – 1970

The bus, leaving from Richmond at 9.27 am, would pass through Hornby and Hackforth on its way to Bedale to the local market. The bus returned from Bedale just after 1 pm, allowing the local residents time for shopping, meeting friends, and any other business.

Severe weather conditions in the 1960s affected school attendances on several occasions:-

Feb 2nd 1962:

"A very stormy morning, after a very stormy night, much damage has been done locally. All the roads are blocked by fallen trees."

Nov 25th 1965:

"Heavy snowfall during the night, it continued (to snow) all day until there was 12-14 inches."

Public transport proved an asset, when on November 30th 1965: "Icy gale force winds persisted all day, Hornby children were allowed to go home on the 2 p.m. Bedale Market bus."

Quote from newspaper 'The Northern Echo,' Tuesday Oct 20th 1966 (How Langthorne village is losing its houses).

Dying village makes its last stand

Our Bedale correspondent

THE tiny village of Langthorne near Bedale is dying.

Year by year more of the 21 houses in the village are condemned and families move out. Already ten houses are under closing orders.

But now two villagers at least are trying to get Langthorne resurrected by urging the Bedale Rural Council to build houses in the village.

Mr. Ronald Murfin, a 41-year-old garage proprietor, wrote to the Bedale RDC asking them to consider building in the village and, at its last meeting, the Council instructed its Housing Committee to look at the problem.

Mr. Murfin said yesterday, "People who used to live in Langthorne years ago, or knew it as children, are shocked when they come back to visit it. Langthorne used to be a pleasant little village. Now everywhere you look there are condemned houses, or others which are falling apart.

"If the Council cannot do anything to help the village you might as well call it dead and all that is left is to bury it."

1960 – 1970

Farmer acts

A farmer, Mr. Peter Goldiee, said, "Several times I have organised meetings at my house trying to plan action. Each time they have been well attended. There is no apathy in the village. It is just that there is very little we can do."

One of the village's oldest residents, who is living in a condemned house, is 68-year-old Mr. Fred Pocklington, a retired farmworker. He lives next door to two houses already empty. One was once the village pub. But the pub closed about four years ago.

"This old house will suit me for the rest of my time. But it's a pity the way the village has gone down like it has. I remember it from when I was a lad, when it was a pleasant place. Now most of the houses are tumbling down," he said.

The village has no main sewerage system and 95 per cent of the houses have earth closets. Water borne sewage can only be made possible by individual septic tanks.

Even the road to the village is unclassified, says Mr. Murfin, who feels bitterly that the village has no nameplate. "We think that the County Council are making some name plates for Langthorne. It is one step forward I suppose, but probably a bit late."

At the recent Bedale RDC meeting, when Mr. Murfin's appeal for new houses was considered, Maj.-Gen. W. E. Clutterbuck said that the Council had made two visits to try and find building sites, but no one wanted to sell the land.

"We know that there is one site in the village where the owner says he won't sell the land.

Entrance (above) to the lost village of Langthorne. Top: A signpost stands near the village without pointing to it.

But there are certainly other sites," said Mr. Murfin.

Mr. John Hobson, 63, of Town End Farm, remembers Langthorne "as a place that was full of life, when I was a young lad. It is a sad disgrace that it is going down the way it is."

A signpost at the end of the village points towards Langthorne. Its message could be grimly prophetic, because it says Hackforth 1. No one seems to have noticed that Langthorne lies between the signpost and the village of Hackforth.

New Millennium ~ The 'stand' must have worked – Langthorne is still there and new houses have been built.

The W.I. and their families at Hornby Castle (3-7-68)
In the 1960s Mrs Clutterbuck was the President of the W.I, and Hornby Castle became a regular venue for summer activities.

1970-1980

St Mary's Church Anniversary

1970 was an important year for St. Mary's Church in Hornby, as celebrations took place to mark its 900th anniversary. (1070 -1970)

The Vicar, Canon B.W. Crawford was pleased that the Archbishop of York was able to preach at Hornby Church on July 5th 1970.

View of Nave and North Aisle from South door"
(Mrs Bardon)

1970 – 1980

A concert was held the following Tuesday at St Mary's as part of the celebrations. An ambitious programme of music was performed, including (from Hornby Castle) Mrs. Gwen Clutterbuck conducting the local choir, with Miss Juliet Clutterbuck as soprano.

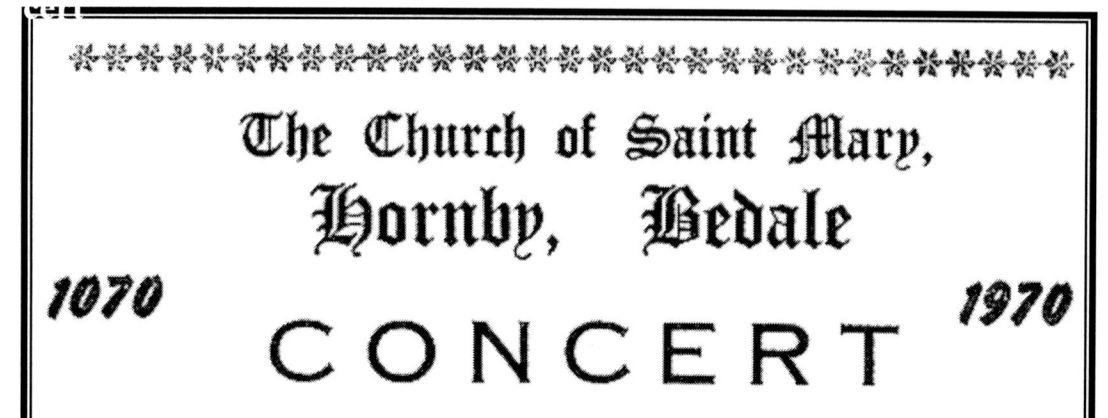

The Church of Saint Mary, Hornby, Bedale

1070 — CONCERT — *1970*

Tuesday, 7th July in the Church at 7-30 p.m.

Miss Juliet Clutterbuck, Soprano, accompanied by Lois Phillips, Piano, in songs by Tinto, Schubert, Brahms, Wolf, also folk songs.

The Wath Women's Institute Choir will sing songs by Baker, Reineike Nils.

Admission by Programme only.

These will be available locally and at the Church. *Price— Two Shillings*

ST. MARY'S CHURCH, HORNBY

Tuesday, July 7th 1970

JULIET CLUTTERBUCK (Soprano.)

LOIS PHILLIPS (Piano)

WATH WOMEN'S' INSTITUTE CHOIR (CONDUCTED BY GWEN CLUTTERBUCK)

SOLO SONGS

HAPPY IS THE LAND	J. S. BACH
MY HEART EVER FAITHFUL	J. S. BACH
ELOISE TO ABELARD	G. F. PINTO
LITTLE WARBLER CHEERFUL BE	G. F. PINTO

GEORGE FREDERICK PINTO was a young English composer who died in 1806 at the early age of 21. The English musician Samuel Wesley said of him "Had he lived he might well have been the English Mozart."

WATH CHOIR

NEVER WEATHER-BEATEN SAIL	CAMPION
SIMPLE GIFTS	arr. COPLAND
BROTHER JAMES' AIR	arr. GORDON JACOB

The Bedale Hunt was active in the area in the 1970s

Mrs Betty Craggs presents the Stirrup Cup, outside the Greyhound Inn, Hackforth.

The Northern Echo 21 Feb 1973

The Bedale Hunt passing through Hackforth, going towards North Road.

D&S 22nd Feb 1972

The Bedale Hunt at Hackforth, Bedale, yesterday setting out for open country.

1970 – 1980

In May 1972, a stagecoach and horses, passed through Hackforth as part of the enactment of the Edinburgh to London journey, which last ran 127 years previously. The school log book quotes: "This morning at 10.15am, we assembled the children on the green triangle in the village, to watch the passing of the stage coach. The children were most excited."

Soon after, on 6th June 1972, "There was great excitement this afternoon when delivery men brought our television set."

Farming

"Harvesting the Mangolds"   *(Mrs. J. Pybus)*

Below:
   A *Fordson* tractor collects in the potatoes   *(Mrs. J. Pybus)*

1970 – 1980

Farm sales were held from time to time, as farms were sold up. The sales were always well supported as local farmers bought items to support the farmers in their retirement.

Street House Farm
Leeming Bar

3 miles Leeming Bar Motel
3 miles Catterick
10 miles Northallerton

T. MURRAY LTD.

In conjunction with

R. & W. HEDLEY,
AUCTIONEERS

are Instructed by J. Ingledew Esq., O.B.E.,
to sell by Auction on

FRIDAY, 4th MAY, 1973

The whole of his valuable
LIVE & DEAD FARM STOCK

Sale to commence at 12-30 p.m.

Note:

The cattle have all been reared on the farm and are a grand lot with a number requiring only short keep. The Ewes have wintered well and have a grand crop of lambs at foot.

The implements and machinery have been well cared for and include a number of items of interest to collectors.

The entrance to the farm is on the west side of the A1(M) Road approximately midway between the Leeming Bar Motel and Catterick Roundabout.

Auctioneers Offices: T. Murray Ltd.,
Estate Offices, Haswell,
Durham.
Tel. Haswell 322/5 & 405

R. & W. Hedley,
High Street, Yarm.
Tel. Eaglescliffe 781214

A good example of a farm sale was the sale of Street House Farm by the Ingledews on May 4 1973. Some of the more interesting items sold were: Telegraph poles (3 for £7); A turnip snagger (£82); A straw chopper £ 6-50

The List of items sold, gave an insight into the type of farm being sold up. Apart from combines, tractors and trailers, some £3000 worth of rams, ewes and lambs, and over £1000 worth of Charolais, Friesian and Hereford calves, heifers and bullocks were sold. Then, there were medicines, netting, troughs, stakes, water tanks, potato and turnip implements, and a variety of small tools such as saws, grease-guns and gripes.

1970 – 1980

95 HEAD OF GRAND HOMEBRED BEEF CATTLE

27 Fries. x Bullocks 18-22 months; 6 Char. x Heifers 18-22 months; 17 Fries. x Bullocks 12-18 months; 4 Char. & Hereford x Ayrshire Bullocks 12-14 months; 5 Char. x Heifers 12-16 months; 15 Fries. x Bullocks 6-12 months; 4 Fries. x Hereford Heifers 7-10 months; 6 Char. x Heifers 6-10 months; 8 Fries. x Bullocks 5-6 months; 1 A.A. x Friesian Heifer 7 months; 2 Ayrshire x Heifers 4-5 months.

121 BREEDING SHEEP

70 Masham Ewes and Lambs' 48 Mule Ewes and Lambs; 3 Suffolk Rams.

TRACTORS and COMBINE HARVESTERS

1969 Massey Ferguson 168 Tractor; 1964 Fordson Dexta Tractor; 1956 Fordson Major Tract or; 1948 Allis Chalmers Model 'B' Pet /Par. Tractor with row crop equipment; 1964 Ransome 902 Combine Harvester; 1964 Ransome 801 Combine Harvester; 1959 Ransome 902 Combine Harvester; Massey Harrison Combine Harvester-bagger.

IMPLEMENTS, MACHINERY ETC

Ford Ransome 2-F reversible digger plough; Ford Ransome 3-F semi-digger plough; Howard Selectarilith Rotavator; Bentall Disc Harrows; Triple K Cultivator; set of four chip harrows; set of to 5 seed harrows; Ripper harrows; toolbar and ridging bodies; Gill Cambridge rotor; Wallace Oliver manure spreader; Ogle gearrings Manure spreader; Cameron Gardner hydraulic mounted loader with fork and earth sheer; Massey Ferguson fertiliser distributor; Amazon Fertiliser Broadcaster; Massey Ferguson Flail Mower; Cock Pheasant Hay Tedder; Lister Blackstone Tractor Rake; Blanch Acrobat Hay Turner; Jones Superstar Pick-up Baler; Trojan Bale Transporter; Barford Bale Collector; Tye hydraulic double tipping Tractor Trailer; Wheatley hydraulic tipping Tractor Trailer; Grain Tank; Gilson Trailer; Lister Blackstone Bale Elevator; Frost & Wood P.D. Binder (as new); Fieldmaster High/Low volume Crop Sprayer; Aldersley Weeders; Old type Rotavator; Johnson 2 row Potato Digger; Ford Ransome mounted Potato Spinner; Edlington Potato Riddle with Villiers Engine; Weigh and Weights; Ord & Teesdale 2 row mounted Turnip Drill; Harrison McGregor Pulpet with 1½ h.p. Petter Engine; Turnip, Snagger; Sellarc Hedge Cutter; Ransome Com Dresser Screen; M/H. Post Hole Borer; Portable cattle Crush; Lamb Creep; Ewe Adopter; 3 Sheep Racks; 20 Sheep Troughs; 400 Sheep net Stakes; 16 Sheep Nets; 9 Rolls Rylock Fencing; 3 Ewe Trusses; 3 Infra Red Heaters; 12 round metal cattle troughs; Various metal and timber troughs; 5 Ladders; Tarpaulin Sheets; 17 Telegraph Poles; 3 Tubular Steel Gates; 2 Iron Gate posts; 150 Breeze Blocks; 2 Fuel Tanks; Large Water Trough; Straw Chopper; winnowing machine; Bamlett Horse fertiliser distributor; oak scrubber; wheel strake; Corn scoop; 4 corn bins; 500 Corner sacks; 2 wooden corn shovels; sack hoist; 24 potato backets; sundry medicines; Bull tether; lead bacon curing bowl; 2 sack barrows; 4 sections of larch lap fencing; Evans deep well pump with electric motor; small tools etc.

1970 – 1980

Inspecting sheep

John Pybus and Dusty the dog

A potato picker

Local farmers at the sale

(photos: Mrs J Pybus)

202

Hackforth School

One March 19th 1975, the inaugural meeting of the 'Tufty Club' took place at Hackforth School. This road safety club, for infant and pre-school children was started up by Mrs Shirley Webster and Mrs. Margaret Johnson.

The following year Hackforth School, won a local road safety competition. The article shows Michael Johnson and Olwyn Gregg holding the winning poster, whilst Leanne Pounder holds the trophy, presented by the Road Safety Officer, Mr Peacock. The remaining school pupils look on.

THE NORTHERN ECHO. Thursday, October 7, 1976

PUPILS of Hackforth and Hornby C. of E. School, Leane Pounder and Michael Johnson, receive from County Coun. C. H. Hoare, chairman of the County Council's No. 1 Area Highway Sub-committee, the Bedale Road Safety trophy won by the school in a competition organised by the authority.

(The Northern Echo, 7-10-76)

Fifteen pupils there might only be at Hackforth and Hornsby Church of England School near Bedale — but they clinched the trophy in a local road safety competition.

1970 – 1980

Queen's Silver Jubilee ~ 1977

A Committee was established to organise the Village Silver Jubilee Celebrations.

Standing:
Bill Gregg, David Gargett, Martin Webster, Jim Ingledew, Frank Smith

Sitting:
Margaret Johnson, Kathleen Smith, Heather Robinson, Mrs Bardon, Jean Metcalfe

Despite the rain, there was an open-air performance of the Kirby Londsdale Mummers Play. This was followed by sports, a treasure hunt and a sit down meal at the village hall.

(Mrs. Bardon)

1970 – 1980

Jubilee Day was celebrated in June 1977 to mark the Silver Jubilee of H.M. Queen Elizabeth II. The school, in which the children had prepared displays of local natural history, was open to the public.

HACKFORTH & DISTRICT JUBILEE CELEBRATIONS
Tuesday 7th June, 1977 - Proposed Events

10 a.m. - 12 noon	Swimming for all school children by kind permission of Mr. & Mrs. Staniland.
1.30 p.m.	FANCY DRESS PARADE
2.00 p.m	Hackforth & Hornby School present a MUMMERS PLAY in the school grounds, followed by: DISPLAY OF ENTRIES in the following competitions, open to all children: Jubilee Hat - Miniature Garden; Cake - Child's flower arrangement; Painted Stone - Cardboard box model

ENTRY FORMS AVAILABLE AT HACKFORTH POST OFFICE.

2.30 p.m - 4 p.m.	SPORTS, COMPETITIONS, ETC.. in the field opposite the Hall, by kind permission of Mr. Johnson.
4.00 p.m.	TREASURE HUNT - to continue during tea.
4.00 p.m. to 6.00 p.m.	TEA in the Village Hall. Please bring your own knife, fork and spoon.
7.30 p.m. - 9.00 p.m.	"DISCO" in the Hall.
8.00 p.m.	DOMINO DRIVE, in the School.
9.30 p.m. – midnight	SOCIAL EVENING for all.

* * * * *

It would be appreciated by the Committee if householders who are able, would decorate their houses, in order to add to the festive occasion.

In order to help with catering and for arrangements to be made to deliver teas to people unable to attend the celebrations, please fill in the form below and return to the Post Office at Hackforth, as soon as possible.

CHILDREN'S JUBILEE COMPETITIONS

each in three age groups

4 - 7 yrs.   8- 11 yrs.   Over 11 yrs.

PRIZES FOR ALL AGE GROUPS

* * * * * *

1. JUBILEE HAT - decorations of own choice.

* * * * * *

2. CARDBOARD BOX MODEL - cardboard only to be used for the structure and trim. Adhesive materials of own choice. The model may be painted.

* * * * * *

3. PAINTED STONE - painted to own design and covered with clear varnish.

* * * * * *

4. VICTORIA SPONGE CAKE - plain sponge, jam filled.

* * * * * *

5. FLOWER ARRANGEMENT - wild or garden flowers or a mixture of both. Dried or artificial flowers should not be included.

* * * * * *

6. MINIATURE GARDEN - biscuit tin lid (not more than 25 cms x 25cms) - not growing flowers.

* * * * * *

+++++ COMPETITIONS 1, 2 and 3 to arrive at HACKFORTH & HORNBY SCHOOL between 3.30 and 5.0 p.m. on WEDNESDAY 1st JUNE.

+++++ COMPETITIONS 4, 5 and 6 to arrive at HACKFORTH & HORNBY SCHOOL on Jubilee Day between 10 a. m. and 11 a.m.

1970 – 1980

The children's fancy dress competition for the Jubilee
(Mrs Bardon)

Mrs Ollie Johnson wearing her crown made especially for the occasion… *(Mrs C. Flowers)*

Right: …and Mrs. Farnaby - in her crown
(Mrs C. Flowers)

Left:

The adult fancy dress competition.

(photo: Mrs Carol Pringle)

1970 – 1980

Hackforth School

The school usually held a concert every Christmas for the parents.

Christmas 1977 *(Mrs Carol Pringle)*

Christmas 1979 *(Mrs C Flowers)*

Christmas 1979 *(Mrs Carol Pringle)*

(Mrs E Greensit)

1970 – 1980

There were only 16 children on the school role in 1978.

Junior Class ~ 1978

Olwyn Gregg, Victoria Greensit, Angela Pilkington, June Gargett, Eleni Casey, Liane Pounder, Mark Webster.

(Mrs E Greensit)

Infant Class ~ 1978

Caroline Robinson, Alan Gargett, Simon Pringle, Robert Young
Mrs Taylor
Rachel Pybus, Johnson Ramsay, David Greensit, Craig Thwaites, Louise Robinson

(Mrs E Greensit)

Village Day ~ 1979

Each June in Hackforth, for a few years after the Queens Silver Jubilee, a Village Day was held, which included a fancy dress competition, games in the village hall, home made teas and a domino drive. Hornby held a village fête for the surrounding area. Among the attractions were a variety of stalls, refreshments, country dancing and a display by the majorettes.

Newspaper Article

Fancy dress. – Despite poor weather the fancy dress parade was well attended. Winners: 1 Craig Thwaites (the Incredible Hulk); 2 Julie Thwaites (Wonder Woman); 3 Sarah Pringle (Jack in the Box).

<u>6-10 years</u>: 1 Simon Pringle (Time Flies); 2 Katie Johnson (Gipsy); 3 June Gargett (Bride Doll).

<u>10-14 years</u>: Eleni Casey (tortoise); Olwyn Gregg (sport for all); Carol Frost (Bunny Girl).

<u>Adults</u>: 1 Mrs O. Johnson, Mrs D. Farnaby (Quality Street); 2 Steven Robinson (Departed Spirits); Mr B. Gregg (nun); Mr M. Webster (monk); Mr J. Metcalfe and Mr K. Robinson (Girls of St. Trinians).

Judges: Mr and Mrs Russell (Scotton); Mr and Mrs Gibbins (Hornby); the Rev. and Mrs W Greetham (Patrick Brompton).

Games were organised in the village hall and homemade teas provided by the sports committee.

A domino drive ended the day's events.

Children's Fancy Dress *(Carol Pringle)*

Spectators *(Carol Pringle)*

1970 – 1980

Left:
Country Dancing at Hornby Village Fête
(Anita Thwaites)

The end of the 1970's saw more bad weather. Roads were closed by heavy snow, but the children didn't seem to mind.

(Photos: Carol Pringle)

The Women's Institute

The W.I continued to flourish in the 1970s. In 1972, Mrs Joan Chapman was elected president, and in 1977, Mrs Audrey Staniland was elected as her successor.

HACKFORTH WOMEN'S INSTITUTE

1977 – 1978

President:
Mrs. Staniland

Vice-Presidents:
Mrs. Howard, Mrs. Metcalfe

Secretary:
Mrs. Ramshay

Treasurer:
Mrs. Barker

Home Economics:
Mrs. Dodd, Mrs. Pringle

Press Correspondent:
Mrs. H. Robinson

Mesdames J. Chapman, Heeley, Johnson.

Meetings at 7.15 p.m.

Above: Miss Mowbray speaking at the Hornby Castle Garden Party organised by the W.I.

Right: The W.I. serve tea at the Garden Party.

Hornby Park Chase

The Walled Garden. This is the description for the Auction in 1930 of the gardens that supplied the Castle.

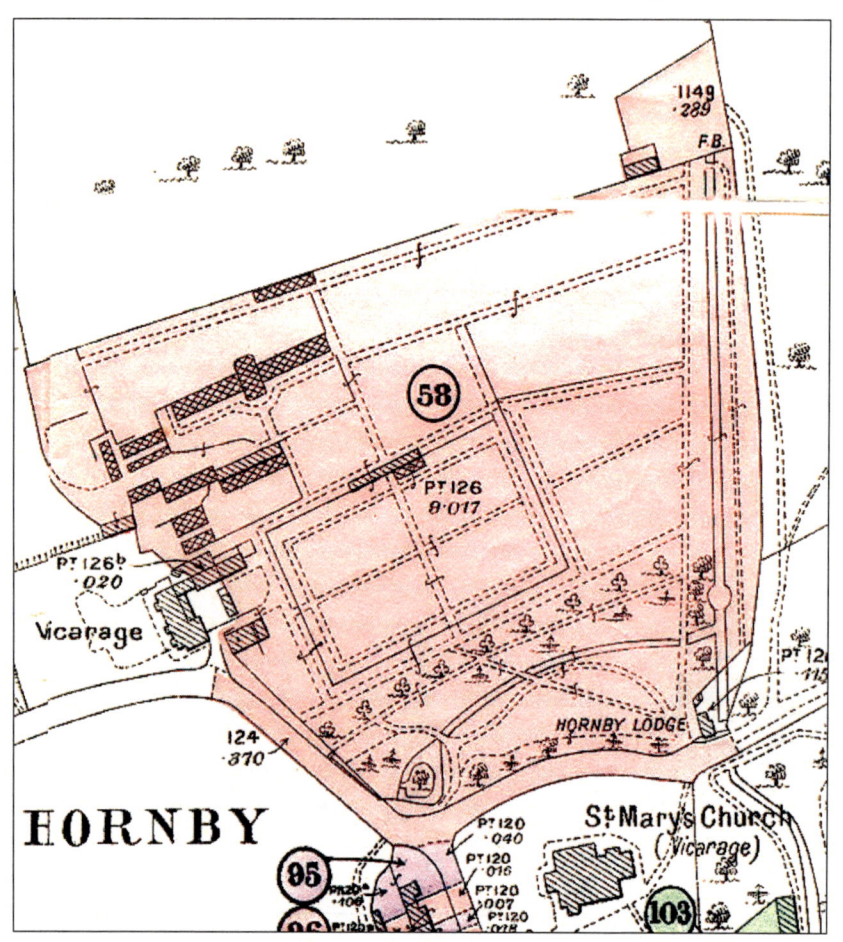

The Gardens adjacent to the house are well laid out in **three sections**, thus forming an economically worked Holding, eminently suitable as a **MARKET GARDEN**, being situated as it is in close proximity to Catterick Camp and within easy reach of Richmond and Darlington.

The high brick wall which surrounds the whole of the property is well stocked with **mature Fruit Trees**, including Pears, Apples, Plums and Cherries. **The South Wall**, of some 850 feet, being a special feature.

The three sections are laid out as follows:

Section one contains Fruit Room with Shelving and Loft over, Coke Shed, **Glass House**, 65-ft. by 15-ft., with piping throughout, adjacent is a Boiler House with 2 Boilers, a **16-Light Crick Frame**, 3 good Store Rooms, **Cold House**, 45-ft. by 12-ft., with span roof, **large Glass House, 54-ft. by** 12-ft., three-quarter span **Carnation House, 81-ft. by** 21-ft., heated throughout, **Conservatory**, a large oval-shaped building stocked with hothouse plants, span **Plant House, 78-ft. by** 21-ft., heated with pipes, Mushroom and Rhubarb House, Potting Shed and Store Room with Fireplace, capital lean-to **Vinery, 90-ft. by** 15-ft., well stocked with Vines of good variety, and heated throughout.

Section two is laid out as a **Vegetable Garden,** divided by fine box hedges, well stocked with **Fruit Trees**. There is a Nectarine House, 33-ft. by 9-ft., and 2 large Store Rooms.

Section three is laid out as a **Vegetable Garden,** well stocked with **Fruit Trees,** there being also a full-sized **Tennis Court.**

The stream, which runs the entire length of the property, is an attractive feature, both from a point of view of beauty and for commercial purposes.

The Glass Houses have, in almost every case, **Water Laid On,** and there are numerous taps throughout the whole of the Garden.

There is a large **ROSE GARDEN**.

1970 – 1980

In the thirties when the estate of Hornby Castle was sold, the castle kitchen gardens were acquired by the Wilson family. The gardens consisted of a small inner one surrounded by a peach wall on the south facing side and a larger garden enclosed by a brick wall. The gardens were run by the family as a market garden for the next forty years. Produce from the gardens was sold at Richmond and Leyburn markets. In the seventies the smaller inner garden was bought by *Tarmac*. Building consent was given for six detached dwelling properties and these were completed in the summer of 1979, and by the end of that year all the houses in 'Park Chase' were occupied.

The original garden walls enclose the houses and these now have a preservation order on them. The wall behind the first four houses in the Chase is a peach wall and still has some of the original chimneys that were used when it was heated in the winter to protect the peach trees. Thousands of nails still remain in the wall.

Families on the whole occupied the houses, the Chase providing a safe playing area for children. Apart from all the children growing up and fleeing their nests, there has only been a very small change in the inhabitants of Park Chase over the last 25 years – Ann Spirit

(photo: John Morris ~ present day)

1979

1980-1990

1980 – 1990

Summer 1980

Fancy Dress Competition at the Village Activity Day held in the field adjacent to Village Hall, Hackforth.   *(Carol Pringle)*

Above:
The Infant class, Hackforth School, Christmas 1980

Left:
The Junior Class, Hackforth School, Christmas 1980
(Carol Pringle)

Diana Day ~ 1981

The School Log Book on July 11th 1981 recorded "Diana Day" at Hackforth, (for Diana, Princess of Wales): "The weather brightened in the afternoon for us, and all went well. Included in the day's events were a fancy crown competition, Maypole dancing, stalls and sideshows, sports, a quoits match, and a domino drive. Teas were served in the Village Hall, and the children were presented with a commemorative mug and crown piece."

Crown Competition at Hackforth

Junior Class
(Mrs Bardon)

Infant Class
(Carol Pringle)

1980 – 1990

Mrs Val Ramsay collecting a mug for Marco her son

(Mrs C. Flowers)

Caroline Robinson collecting her commemorative mug

1980 – 1990

School children Maypole dancing on Diana Day
(Carol Pringle)

The Men's Race
(Carol Pringle)

Hornby Fête 1982

Fêtes were held regularly at Hornby Castle, often for the Church, but also for the school.

Children Country Dancing on July 3rd 1982 at the Church Garden Fête held at Hornby Castle. *(Mrs. C. Flowers)*

Dancing around the Maypole *(Mrs. Bardon)*

The Fancy Dress Competition *(Mrs. Bardon)*

1980 – 1990

1982

Hackforth School

Mrs Flowers, Matthew Ryans, Mark Dodd, Andrea McKinlay, Rachel Gibson, Wendy Metcalfe, Susan Allan, Johnson Ramsay
Jonathan Ryans, Louise Robinson, Allan Gargett, Katie Johnson, Caroline Robinson, Robert Young, Craig Thwaites, **Mrs Thomas**
Charles Dodd, Nigel Parker, Gaynor Ramsay, Zoë Pounder, Julie Thwaites., Andrew Dodd, Wayne Metcalfe
Scott Metcalfe, Layla Ramsay, Scott Spirit

1980 – 1990

School trips

Scarborough ~ 1982 and Clarke Hall, Wakefield
(photos: Mrs C. Flowers and Val Ramsay)

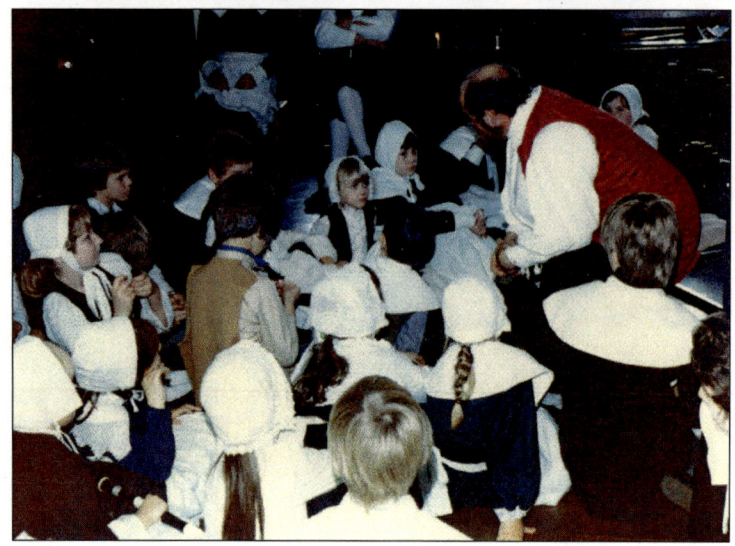

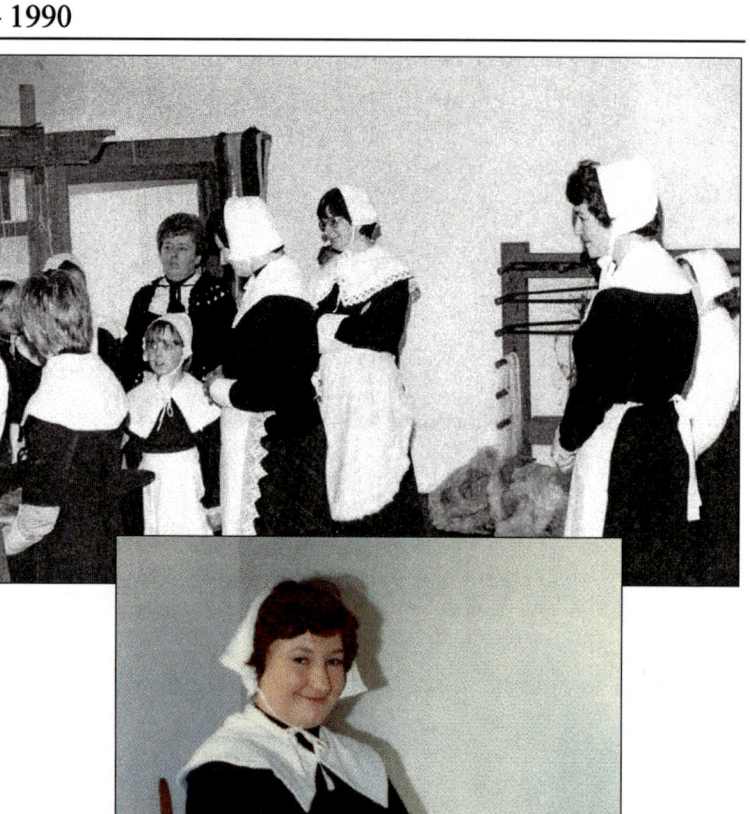

222

1980 – 1990

1983

1984

1985

1987

Photographs (Carol Pringle)

1980 – 1990

Hackforth School ~ 1986

Andrew Dodd, James Jackson, Charles Dodd, Wayne Metcalfe, Joseph Howard, **Mrs Kirby**, **Mrs Sutcliffe**
Mrs Flowers (Head Teacher), Elizabeth Robinson, Georgia Ramsay, Layla Ramsay, Sharon Brown, Rachel Breeze, Rachel Willis, Amanda Brown
Claire Spirit, Marco Ramsay, Gemma Metcalfe, Andrew Percival, Joanna Dodd, Rebecca Russell, Rachel Craggs, Scott Metcalfe, Anna Fish, Timothy Gibson, Lindsay Ramsay

1980 – 1990

Left:
Mrs. Christine Flowers, headteacher, presents flowers to Mrs. Farnaby on her retirement as school caretaker.

A computer evening at the School

Below: Martin and Shirley Webster, George and Val Ramsay

Malcolm Percival, with Christine Percival, Mrs. Thomas (teacher) and Mr. Ken Pounder

Right:
Dennis Smith with Shirley Allen

(photos: Mrs C Flowers)

1980 – 1990

"Only a Baby" ~ Christmas 1984

(photos: Mrs Anita Thwaites)

Gaynor Ramsay, Rachel Gibson and Sophie Howard

(Mrs Heather Robinson)

Medieval Banquet at Richmond Castle ~1985

Hackforth School organised a trip to take part in a Medieval Banquet at Richmond Castle.

(photos: Mrs Anita Thwaites)

1980 – 1990

Domesday Survey

All the schools in North Yorkshire were asked to complete a "Domesday" type survey about their local area in 1985. The Survey (See Appendix 1 for complete survey) by Hackforth School gives an interesting insight into the local area. Subjects covered, included housing, employment, shopping, heating, cooking, the youth club, and entertainment.

Sue Butler teaches the children baseball. With bat and gloves are left to right: Matthew Ryans, Lindsey Ramsey and Sophie Howard

Hackforth School & playground ~ present day

(Sandra Webb)

America at home

VILLAGE schoolchildren went on a day trip to America yesterday without leaving the playground of their tiny school.

Hollywood, was transported to sleepy Hackforth, near Bedale, for a real "Have A Nice Day" July The Fourth Stateside celebration with a genuine USA guest.

The 26 five to 11-year-old North Yorkshire youngsters dropped their cricket bats in favour of baseball ones and followed up with a snack of chocolate chip cookies.

"It's just like a real July 4, although it seems a bit unusual around here. Even the weather is right," said American guest, Susan Butler, an 18-year-old college student from Quincy, Illinois.

Susan is on a three-month exchange visit staying with school headteacher Mrs Christine Flowers, who thought a July 4 children's celebration was too good an opportunity to miss while Susan was here. It also tied in with an infants projects on the Plains Indians.

1980 – 1990

Hackforth School Christmas Meal ~ 1986

(Mrs Heather Robinson)

Mrs. Heather Robinson, Mrs. Farnaby and Sue Bishop (Part-time teacher)

1980 – 1990

Hackforth Juniors complete a Zoo Project ~ 1988

1980 – 1990

Hairdressing ~ 1st March 1989

NORTH YORKSHIRE News

Pupils are a cut above the rest

● HAIRDRESSING was all cut and dried for these pupils. (7250-16)

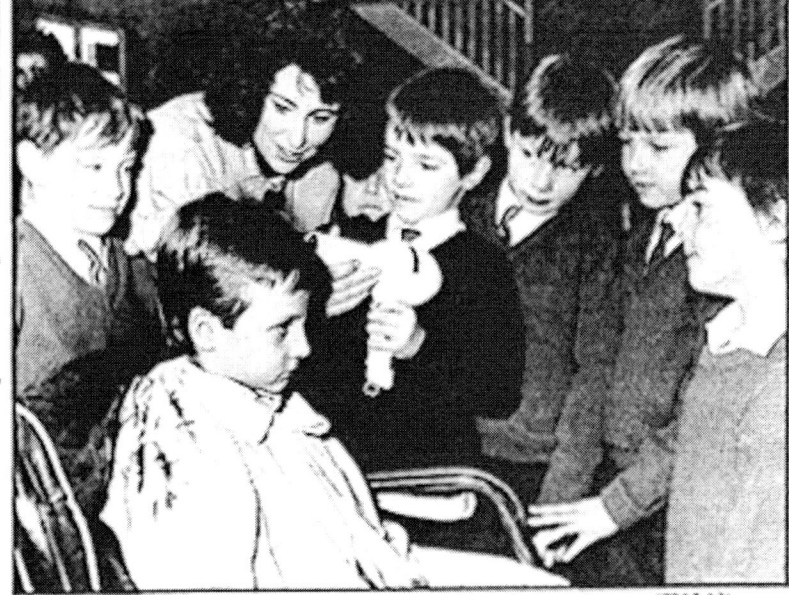

● HACKFORTH schoolchildren getting to grips with hair drying techniques. (7250-13)

Top left:
Laura Metcalfe, Graham Dodd, Geraldine Potts and Kate Jackson

Right: Martin Armstrong, Martin Ramsay, Richard Blanchard, Robert McKinlay, Chris Dodd and Alex Breeze

Rudd Hall Fire
Blaze hides clues to theft

By JOE WEBER

DETECTIVES were investigating a blaze which badly damaged a 300-year-old historic hall – only hours after burglars escaped with valuable antiques!

Police were searching for clues in a bid to discover if the large country house had been set on fire by thieves trying to cover the traces of their break-in.

Last night a fire brigade expert said the cause of the blaze was unknown, but the fire was believed to have started in a waste paper basket in a room with a closed door.

Gutted

But last night the elderly owner, Mrs Connie Tyson, was sleeping peacefully in a nursing home unaware that police and firemen had spent hours sifting through the charred remains of her home.

Worried staff at the home in Ripon fear the shock could be too much to bear for the 87-year-old widow, who has lived for many years at Rudd Hall near East Appleton a few miles from Richmond.

Yesterday 20 firemen spent nearly two hours fighting to save the building after flames completely gutted one room and then burnt through the ceilings and spread into the house.

Firemen wearing breathing apparatus searched the smoke-logged house while others hurriedly started pumping water for their hoses from an ornamental lake.

Four fire engines raced to the blaze after a farm worker raised the alarm as smoke and flames billowed out of the building, which has been empty for nearly a year.

Forensic experts were trying to discover if missing antiques and valuable pictures had been destroyed in the blaze, or stolen during the break-in.

A gardener explained that antique silver had been found piled in the kitchen and that paintings had been kept on the walls of the morning room where the fire started.

CID officers were checking on a suggestion that the thieves could have learned the house was unoccupied from a radio news report earlier this year, which revealed the house was standing empty,

Valuables

Police discovered valuables in one upstairs dressing room were untouched. The room had been left undisturbed since Lieut. Col. Charles Tyson died several years ago.

His loose change was neatly piled on top of the dressing table and silver backed hairbrushes and a cut-throat razor were nearby.

His trousers were still hanging over the back of a chair and his uniform still hanging in a wardrobe and his shoes and boots were placed neatly in a rack.

His name is still listed in the telephone directory and nearby villagers explained his car had been carefully preserved in a garage for several years after his death.

A Police spokesman said relatives were travelling to the house to help discover what was missing. "Our inquiries have revealed that the premises had been forcibly entered during the night and an unknown amount of antiques stolen."

"A considerable amount of damage has been caused to the house by the fire but we can't put a figure on it," he added.

Mrs Tyson

Rudd Hall — scene of the weekend fire

1980 – 1990

Rutex

When the weekly market bus service finished in the early 1980s, it was decided to introduce a car sharing service. Each village was represented, but the service was under-utilised.

WHAT IS THE CAR SHARING SERVICE?
A committee of local volunteers has organised a car service to provide lifts where journeys cannot be made by bus or any other means. New legislation* allows drivers (whose vehicles must be specially authorised by North Yorkshire County Council) to accept payment in return for lifts.

The service is not intended to supplant private arrangements made from time to time between friends and relatives, but to help people, who may not have access to such arrangements, to make journeys on their own initiative.

WHERE MAY I TRAVEL?
Lifts can be given anywhere within the parishes of Hackforth, Hornby, and Langthorne (the experimental area) or from one of these parishes to:
BEDALE
LEEMING BAR MOTEL
CATTERICK VILLAGE

HOW MUCH WILL THE LIFT COST?
If the driver is making the journey anyway (apart from a slight diversion):
7p per mile when the passenger is in the car.

If the driver is making a special journey.
10p per mile when passenger is in the car;
5p per mile when car is empty.

If more than one passenger is travelling the charge should be shared between them.

WILL A LIFT ALWAYS BE PROVIDED?
Passengers will, wherever possible, be matched with drivers who are already making a journey for their own purposes and this may require a little flexibility in the passenger's time of travel.
If a request cannot be satisfied in this way a driver may be asked to make a special trip, but passengers must accept that, since all the drivers are volunteers, it may not always be possible to provide a lift. However, in an emergency or for a very important trip (e.g. to a doctors surgery) every effort will be made to find a driver.

BUS SERVICES
To avoid wasteful duplication of services, lifts will not be given from Hackforth or Hornby at times when the market day bus is running.

HOW IS A LIFT ARRANGED?
Passengers requiring lifts and drivers offering to give lifts should contact one of the co-ordinators who will try to match supply and demand.
CO-ORDINATOR FOR HACKFORTH & HORNBY
Mr E. C. Holman
The Shieling
North Road
Hackforth
Tel. Richmond 811773

CO-ORDINATOR FOR LANGTHORNE
Mr K. Pounder
The Stelling
Langthorne
Tel. Bedale 3276

*Passenger Vehicle (Experimental Areas) Act 1977

---

rutex

INTRODUCING YOUR HACKFORTH and DISTRICT CAR SHARING SERVICE

for the parishes of HACKFORTH HORNBY and LANGTHORNE

SERVICE STARTS MON 2ND OCTOBER

The Village Hall

In June 1980, there was a proposal to build an extension to the village hall, and to put a new roof on the kitchen area. Grants were applied for, and £325 was obtained from Hambleton District Council, and £650 from Yorkshire County Council towards the total cost of £8,000. Hambleton District Council also provided a grant of £1,000 to re-roof the main hall. In 1981, after all the work was completed, the car park was surfaced with tarmac. A tradition of domino drives was established on the second Saturday of each month, to provide a regular income for the Village Hall. Hire charges were set at £12 for the main hall and £5 for the small hall. With the installation of Calor gas heating, the hire charges were raised to £14 for the main hall, and £7 for the small hall. Despite these increased charges, it was noted that the village hall account was overdrawn in 1985, so a sponsored walk that summer raised £321-50. Mr. Hutchinson offered to graze his sheep around the village hall in an attempt to keep the area tidy, whilst inside, the hall was decorated.

The village hall was now used regularly for local activities. Whist and domino drives raised funds, whilst a table tennis club was started up on Monday evenings, and Hackforth School used the hall twice a week for P.E.

The W.I.

After 50 years, the image of the W.I was beginning to change, both locally, and nationally and its popularity was in decline. However, many small communities still looked upon the W.I as an integral part of rural life, and in Hackforth, the monthly meeting night was changed from a Thursday to a Wednesday. As membership was slowly falling, new sources of income were sought, and the Annual Christmas Domino Drive was instigated.

In the 1980's Mrs. A. Staniland was President until 1985, when Mrs Young took over. The annual subscription was £4 a year. A cup of tea and a raffle ticket cost 10p, payable at each meeting.

In 1981, Hackforth W.I celebrated its Golden Jubilee. Invitations were sent out to members past and present to mark the notable occasion.

The President and Members of
Hackforth Women's Institute

have much pleasure in inviting you to the

Golden Jubilee Meeting

on *Wednesday, 9th September 1981*

Sherry Reception 7-0 p.m.

Mrs. Ramshay
Whiteways
Wooden Hill Lane
Northallerton

R.S.V.P. by
1st. September

Menu

Sherry

Turkey and Tongue
Salads

Cheese Cakes
Apple Pie and Cream
Fruit Salad
Trifle
Mousse
Souffle

Cheese and Biscuits

Coffee

Entertainment

by
Mr. & Mrs. Clough
of Ponteland

Toast

The Institute

Proposed by: Mrs. Kate Simpson

Response by: Mrs. A.M. Staniland
President

Display of Mementoes

Snow at Church View, Hornby
(Mrs Bardon)

1990-2000

1990 – 2000

December 1990 ~ The snow collected on the electricity wires and the weight of the snow brought down the poles. It was 4 days before the electricity was reconnected.

(Mr. Towler)

The Post Office, located in Silver Street, Hackforth, was run by Mrs. Kay Moss. Newspapers could be ordered, and were left out for collection every day.

(J. Brown)

On 29th April 1997 the Post Office was sold, and Audrey Plews took over the running of the Post Office, from North Road, Hackforth.

The Village Hall

At Christmas 1990, Hackforth Village Hall was the venue for the local residents to put on a production of "'Allo 'Allo, it's Christmas," written by Jim Pringle and arranged by the Village Hall Entertainments Committee.

(Mrs. C. Pringle)

'The audience'

(Mrs C. Pringle)

1990 – 2000

It was agreed in the late 1990's, that the Village Hall needed to be updated, ready for the year 2000. Grants were sought and obtained from Yorventure (£17,300) the Rural Development Council (£4,000) and Hambleton District Council (£1,850). The work, included a new kitchen and storage room, double-glazing and new doors. Finally, the Village Hall was decorated throughout, and new curtains and light fittings installed.

Delight as Village Hall gets face lift

VILLAGERS at Hackforth near Bedale, have celebrated the completion of a £21,000 refurbishment scheme at their village hall.

The hall serves a 150-strong community and has been given a complete overhaul and now boasts new windows, wiring and heating, a vastly improved kitchen and smart new decor.

On Saturday, residents were invited to an official opening of the hall, carried out by chairman Arnold Butler.

The improvement scheme has been funded by £17,300 from environmental body Yorventure, which receives land-fill tax credits from Northallerton-based waste management company Yorwaste Ltd.

The Rural Development Commission provided a further £4,000 and Hambleton District Council also contributed £1,850.

A bequest of £1,000 was also made to the project by the late Mr James Ingledew, a former chairman of Hackforth Village Hall Committee.

Mr Butler said: "Improvements to the hall were long overdue and it's been a long haul to get this far but we're delighted with the end result. The hall is a valuable resource for our small community and neighbouring ones.

"One of the most pleasing aspects of the improvement project was that it provided work for local contractors."

Hackforth Village Hall was built by local people on land donated by the late Duke of Leeds in 1937.

Among its many other uses, the building is used for gym lessons by pupils at the adjacent Hackforth and Hornby Primary School and is a regular base for local domino and whist drives, as well as providing a base for social functions.

~ North Yorkshire News 2 February 2000

Local Residents gather after grant is obtained for the Village Hall ~ 1998
(John Brown)

Extended hall to reopen

HACKFORTH will tomorrow celebrate the official opening of its refurbished village hall, built 63 years ago.

What began as a relatively small project involving a £7,000 extension grew to include new windows and doors for the main building as well as replacement heaters and a kitchen, internal redecoration and new furnishings, with a final price tag of just over £25,000.

Grants totalling £21,420 came from Yorventure, the Northallerton company which receives substantial funding through the landfill tax credit scheme, the Rural Development Commission and Hambleton District Council.

The rest of the money came from funds raised by the village hall committee and a legacy of £1,000 from Mr James Ingledew, of Street House, Little Holtby.

His father, William, was one of three people who set up an account in 1921 to build the hall. The foundation stones were laid in 1937 on land given by the late Duke of Leeds, who then lived nearby at Hornby Castle.

Funds available at the time were about £700 and these, combined with a grant and a loan from the National Trust, enabled the building committee to complete the hall in seven months for about £1,200.

The army requisitioned the hall in September, 1940, and stayed until the end of the war.

A small meeting room costing £8,500 was added in 1980, but the hall committee recently decided that a further extension was needed.

Committee chairman Mr Arnold Butler said: "We found that hardly anybody wanted to book the small room because it was also being used as a store room and was getting so full of stuff.

"Originally we were only going to do the new extension as a way of coping with the storage problem, but as we began applying for grants we heard about Yorventure and decided to approach them.

"They made a grant of just over £17,000 which enabled us to replace the windows, doors and heaters, which were about 20 years old.

"It would have been a shame to let the hall deteriorate and we feel there has been a 100pc improvement. It has been worth all the effort we made to get the grants.

"The hall is warmer because the windows are double glazed, the new kitchen is much better, more people can be accommodated in the meeting room because some of the things have been moved out, and the redecoration makes the hall more welcoming."

Villagers will be shown round the refurbished hall when it is opened tomorrow night by Mr Roger Clutterbuck, of Hornby Castle.

WELCOME: Outside the hall are, from the front, chairman Mr Arnold Butler, vice-chairman Mr Jim Pearson, treasurer Mr John Brown, and committee member Mr Malcolm Percival. – DST

1990 – 2000

Hackforth Village School

There were about 25 pupils in 1990:
<u>Back Row</u>: **Mrs C Jenkins, Mrs D Millward,** Gemma Metcalfe, Rebecca Potts, Joanna Dodd, Laura Blanchard, Robert McKinlay, Marco Ramsay, **Mrs Sue Kirby, Mrs A Thwaites.** <u>Middle Row</u>: Christopher Peacock, Paul Noone, Rachel Iveson, Kate Jackson, Christopher Dodd, Richard Blanchard, Michael Smith, Sally Metcalfe. <u>Front Row</u>: Geraldine Potts, Martin Ramsay, Adam Peacock, Stuart Jackson, Lindsay Ramsay, Robert Armstrong, Daniel Poole, Peter Armstrong, Helen Robinson.

1990 – 2000

Laura Blanchard and Lindsay Ramsay working on their transport project ~ Jan 1991.

Joanna Dodd and Holly Coxson at York Railway Museum ~ 1991.

Robert McKinlay, Kate Jackson, Stuart Jackson at the Village Hall for a Transport Drama Day ~ 1991

A visit to Steetley Quarry ~ 1991

In 1994, the school was threatened with closure due to declining numbers, but managed to avert this.

1990 – 2000

A trip to Ingleborough ~ 1991

1993 Sports Day action

1993 Sports Day action

1990 – 2000

Christmas 1993 ~ Adam Peacock, Geraldine Potts, Kate Jackson, Richard Dodd.

Adam Peacock reads to Katy Hurworth ~ 1994

Anne Gargett helps with the Teddy Bears Picnic ~ 1996

A School visit to How Stean Gorge

1990 – 2000

Geraldine Potts, Claire Metcalfe, Ben Durrans, Graham Dodd, Tony Mableson, Michael Smith, David Bowers ~ 1994

Santa's Grotto at Hackforth School Fayre 1996 – Lindsay Brown with Colin Blanchard

The Christmas Play ~ 1996

Polyanna Mitchell, Chelsea Horn, Lindsay Brown

1990 – 2000

Hackforth School ~ 1996

<u>Back row</u>: **Mrs. P. Durrans**, Thomas Anderson, Laurence Crate, Kayleigh Poole, Richard Dodd, Claire Metcalfe, Ben Durrans, Lee Williamson, **Mrs. C. Brown**. <u>3rd row</u>: Sean Webb-Collins, Barnabus Knights-Johnson, David Bowers, Pollyanna Mitchell, Colin Field, Sharon Mellor, Barry Horn, Chelsie Horn, John Blows, Matthew Larby, Scott Norman. <u>2nd row</u>: Henrietta Niekirk, Lindsay Brown, Tanya Stirk, Sarah Potter, Sophie Bolton, Katy Hurworth, Charlotte Hurworth, Sarah Larby, Dean Norman. <u>Front row</u>: David Field, Michael Metcalfe, Edward Blows, Andrew Coulter, Joshua Walker, Thomas Lockhart, Henry Anderson, Matthew Donaldson.

Big praise for tiny school

A SMALL village school has been given top marks by a team of Government inspectors.

The 20-pupil Hackforth and Hornby Primary School was praised by inspectors from the Office for Standards in Education (OFSTED) who said the quality of teaching was good and the children well behaved.

Situated in the village of Hackforth, near Bedale, North Yorkshire, it is the second small school in the county to be patted on the back by Ofsted.

Recently, Kell Bank Primary School, near Masham, which also has only 20 pupils, was described as "outstanding".

Hackforth and Hornby governor Marie Larby, said: "It is rewarding to have independent confirmation of the high standards we believe this school achieves.

"This has been achieved by the hard work of staff, governors and the support of parents and the community."

Newspaper article 1996

The successful OFSTED inspection at school meant that parents were prepared to bring their children to Hackforth from the surrounding area. An extension, and alterations to the school in 1998 improved facilities, both for the children, and staff.

School turns to DIY and gives itself a new face –

STAFF buckled down and mucked in to do their bit when it came to giving their village school a face lift.

Hackforth and Hornby CE Primary was among a number of North Yorkshire schools to benefit from a £90m national improvement package announced by Education Secretary Mr David Blunkett last year.

The 160-year-old school, which escaped a closure threat in 1994 and now has almost 40 pupils, has a new look described as "dramatic" by Mr Simon Ashby, its head teacher for two years.

The improvement project, which cost almost £24,000 including a £400 contribution from school funds raised mainly by parents, included making an indoor route to the boys' toilets, which have new urinals, installing wash basins for both boys and girls and moving the school office from behind a partition into what was the front entrance.

An extension porch built over a recessed alcove has become the main school entrance and children's cloakroom, and sinks have been fitted in the infants' classroom.

Work on the toilets was done by a professional building firm from Northallerton but Mr Ashby, his staff and a helper were responsible for improvements to the classrooms and office.

Mr Ashby worked with teachers Mrs Mary Hutchinson and Mrs Cynthia Spencer, classroom assistant Mrs Sue Williamson, school secretary Mrs Sue Kirby and Mr Arthur Kirby during the summer holiday and autumn term.

He said work on the boys' toilets would mean improved security and hygiene and added: "The transformation in the school has been fairly dramatic. The whole place has changed.

"When it came to the staff contribution we had to do just about everything from putting in sinks, drilling and joinery to plumbing, shelving and redecorating. It involved quite a few DIY skills.

"We are very pleased with how it all looks. There are still some things we would like to do, but we have got the main fabric of what we want."

Pictured above: Mr Ashby takes a back seat to a workmanlike Lindsay Brown, aged 8.

Newspaper article 1998

The Women's Institute (W.I.)

From left: Joan Chapman, Jean Ramshay, Ann Harrison, Mabel Barker, Mrs. Janet Bardon

Article: **Half a century in Hackforth WI**

Presentations have been made at Hackforth to four women with 200 years of WI service between them

Mrs Joan Chapman, Mrs 'Bardie' Bardon, Mrs Mabel Barker and Mrs Jean Ramshay have been members of Hackforth WI for 50 years, and the annual meeting was a time for reminiscing.

They were presented with 50-year certificates by Mrs Ann Harrison, Chairman of the North Yorkshire (West) Federation, who is pictured with them above, and received bouquets from their WI colleagues.

Hackforth WI, which has about 20 members, has always met in the village hall. It was founded almost 70 years ago and Mrs Chapman joined it at the age of 16, having been taken to a meeting by her mother.

WI President Mrs Betty Burke said, "We like to think that, to have four ladies with 50 years' membership each in such a relatively small institute, is quite an achievement.

"Such presentations can be made at federation meetings in places like Skipton, but the ladies decided they would like their presentation at their own WI.

"They had many memories of the past 50 years and have seen many changes from the days when there were many more competitions.

"Today the WI plays darts and table tennis, and we have 22 women from all over the federation coming to play table tennis in the village hall."

1990 – 2000

The Annual Domino Drives are now a main source of funding for Hackforth W.I. and are well supported by people in the Richmond and Bedale area. Members very generously donate prizes for the raffle.

Mrs. Maisie Newcombe

Mrs. Barbara Pearson, Mrs. Anne Pace and Mr. Derek Hutchinson prepare the raffle ~ 1999.

The Millennium

The Millennium

In 1998, a committee was formed to raise money to celebrate the Millennium in the Hackforth, Hornby and Langthorne area. A questionnaire was sent out to each household to find out how they would like to commemorate the Millennium.

HACKFORTH AND AINDERBY MIERS PARISH COUNCIL
MILLENNIUM CELEBRATIONS

It has been proposed that it would be fitting for the village to organize something to mark the Millennium. Colin Blanchard, Jim Pearson and Jim Pringle started off the idea and, to this end, Stewart and Linda Burrows have donated £200 from the Harvest Auction. The matter was discussed at the Parish Council meeting and it was agreed that a public meeting be held to see what support such a project might receive.

It was agreed that, as well as inviting Hornby, Langthorne, and East and West Appleton, the Church, the School, the Women's Institute, other interested parties should be asked to send representatives. It was proposed that the meeting should elect a committee and a chairman who, in turn, could form subcommittees to run various aspects of the celebrations such as finance, events etc. The entire project depends on the enthusiasm of yourself and your families to commemorate this notable event.

The meeting will take place in Hackforth Village Hall at <u>7.30pm on Wednesday. 17th June</u>. Please make a note of the date, turn up and let us have your views.

John Cowley, Vice-chairman.

"The meeting held in Hackforth Village Hall was very well attended by a cross section of the villages and it was obvious that people want a memorable millennium. To this end a committee has been formed to oversee the organisation of events.

"We need bright ideas and sparkling suggestions as to what YOU want for the year 2000. Please let us know what you want to happen be it an event, commemorative project or any other way of marking this historic year.

"Ideas are also required for fundraising, remembering that we only have 18 months left before the beginning of the year 2000."

As a result, several fund raising events were arranged during 1999 to finance the celebrations in the year 2000. A wide range of events took place, involving as many local people as possible. The events in 1999 included a New Year's Walk, a Sketch Show, a Fashion show, a Treasure Hunt, and a Yorkshire Day. A calendar for the year 2000 was produced, using local old postcards.

A self-financing '100' club was set up to run for 2 years and ending in December 2000 to assist with prize draws.

The Fundraising Events in 1999

3rd Jan 1999

WALK FOR THE MILLENNIUM
(in aid of the Hackforth, Langthorne and Hornby millennium fund)

**On Sunday 3 January 1999
From Blacksmith's Farm, Silver Street
Hackforth**

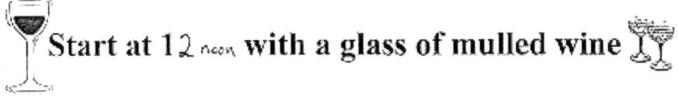

Start at 12 noon with a glass of mulled wine

**Followed by a walk for all the family.
approx 1hour's walk on hard tracks**

Grannies, Grandpas, Mums, Dads, boys,
girls, cats and dogs all welcome

£1 for Adults, 50p for children

Why not have lunch in the pub afterwards?

(Mrs C. Pringle)

The Millennium

On 20th March 1999, The Village Hall in Hackforth was the venue for the "Millennium Farce!" written and produced by Jim Pringle.

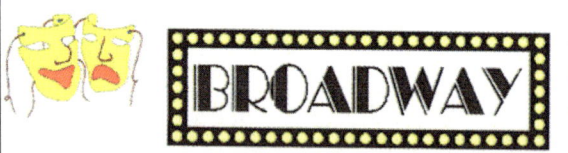

BROADWAY

MILLENNIUM FARCE

IN HACKFORTH VILLAGE HALL
SATURDAY 20TH MARCH AT 7.30 PM
£3 ADULTS £1.50 16 & UNDER
REFRESHMENTS INCLUDED BAR AVAILABLE
PROCEEDS TO MILLENNIUM FUND

TICKETS FROM:
GREYHOUND INN
HACKFORTH POST OFFICE
MILLENNIUM COMMITTEE
CRAKEHALL POST OFFICE

BRING MUSIC TO YOUR EARS
BRING MUSIC TO YOUR EARS

SATURDAY 20th MARCH 1999

MILLENNIUM FARCE PROGRAMME

ENTERTAINMENT

1. 'WONDERWALL' & 'IRISH JIG' — Johnson, Georgia and Marco Ramsay
2. 'A ROAD WARNING' — Roger Clutterbuck and Melvyn Peacock
3. RECITATIONS — Nick Broadwith
4. 'ANNIE'S SONG' — Jenny Durrans and Kayleigh Poole
5. 'HOVIS' TUNE — Jenny Durrans
6. 'SCARBOROUGH FAIR' — Kayleigh Poole
7. 'POETRY READING' — Doreen Howe
8. 'EXTRACTING THE LAST DROP' — Arnold Butler Simon Butler, John Cowley, Brian Dobson. Audrey Plews and Bob Walker
9. 'A FRENCH FOLK SONG' — Chelsie Horn and Lindsay Brown
10. 'LITTLE JOHN' & 'OH WHEN THE SAINTS…' — Tanya Stirk and Jonathan Stretton-Downes
11. 'ELVIS…I'M WANDERING ALONG' — Katy Hurworth and Scott Norman
12. 'OLD SPICE' — Simon Butler, Sue Hurworth, Pat Moate and Melvyn Peacock

BUFFET SUPPER

DANCING TO MUSIC PROVIDED BY DENNIS HURWORTH

The Millennium

Roger Clutterbuck talks about the problems of mud on the roads. Right: Nick Broadwith recites an "Ode to Farmers"…

…and right: Doreen Howe wrote a poem especially for the occasion.

Above: Kayleigh Poole and Jenny Durrans play the flute.
Right: The Ramsay Family Group from Hornby.
(Photographs by Mrs C Norman)

The Millennium

"Yorkshire Water Bored Meeting": Audrey Plews, Bob Walker, Simon Butler.

Top right: Tom Myers 'interrupts' the proceedings.

Right: John Cowley speaks at the 'Bored' Meeting.

Left: Speakers at the 'Bored' Meeting ~ Brian Dobson & Arnold Butler..

The Millennium

Top Left: Lindsay Brown and Chelsie Horn play the violin.

Top right: Elvis Presley, alias Scott Norman, sings and Katy Hurworth plays the tambourine.

Left: The Spice Girls!
Pat Moate, Mervin Peacock, Simon Butler, Sue Hurworth.

The Millennium

The audience ~ a full house!

HACKFORTH MILLENNIUM ASSOCIATION

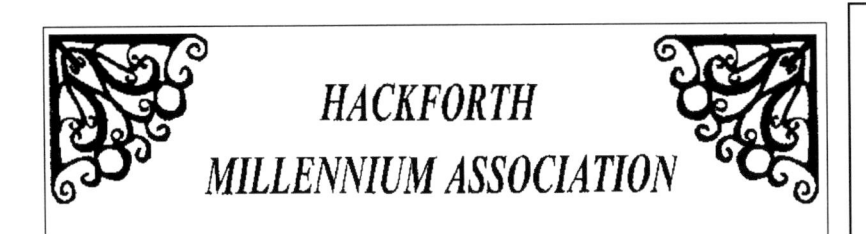

PRESENTS

An evening of

FASHION and BEAUTY
at
HORNBY CASTLE

Wednesday 28th April at 7:30p.m.
(by kind permission of Mr & Mrs R Clutterbuck)

Admission by programme
price £5
(to include a glass of wine)

MODEL'S HAIR STYLED BY

SCRUPLES

The Courtyard
Market Place
Bedale   01677-422293

CLINIQUE

and

ESTEE LAUDER

Barkers (Northallerton) Ltd
198/202 High Street
Northallerton   01609-772303

FASHION BY

GILT EDGED

21 Market Place
Leyburn
Nth Yorks   01969-624811

CYCLE TREASURE HUNT

*BUT
IF YOU REALLY HAVEN'T GOT A CYCLE
THEN A WALKING TREASURE HUNT !!!*
(Length of cousre approx. 3.5 miles)

SUNDAY 4th JULY

Starting Point:
Hackforth Village Hall
at 3.00pm

Followed by:-
SAUSAGE BARBECUE
and
fun and games at Street House Farm
(just follow the clues to find your way!!!)

TICKETS:-   £2.00 per adult
£1.50 per child
£5.00 per family of four

Available from: Jenny Pybus
Ann Spirit

ALL proceeds to go to Hackforth Millenium Association

Following the clues

The Treasure Hunt finishes at Street House Farm with a barbeque and quiz

The Millennium

The Millenium Committee invite you to 'YORKSHIRE DAY'

Sunday 1st August 1999, 2pm onwards, at the Greyhound Country Inn, Hackforth.

Adults Competition for the best garden 'Yorkshire Rose'

Childrens Competition for the best home-made or painted 'Yorkshire rose'
Age categories; under 10 years old & 10 – 16 year olds.

Yorkshire Cake Stall

Quiz

Childrens Games

Come & try Quoits – beginners welcome!

+23.7.99

HACKFORTH, HORNBY AND LANGTHORNE MILLENNIUM CELEBRATIONS.

SUNDAY 1ST AUGUST 1999 2PM ONWARDS

'YORKSHIRE DAY'
at
THE GREYHOUND COUNTRY INN
HACKFORTH

Dear Friends,

We hope you are able to join the fun and participate/contribute in the following:

YORKSHIRE ROSE - Bring your home-grown Yorkshire rose (any colour!) between 2.30pm and 3.00pm, judging will take place at 3.15 pm approximately, with a prize for the winning entry.

CHILDREN'S YORKSHIRE ROSE - This competition is for the best home-made rose or painted picture of a rose. There are three age categories: 5-7years.
8-10years.
11-16years.
Entries (labelled with name and age) should be brought between 2.30pm and 3.00pm, judging will take place at 3.15 pm approximately, with a prize for each age category.

YORKSHIRE CAKE STALL - **All** contributions for the cake stall will be gratefully received (any traditional Yorkshire cakes?). Please label your contribution with type of cake and an approximate price.

QUIZ - From 2.pm onwards there will be a Yorkshire-related quiz sheet for sale in the Greyhound, cost 50p.

CHILDREN'S GAMES – These will take place from 2pm outside the Greyhound

QUOITS 'PRO/AM' – From 2pm onwards you can enjoy yourself trying out the traditional game of quoits. No previous knowledge or skill necessary! - you will be partnered with an experienced quoits player who will explain everything you need to know.

ICE CREAM/REFRESHMENTS will be sold.

ALL ACTIVITIES WILL TAKE PLACE OUTSIDE, UNLESS IT IS RAINING.

Best Wishes, Jim Pringle.

Hackforth Millennium Association

AUTUMN FAIR, PRODUCE SHOW AND BARBECUE

**Saturday 11 September 1999
12 noon onwards**

Refreshments

at Hackforth Village Hall

Grand Raffle

Quiz?

Competitions

Ice creams

Balloon Race

For information on "classes", see any committe member, or look out for the schedule coming through your door soon!

The Millennium

2000 Events:

> 1.5.2000
>
> HACKFORTH, HORNBY AND LANGTHORNE MILLENNIUM CELEBRATION
>
> Dear Friends,
> **Diary alert!!**
> At a recent meeting of the Millennium Committee it was decided to organise the following activities / events:
>
> | Date | Event |
> |---|---|
> | 9th July 2000 | Proposed **'Open gardens'** in Hackforth. If you wish to be involved by opening your garden, helping to organise, or would be a visitor, please let one of the Committee members know. |
> | 6th August 2000 | 'Yorkshire Day' – with free B.B.Q. This is a repeat of an enjoyable event held last year. |
> | 9th September 2000 | Produce Show - prospectus detailing the sections out soon.! |
> | 2nd December 2000 | ' An evening in the Village Hall '– party/ presentation etc. |
> | 7th January 2001 | Village Walk |
>
> Commemorative Millennium village sign. Please look at the Noticeboard to see the design chosen - if you have any comments to make regarding the design, please contact Jim Pringle a.s.a.p.
>
> Best wishes
> Jim Pringle

Among the many suggestions made, it was decided to fund the following:

- Bulb planting and a wrought iron Village sign in Hackforth.
- Bulb planting and the installation of 2 stone-faced village signs in Langthorne.
- A Yew tree to be planted, and a wooden seat installed in the Church Yard at Hornby.
- A local History Book to collect together maps, photos, memories and any other relevant information of the local area.

It's Your Party

Join together to celebrate

Yorkshire Day

with a fun afternoon for all the family

Sunday 6 August 2000

at The Greyhound Country Inn, Hackforth

from 3.00pm onwards

- Activities and Games Galore!
  - Free Barbecue Tea!

full details of attractions overleaf

with the kind permission of Linda & Stewart Burrows, The Greyhound Country Inn and Paul and Ann Dyer, The Mill, Hackforth

Whilst the Millennium Committee strives to ensure a safe and successful event please note that attendance and participation is strictly at your own risk

Organised by the Hackforth, Hornby & Langthorne Millennium Committee for the Millennium Celebrations

---

It's Your Party

* * * * Attractions * * * *

Tug of War
3.00 - 3.30pm. Men's, Women's, Children's and Mixed classes (bring old clothes!)

Followed by:

Children's and Adult Sports Races
3.30 - 4.30pm. Egg & Spoon, 3 Legged, Sack races etc, Wellie Wanging

Quoits Pro-Am
All afternoon from 3.30pm All welcome, tuition a pleasure for non-players

Bring and Buy Cake Sale
On sale from 3.30pm. Please bring cakes on the day or beforehand by arrangement with Grace Stretton-Downes, Meadowcroft, Langthorne. ☎ 01677-423260

Dominoes Pro-Am
All afternoon from 3.30pm. All welcome, tuition a pleasure for non players

Yorkshire Pub Quiz
From 3.30 - 5.30pm. Take a quiz sheet and complete at your leisure during the afternoon 25p per sheet

Best Yorkshire Mouse Competition
In the tradition of the Yorkshire "Mouse Man" furniture maker
Make and enter your mouse. Any medium. Under 11 years, 11-18 years and adult classes
Adult entry 50p. Under 11 years and 11-18 years - free entry. Judging at 4.00pm

Best Yorkshire Hat Competition
Decorate and enter a hat, celebrating the best of Yorkshire
Under 11 years, 11-18 years and adult classes
Adult entry 50p. Under 11 years and 11-18 years - free entry
Judging at 4.00pm followed by Hat Parade at 4.30pm

Available all afternoon from 3.30pm
Yorkshire Ice-creams - 50p each
Raffle - tickets 20p each

Free Barbecue tea from 5.00pm

All activities are free entry unless otherwise stated
Wet weather arrangements - Tug of War, Quoits and Sports will not take place

All enquiries:
David & Linda McKnight - ☎ 01748 811128; E-mail: david.mcknight@cropwise.co.uk
Simon & Grace Stretton-Downes - ☎ 01677 423260; E-mail: simon@stret-d.totalserve.co.uk

Whilst the Millennium Committee strives to ensure a safe and successful event please note that attendance and participation is strictly at your own risk

The Millennium

Left:
Jim Pearson and Martin Webster enjoy a chat.

Right:
Linda McKnight with hats and mice

Below: Children's Races

Below: The cake stall

Yorkshire Day marked by celebration

THE millennium committee of Hackforth, Hornby and Langthorne organised a celebration to mark Yorkshire Day.

There were competitions for adults and children, ice cream and cake stalls, quoits for beginners and the prize for a Yorkshire-grown rose was won by Mr Peter Knox. The events in fine and warm weather raised £121.

The millennium fund is growing steadily thanks to those who supported the 100 Club and to Mrs Jenny Pybus and Ann Spirit who organised a cycle ride, treasure hunt and barbeque and gave the £140 proceeds to the villages' fund

Plans for commemorative projects should be completed soon and there will be an open meeting in the autumn for people to approve them or make further constructive suggestions.

The next millennium event is an autumn fair in Hackforth village hall on September 11, starting with a barbeque at noon.

Newspaper article

Hackforth Millennium Association

Craft and Produce Show

Saturday 9th September 2000
11 am onwards

Hackforth Village Hall

The Millennium

Craft Produce Show **2000**

Garden Produce

Photographs: Mrs Tracey Snowdon

Children's class - edible necklace and (below)
Flower arrangement in unusual object

The Millennium

9th July 2000 ~ Six gardens in and around Hackforth were opened to the public.
Viewing Mill Cottage.

(Jenny Walker)

Bulb Planting outside Hackforth

(photographs Mrs C Pringle)

Colin and Kath Blanchard, Linda and David McKnight, and Jenny Olivant

Left:
Mr Tim Easby with his daughters Olivia and Camilla.

Right:
Jenny and John Pybus

Hornby Yew

A Yew tree was planted in St Mary's Church Yard at Hornby, to commemorate the Millennium.

The service was conducted by Rev. David Christie, and involved the youngest and oldest resident in planting the tree. (Camilla Easby and Jack Metcalfe.)

(Darlington & Stockton Times)

Millennium seat: Villagers near Bedale have been given a little extra comfort to mark the millennium.
Anyone with weary legs can rest on a seat presented to the parish of Hornby by the millennium committee for Hackforth and Hornby. It has been given pride of place in the grounds of St Mary's church.
Pictured at the presentation are, standing, left to right, Malcolm Percival, the Rev David Christie, Martin Cawood, Christine Brown and Ronald Richardson. Seated are Jim Pearson, who made the presentation, and Val Ramsay. BR/DST

The Millennium

Village Millennium Projects

Hackforth Millennium Association Newsletter

As we draw to the end of the Millennium year the Hackforth Millennium Association would like to invite you to **'A Bit Of A Do'**. We are holding a party on Saturday 2nd December from 7.30pm to 1.00am in Hackforth village hall to celebrate all we have achieved over the last 2 years since the Association was formed, and to say thank you for all your support. There will be a bar, food and entertainment will be provided. The programme of events will include:
- Disco and live music by Rodney Gee and his band
- Presentation of the signed village photograph to the village hall, - preview of the history book presently being compiled, - a raffle and the final draw of the 100 club,
- A review of all that has been achieved over the last 2 years including -
    highs and lows, bulb planting, village walks, Yorkshire Day, produce show, open gardens, fashion show, village signs and seat etc.,

We would appreciate any photos you may have of any of the Millennium activities so that we can make a visual presentation, recording the events, to put on display on the night. Please pass any such photos to a member of the committee listed below as soon as possible, in an envelope with your name on the back of all photos so that we may return them.

In order that the catering requirements can be organised please fill in the slip below with your intention to attend the party and return to a member of the committee by Friday 17th November. Your prompt response will be most appreciated.

We hope to see you all on the 2nd December and aim to give you a very enjoyable evening.

Committee members:

Jim Pringle	Simon Butler	Jim & Barbara Pearson
Colin Blanchard	Malcolm Percival	Tracey Snowdon
Christine Brown	Pat & Richard Moate	Jenny Olivant

The Millennium

Hello 2000!

HELLO 2000 — Villagers turned out on force to mark the new Millennium in the village of Hackforth near Bedale – some of the 150 residents gathered at the heart of the village for a commemorative group photograph snapshot of village life at the beginning of the 21st Century.

Northern Echo

The Millennium

When the *Northern Echo* featured Hackforth in its series 'Hello 2000', the Millennium Committee asked all the residents to sign the border surrounding the photograph. At 'A Bit of a Do' – the framed photograph was presented to the Chairman of the Village Hall (Jim Pearson) by the Chairman of the Millennium Committee (Jim Pringle)

The Audience.

After 2000

Some of the events introduced for the Millennium Celebrations have become an established part of Village Life. In particular, the News Year's Day Walk and the Autumn Produce Show have proved popular.

Perhaps we should look to the children to see what they think the future will hold. "I think Hackforth will have developed and be much bigger. There will be a few shops and more houses built on some of the fields. Any farms that remain will use hi-tech farm machinery. The school will either be bigger and modernised, or not there at all."

The Millennium

Hackforth & Hornby C of E School

Far Left: Village Hall ~ Centre: School ~ Right: School House   *(Sandra Webb)*

Appendix 1 ~ Domesday 1985

Appendix 1 – Domesday 1985

GENERAL DESCRIPTION Page: 01

This is a predominantly agricultural area with many farms on it. The farmland is fertile and is used mainly for dairy farming and crops or grass, corns (especially barley) and potatoes. Many of the farms are old established farms. The largest centre of population is Hornby village. This small village developed around the castle and many of the buildings are associated with the castle. There is quite an expanse of woodland near the castle – some of this is newly planted with conifers and is reserved for rearing pheasants.
There is also a series of lakes running south and east from the castle. On one of these lakes is a duck decoy.

Keywords for Indexing:
- LANDSCAPE
- FARMING
- CASTLES
- VILLAGES

HORNBY VILLAGE page: 02

Hornby Is a very small, quiet village set amongst farmland. The main building in Hornby is the castle. The village was built around the castle.
There is a church. It probably came with the castle along time ago. There is a new Estate next to the old vicarage. It is called Park Chase. There are 6 houses in it and 23 people live there. Hornby Castle has got its own water supply. It comes from the fields and goes to the castle and some of the estate houses. There is an old gas house. It is where they used to make gas. There are some very old cottages in front of the church. One of them is the castle's old laundry. Much of the life today in Hornby still centres round the castle and the church.

Keywords for Indexing:
- LANDSCAPE
- VILLAGES
- LOCAL HISTORY
- CASTLES

GENERAL DESCRIPTION Page: 01

This is a rolling agricultural area bisected by the A1 trunk road (the main London to Edinburgh road which follows the route of the Roman Dere Street).
There is little high land and most of the fields are cultivated though some are grazing land for sheep or cattle. The main crops grown are cereals, potatoes and grass for hay or silage.
Hackforth Village is the largest settlement having about 40 houses and a population of about 120. Here there is a school, village hall, public house and a sub-post office/shop.
Ainderby Miers and Gyll Hall are farmhouses of historic interest. On the east side of the A1 road there is a stud farm and a haulage contractor.

Keywords for Indexing:
- LANDSCAPE
- FARMING
- HACKFORTH VILLAGE
- HISTORIC BUILDINGS

HACKFORTH VILLAGE Page: 02

Hackforth village is a quiet village just west of the A1 road. It consists of 39 houses and a lot of farmland.
There are 2 farms in Hackforth itself. There is also a school, Village Hall, a Post Office and a Public House. There are some Council houses and some modern stone houses. Some of the detached houses are quite large. One has its own swimming pool. One or two of the houses are old – Manor Farm dates back to the sixteenth century. There are allotment gardens in the village. People use a patch of garden to grow vegetables and fruit in.
The village shares a policeman with other villages and a vicar with 3 other villages. Local service vans such as fish 'n chips and county library vans visit regularly.

Keywords for Indexing:
- LANDSCAPE
- VILLAGES

Appendix 1 – Domesday 1985

THE CASTLE, HORNBY — Page: 03

The castle was built in the 13th Century. It was built by the St. Quintens. It was built as a stately home not as a fighting castle. At that time lots of stately homes, churches and manor houses were built with battements. In the 18th Century the castle was altered. In these days it belonged to the Duke of Leeds. He owned it until 1930 when it was sold. Then some parts of it were pulled down, as they were unsafe. The castle has many fields and gardens around it. Today the castle is lived in by Major-General Clutterbuck and his family. It is not at present open to the public but it is used for special village occasions, especially those associated with the church

Keywords for Indexing:
  LOCAL HISTORY
  CASTLES
  GARDENS

CASTLE EMPLOYMENT, HORNBY — Page: 04

Major-General Clutterbuck lives in the castle with some of his family. The castle gives employment to several people. Mrs. Bardon works in the castle. She cooks the dinner for the family. Mrs. Jopling cleans the rooms. Mrs. McKinlay helps Mr.& Mrs. Michael Clutterbuck with the domestic work in their part of the castle. Mr. Errington is the gardener and odd job man at the castle. He looks after all the castle gardens. He also looks after the General and acts as his chauffeur. Mr. Smith is the farm foreman. He helps to organise the farm men. Mr. Jopling works on the castle farm. He is also the estate gamekeeper. Mr. Atkinson is the stockman on the farm. Mr. Fullerton provides additional help three days a week. He is a long serving employee. Mr. Hurworth is a farm worker. Mr. Roger Clutterbuck is in charge of the farm.

Keywords for Indexing:
  EMPLOYMENT
  FARMING
  HISTORIC BUILDINGS
  DOMESTIC WORK

POPULATION SURVEY, HACKFORTH — Page: 03

We conducted a survey to find the population of Hackforth village. These are our results.

{Adults}	82 (including 16 pensioners)
{Children:}	
Primary school	15
Secondary school	10
Pre School	7
Further education	6

This gives a total of 120

The population has stayed at between 100 and 160 for about 150 years.

{CHILDREN'S SURVEY 1985}

Keywords for indexing:
  POPULATION
  SURVEYS
  STATISTICS EDUCATION

THE SCHOOL, HACKFORTH — Page: 04

Hackforth School has been standing since Victorian times. The school once had 82 pupils, now there are 26. There are 15 juniors and 11 infants. I am a fourth year junior. There are two classrooms. The school has a small garden along the front. The canteen stands in the middle of the play area. Mrs. Thwaites, our cook, cooks school Dinners for us here. They cost 67p a day. There is a lawn and a yard for us to play on. Mrs. Flowers and Mrs. Skinner are our teachers. Mrs. Robinson is our dinner lady; she looks after us at dinner time. Some children bring a packed lunch but I have school dinners. The P.E. shed is attached to the school. The boys' toilets are outside in the yard. There is a house attached to the school which used to be for the head teacher to live in.

Keywords for Indexing:
  EDUCATION
  SCHOOLS
  FOOD

Appendix 1 – Domesday 1985

WATER SUPPLY, HORNBY Page: 05

Hornby Castle has its own water supply. The supply feeds the castle, the gas works and many of the houses in Hornby village. The water comes from a spring in the field opposite Park Chase. The spring has never dried up even in drought years. The water is very clear and very hard. It is piped across the field to the pump house. A small pipe from here used to feed a standpipe in Hornby village. The two hydrams pump the water to the reservoir which is several fields away on higher ground. The reservoir holds 8,000 gallons of water and is 8 feet deep. The water falls by gravity to the Castle and other houses. Recently the nitrate content of the water has risen as a result of the nitrate fertilizers put on the farmland being absorbed by the rain water.

Keywords for Indexing
  HOME LIFE
  WATER SUPPLY

SUMMER FAYRE, HORNBY Page: 06

A Summer Fayre is held annually in Hornby Castle grounds. Proceeds go to St. Mary's Church, Hornby. This year there was an ice cream stall, a second-hand book stall, and tombola where you picked a ticket from a drum. If your ticket number was on a prize, you won that prize. There was a welly-throwing game where you tried to throw a Wellington the furthest. Raffle tickets, cakes, toffee apples, biscuits, jams etc were sold. A board had jars on and you had to throw ping-pong balls into them to win the money. The entrance fee to the Fayre was 50P. For this you had afternoon tea which was scones, cakes and a cup of tea.
  There was also a pony and trap which you could buy rides in. Everyone enjoys the Fayre Day.

Keywords for Indexing:
  EVENTS
  ENTERTAINMENT RECREATION
  CUSTOMS

HOUSING, HACKFORTH Page: 05

In Hackforth there are about 40 houses. There are only five council houses and two council flats. A few of the other houses are still owned by Hornby Castle estate and the farm workers live in them but the majority are privately owned. Over half of the houses are either detached or semi-detached. Except for the council houses nearly all the others are built from stone. Many are quite old and have been modernised. All the houses have some garden by them and most of them have a garage. There are some 'listed buildings', for example Roundhill Farm and Manor Farm.

Keywords for Indexing:
  HOUSING
  LISTED BUILDINGS

EMPLOYMENT, HACKFORTH Page: 06

From our survey of the people of Hackforth we found that the majority of workers are employed locally. 16 out of the 38 employed are farm workers. Some of the women in the village are also employed locally as cooks or caretakers. Many who travel between 5 and 15 miles worked in shops as assistants. The builders and gardeners travelled from place to place. There are 2 teachers who travel by car to work and 2 wagon drivers, one works at Catterick, the other works at Middlesbrough. A civil servant who works at Pontefract travels farthest. Amongst the other occupations are a Doctor, a Restaurant manageress and an agricultural miller. There is also a stud farm and a haulage contractor in the area. At least 12 of the households asked have retired people in them.

{CHILDREN'S SURVEY 1985)

Keywords far Indexing:
  EMPLOYMENT
  OCCUPATIONS
  CHILDREN'S SURVEY

Appendix 1 – Domesday 1985

ST MARY'S CHURCH, HORNBY Page: 07

The church at Hornby is a Norman church. It is 905 years old. The tower is the oldest bit of the church. Although close to Hornby Castle St. Mary's also serves as a Parish church for Hackforth. Every Sunday there is a service. Once every month there is a Family Service on a Sunday. Some of the school children sing and read prayers. There is also an End of Year service for leavers from Hackforth School. There are special services at Harvest time and Christmas. The caretaker of the church is Mrs. Brunskill. The vicar is called Reverend Pearson. The vicar also looks after Patrick Brompton, Crakehall and Hunton churches.

Keywords for Indexing:
   RELIGION
   CHURCH
   ST. MARY'S
   LOCAL HISTORY

POINT TO POINT, HORNBY Page: 08

Once a year in April Point to Point races are run at Hornby. This is a great social event. It is, organized by the Bedale Hunt and the West of Yore Hunt. Profits are shared between the Hunts.
The Point to Point is the Hunts' Annual Steeple Chase. The longest race is three miles and the jumps are made of bush, are 4 feet high. There are cash prizes for the winners. Both men and women compete but horses must have hunted a specific number of times to qualify. A cup is presented to the horse and rider who wins the most races.

Keywords for Indexing:
   EVENTS
   RECREATION

SHOPPING, HACKFORTH Page: 07

We asked housewives where they did their shopping. Most daily shopping is done at Hackforth Post Office. There are ten different places at which people do their weekly shopping. The most popular is Bedale; twenty people shop there. Ten shop at Northallerton four shop at Darlington and three shop at Hackforth. Richmond, Catterick, Leyburn, Middlesbrough, Masham and Ripon are also used for weekly shopping. Larger items of shopping are bought in Northallerton and Darlington although Richmond, York, Ripon and Harrogate are also used.
(CHILDREN'S SURVEY 1985)

Keywords for Indexing:
   TRADE
   SHOPPING
   LIFE STYLES
   LOCAL TOWNS

HEATING & COOKING, HACKFORTH Page: 08
   Heating
People in Hackforth use 6 different ways of heating their houses. 27 houses use coal, 11 use electricity, 10 use oil, 7 use wood, 4 use coke and 2 use gas. Coal is the most popular as it is cheap and the coal fields are close by. Wood is more popular in the country as it is plentiful. Gas is not piped into the village therefore gas cylinders are used.
   Cooking
The majority of people use electricity to cook with, as it is fairly cheap and reliable and clean and easy to use. Other fuels used were gas (4 households) coke (1 household) coal (2 households) wood (1 household).

Keywords for Indexing:
   ENERGY
   FUELS

Appendix 1 – Domesday 1985

BEDALE HUNT, HORNBY Page: 09

Bedale Hunt meets four Mondays a season at The Greyhound, Hackforth and hunts over Hornby Park which has some of the best hunting in the area. The 2 packs of 40 hound dogs are kept in Little Fencote. The kennel huntsman is G. Cook. There are 2 Whipper-ins who help look after the hounds. Bedale hunt has three Masters: Mr. D.H. Dick, Sir Stephen Furness and Mrs. A. Moore. They look after the country and are in charge of the hounds. At the hunt, the Masters, hunt servants and invited guests wear red coats. The riders have a stirrup cup before setting off – an alcoholic drink to keep them warm. The Master blows a horn to instruct the hounds and the field (hunters). The hounds find the scent of a fox and, as they chase it, the huntsmen follow. Bedale Hunt has 100 horses at each meet. The number of foxes caught varies.

Keywords for Indexing:
   EVENTS
   RECREATION
   HUNTING
   SPORT

HOME FARM, HORNBY Page: 10

My farm is owned by my Grandad and we look after it. My Grandad comes once a week to see how the farm is. Our farm has 80 to 90 cows. In the summer we have lots of cows calving. We milk about 80 of the cows. We have 10 sections in our milking parlour. My dad takes turns at having the weekend off. My dad does the milking. We have about 11 fields and the biggest one is the 20-acre field. We have 4 tractors; one of these is a new one. We grow corn and oilseed rape but this year we are growing corn and maize. We have three dogs and four cats; we have two kittens.

Keywords for indexing:
   FARMING
   EMPLOYMENT
   HOME LIFE

THE SHOP, HACKFORTH Page: 09

Hackforth Village Post Office shop is where the blacksmith's shop was many years ago. The shop is open from 8.15am to 1.pm and 2.pm to 5.30pm on Monday, Wednesday, Thursday and Friday. It is open from 8.15am to 1.pm on Tuesday and Saturday. Mrs. K. Moss is the Post Mistress today. The shop sells groceries, newspapers, sweets and ice cream. About 40 newspapers and about £2.00 of sweets are sold each day. The post office sells stamps and people collect their pension from there. There is also a big board on which local advertisements are displayed. The Village shop is used by many of the local people for their daily shopping.

They also enjoy a good chat to each other here.

Keywords for Indexing:
   TRADE
   SUB POST OFFICE
   LOCAL SHOP

THE GREYHOUND INN, HACKFORTH Page: 10

The Greyhound Inn dates back to the 1740s. It was re-named The Greyhound because of greyhound racing held on the Grass in front of the pub. Today there are 2 bars, a lounge and a public bar. The bars are open at lunch time and again in the evening. Webster's and Newcastle beers and gin, whisky, and brandy are the most popular drinks. Orange and coke are popular non-alcoholic drinks. Bar meals such as scampi, trout, hotpots and sandwiches with a selection of deserts are sold at lunch time and in the evenings. The busiest night is Friday.

There is quoits club which plays matches during the Summer months and there is a ladies' darts team.

Accommodation consisting of one family room, one twin bedroom and two double bedrooms is available.

Keywords for Indexing:
   TRADE
   LIFE STYLES
   RECREATION
   FOOD AND DRINK

Appendix 1 – Domesday 1985

A SATURDAY IN MY LIFE   Page 11

I wake up at 7.30 a.m. I watch T.V.A.M. and The Wide Awake Club. I get up at 9:30 am. For breakfast I have cornflakes. Then I wash. I watch T.V. again. I usually watch a television programme called Number 73 on Saturdays, then I do my jobs. I feed the animals and run errands for Mum and Dad. At 12:15 I give my bedroom a good tidy up and practice on my recorder. Then it is time for dinner.

After dinner we either go to Bedale or we go to Agglethorpe. Later, Tim (my brother) and I play outside then get the cows in for milking. We have tea at 7:30 p.m. We then get ready for bed. We sometimes watch T.V. while Mum and Dad get ready to go out. We go to Grandma's while they go out. We are then collected at 12.00 and go home.

Keywords for Indexing:
  HOME LIFE
  ENTERTAINMENT

GHYLL HALL FARM   Page 11

The farm is 141 acres. On it we keep 270 sheep and 200 hens live in hen houses and the sheep stay in the fields. We also have 85 bulls which live in the foldyard. These are sold for beef at the market. We have 2 heifers and 1 milking cow. We also keep 15 pigs which are fattened and then sold. As well as hens, we have 19 ducks and 9 goslings. We sell the eggs and sometimes sell the hens for meat. On the farm we have 2 goats and 2 kids and 4 dogs and 20 cats. We grow barley, wheat, potatoes, and grass for hay and silage. To help with the farm work we have 5 tractors, 2 ploughs, 2 grass cutters, 2 balers, a combine harvester, a hay turner, 2 muck spreaders and six harrows. The grass is made into silage and stored in silos.

Keywords for Indexing:
  FARMING
  ANIMALS

FOOD   Page: 12

This is what I had to eat yesterday .At eight o'clock I had my breakfast. I had a cup of coffee and two pieces of toast with butter on. I had my lunch at school. I had chicken vol au vent, peas, sweetcorn and potatoes, and for pudding I had yoghurt. I went home and had a biscuit before my tea. Then at half past six I had my tea. I had a beef burger, potatoes, peas and beans. For my pudding I had fruit flan with ice cream and cream.

Sunday meals are often special. For my Sunday dinner I often have roast lamb, peas, Yorkshire pudding beans and roast potatoes. After that I have a biscuit.

For my tea I have lots of different things like sandwiches, sausage rolls, cakes and tarts.

Keywords for Indexing:
  HOME LIFE
  FOOD

YOUTH CLUB, HACKFORTH   Page: 12

Every Thursday at the Village Hall there is a Youth Club. It starts at 6.30 p.m. and finishes at 8.30 p.m. The children that go are mainly from Hackforth and Hornby. They are, aged from about 8 to 16. Approximately 15 children go a week. Entry fee is 15p. There is a selection of sweets to buy such as Mars bars, Chewits, Twix, Polos and crisps. Soft drinks are sold too.

There is always an adult to organize the games. Mr. George Ramsay is organizing the club at present. The games we play are pool, snooker, table tennis, badminton, darts and swing ball.

We also play rounders each week. Everyone joins in this game.

Keywords for indexing:
  CLUBS
  RECREATION
  YOUNG PEOPLE
  GAMES

Appendix 1 – Domesday 1985

PLAYING OUT AT HORNBY Page: 13

In Hornby there are lots of different places we play in. One is a bridge over a beck. There are lots of trees round the beck. We enjoy trying to get across without using the bridge. There is also a tree in one field which has a branch that is bouncy; we have rides on it we call it the Bouncy Branch.

When we play cricket. We play it in Park Chase. We sometimes make secret dens. Sometimes we play hide and seek. In winter we find ice ponds and play Eskimos trying to catch seals. We get sticks and smash the ice. Sometimes we collect ladybirds and put them on slates.

Keywords for indexing:
 LIFE STYLES
 RECREATION
 GAMES

SCHOOL FROM HORNBY Page: 14

Most of the children in Hornby go to Hackforth School but a few go to Private schools. All the children in Hornby who go to Hackforth School go in cars. Sometimes in Summer, children bike to school. Most of the mums who take them to school give lifts to other children. They usually go out at 8.40 and get to school at 8.50. School starts at 9.00 with prayers. We do Number work or English in the morning. Some times we watch schools programmes on the T.V. In the afternoon we do some art or craftwork or sometimes we do P.E. We go home at 3.30 and get home about 3.40: We usually go out to play when we get home.

Keywords for indexing:
 LIFE STYLES
 EDUCATION

QUOITS CLUB HACKFORTH Page: 13

Quoits is a popular revised sport: The point of the game is to throw a quoit (an iron hoop) onto a pin from a set distance. The pin is 3 inches long and is in the centre of a clay square. The pitch is 11 yards long. The quoits weigh 5 pounds each. A ringer (over the pin) scores 2 points and the quoit closest to the pin scores 1 point. Hackforth Quoits Club practises on Sundays. It belongs to the Zetland League and the Lower Dales League.

There are 7 or 8 players in a team. The members take turns to look after the pitch. They cut the grass and soften the clay. The pitches are at the Greyhound Inn.

The Hackforth Club was formed in 1977 – Silver Jubilee Year. Membership costs £1.00 per year.

Keywords for Indexing:
 CLUBS
 RECREATION
 GAMES
 QUOITS

WOMEN'S INSTITUTE, HACKFORTH page: 14

W.I stands for Women's Institute. It is held on the second Wednesday of each month in the Village Hall. There are 25 members, mainly from Hackforth and Hornby. The committee has about a third of the members on it. Mrs. Young is President, Mrs. Spirit is Secretary and Mrs. Poad is Treasurer. The Hackforth Branch is 54 years old. It is in the North Yorkshire West Branch. The annual subscription is £4 a year. A cup of tea and raffle ticket cost 10p each per meeting. Each month a speaker comes to speak about a specific subject. There are outdoor activities in the Summer. There is a competition at each meeting. Points are awarded to winners. The member with the most points wins a presentation cup. Members go to Denham College to do courses like home-craft, cookery and gardening.

Keywords far Indexing:
 CLUBS
 RECREATION

Appendix 1 – Domesday 1985

HORNBY OLYMPICS, HORNBY Page: 15

During the school Summer holidays, Hornby Olympics was organised. This was a fun day for the children. There were lots of races. There were straight running races. There was an egg and spoon race where you had to run carrying an egg in a spoon. There were piggyback races where you carried someone on your back. We also had a dressing up race. You have to run to some coats, put one on, run to some hats, put one on, then run back. There was a long distance race where you run round a big field. There was another race to see how slow you could go on your bicycle. Winners of the races won a chocolate bar. We all had a drink afterwards. About 20 children took part. Results were pinned on the noticeboard.

Keywords for Indexing:
  RECREATION
  SPORTS
  OLYMPICS

PHEASANT SHOOTS, HORNBY Page: 16

Pheasants in Hornby wood are reared especially for the shooting season. The season is from October 1st to February 1st. During the close seasons pheasants are protected so that the young can grow. The young are reared in pens and fed on small grain. At a pheasant shoot there are usually 8 guns shooters with 2 guns and a loader each. There are 20 beaters who beat the ground to make the pheasants fly up. The 6 gun dogs retrieve the shot birds. A well-organised shoot can cost up to £1000. Sometimes food is provided and it is eaten at a shooting lodge.

Keywords for Indexing:
  EVENTS
  RECREATION
  SPORT
  PHEASANTS

VILLAGE HALL, HACKFORTH Page: 15

The Village Hall was built in 1937. It consists of one main hall and a kitchen. Stones round the outside wall give the names of people who donated money to the building. A games room was added in 1982. The hire charges are £14 for the main hall and £7 for the smaller room. Prices include the use of the kitchen. Mrs. B. Robinson is the caretaker. The hall is run by the Village Hall Committee. Mrs. Mss takes the bookings. The regular users include the Youth Club (weekly) the W.I (monthly) and a domino drive is held weekly.
Profits may go to local clubs or charities. The hall is also used for Discos and parties. It is also used annually for such events as Christmas Fayre (for St. Mary's Church sale of goods made by the blind, Harvest Supper, sale of goods in aid of the mentally handicapped.

Keywords for Indexing:
  CLUBS
  LIFE STYLES
  RECREATION
  ENTERTAINMENT

HOME ENTERTAINMENT, HACKFORTH Page: 16

In the Hackforth area, out of twenty-seven children, ten have home computers. Eleven children have their own television, nineteen have radios and sixteen have tape recorders. Fewer children have their own computer because they are quite expensive. Lots of children have tape recorders and radios because children like listening to music especially pop music. Many children have personal radios with little headphones so that they can listen to the music without disturbing anyone else. Quite a lot of children have their own portable T.V. Some use the T.V. as the monitors for their computers. No family has more than one computer. Computers are very popular birthday and Christmas presents this year. *(CHILDREN'S SURVEY RESULTS 1985}*

Keywords far Indexing:
  MEDIA
  RECREATION
  COMPUTERS
  TELEVISION

Appendix 1 – Domesday 1985

POND DIP Page: 17

We did a pond dip in one of the Hornby ponds; these are some of the creatures we found:

Toads	Water fleas
Tadpoles	Daphnia
Water boatmen	Water worms
Caddisfly	Gnats
Stickleback fish	Leeches
Water spiders	Larvae of various types
Water snails	

We know that there are also pond skaters and whirligig beetles in the ponds.
The ducks and birds live on the weed and life in the pond.

CHILDREN'S SURVEY 1985

Keywords for Indexing:
  ECOLOGY
  LAKES

LAKESIDE PLANTS, HORNBY Page: 18

We went for a walk round one of the lakes at Hornby and looked at the plant life. These are some of the plants we found:

Watercress	Indian balsam
Watermint	Speedwell
Marestail	Woundwort
Duckweed	Flowering rush
Watercress	Meadow cranes-bill
Chickweed	Vetch
Water plantain	Jack-by-the-hedge
Marsh thistle	Bugle
Burdock	Cow parsley
Meadow sweet	Buttercup'
Toadflax	Daisy
Great reed mace	Forget-me-not
Bur reed	Bullrush
Arrowhead	Rose bay willow herb

CHILDREN'S' SURVEY 1985

Keywords for Indexing:
  ECOLOGY
  PLANT LIFE
LAKESIDE PLANTS

TRAFFIC CENSUS A1 TRUNK ROAD Page: 17

We took 2-15 minute traffic counts on the Hackforth village road and the A1 trunk road. The first was on Friday June 21st and the next on Wednesday, June 26th. On both occasions the count in Hackforth was very low – 7 vehicles. On the A1 we found more vehicles were travelling south than north and the volume of traffic was much higher on the Friday. It was noted that lorries were more frequent midweek and caravans and cars were more frequent on the Friday.

COUNT 1	N.	S.	COUNT 2	N	S
Cars	229	270		155	206
Lorries	71	79		75	82
Vans	29	39		16	9
Coaches	1	8		7	1
Caravans	9	5		1	4
Motor bikes	8	1		0	4

CHILDREN'S' SURVEY 1985

Keywords for Indexing:
  TRANSPORT
  TRUNK ROAD

THE POLICEMAN, HACKFORTH Page: 18

Our local policeman is called P.C. Martin. He looks after 9 other villages as well as Hackforth. These are Thornton Watlass, Thirn, Newton-le-Willows, Patrick Brompton, Crakehall, Dowling and Burrill, Langthorne, Hackforth and Hornby. He lives at Crakehall. He moves round his beat in a car and he carries with him a radio repeater. This means he can work away from the car, but the police can still contact him. His base police station is at Bedale. He drives between 50 to 60 miles a day in his car. His patch deals with about 45 crimes a year. Most of this is petty theft. Each village policeman has in his home a special telephone for early warning in case of nuclear alerts.

Keywords for indexing:
  LAW AND ORDER
  POLICEMAN
  CRIME
  COMMUNICATIONS

Appendix 1 – Domesday 1985

TOURISM, HORNBY Page: 19

Mill House is a historic farmhouse. It has bed and breakfast accommodation. It is open from Easter until October, but sometimes Mrs. Knox (the owner) doesn't open it all the time. The charges vary according to the guests. There are two double bedrooms. It is difficult to say how many guests stay per year. Most people come again and again. These are mostly friends. Couples enjoy the peace as no children under ten are taken.
As Hornby is in the 'Herriott Country' many tourists drive through the area or walk the rural footpaths. St. Mary's Church also attracts visitors as it has a unique Norman carved archway.

Keywords for indexing:
TOURISM,
WALKS
HOLIDAYS
HERRIOTT COUNTRY

BIOGRAPHY Page: 20

This block of the Domesday Project was researched, written and compiled by the pupils of Hackforth and Hornby Church of England Primary School.
The following pupils were involved:
Susan Allan, Andrew Dodd,
Charles Dodd, Mark Dodd,
Rachel Gibson, Joseph Howard
Sophie Howard, Wayne Metcalfe,
Rachel Plant, Simon Plant,
Gaynor Ramsay, Layla Ramsay,
Matthew Ryan, Julie Thwaites.
Teaching staff – Mrs. C.M. Flowers.
Thanks are recorded to all who answered questions and volunteered information and especially to Mr. & Mrs H. Spirit and Mr. A. Flowers.

Keywords for Indexing:
BIOGRAPHY

TOURISM, HACKFORTH Page: 19

St. Anne's Cross Caravan Site, open April to November, costs £2 a night. It takes 5 touring caravans or tents. There are toilets and showers for public use. In 1985 trade has been affected by poor weather. It can also be affected by road works on the A1.
Ainderby Miers is an historical farmhouse, which offers farm holidays. It is owned by Mrs. V. Anderson. There are 2 double rooms, 1 single room and 1 family room. It costs £56 for a week's bed and breakfast – £98 if an evening meal is taken. There are facilities for making picnics.
In Hackforth village, bed and breakfast accommodation is offered by The Greyhound Inn and Park House. There is also a holiday cottage in Silver Street. This area is excellent as a base for touring the Dales countryside of North Yorkshire.

Keywords for Indexing:
TOURISM
WALKS
HOLIDAYS
ACCOMMODATION

BIOGRAPHY Page: 20

This block of the Domesday Project was researched, written and compiled by the pupils of Hackforth and Hornby Church of England Primary School. The following pupils were involved:
Susan Allan, Andrew Dodd, Charles Dodd, Mark Dodd, Rachel Gibson, Joseph Howard, Sophie Howard, Wayne Metcalfe, Rachel Plant, Simon Plant, Gaynor Ramsay, Layla Ramsay, Matthew Ryan, Julie Thwaites; Teaching staff: Mrs. C.M. Flowers. Thanks are recorded to all who answered questions and volunteered information and especially to Mr. & Mrs H. Spirit and Mr. A. Flowers.

Keywords for Indexing:
BIOGRAPHY

Appendix 2 – 19th Century Census

Appendix 2 – 19th Century Census

OCCUPATIONS in 1851	No. employed from Hackforth Township (29 households)	No. employed from Hornby Township (18 households)	No. resident in Hornby Castle (1 household)	No. employed from Langthorne Township (30 households)
Bootmaker				1
Butler (Under)			1	
Butter Factor				1
Carpenter	1			
Clerk	1			
Cook		1	1	
Cordwainer	1			
Corn miller	1			
Dressmaker		2		1
Farm Bailiff		1		
Farm / Agricultural Labourer	6	2		1
Farm Servant	9	4		7
Farmer	4	4		4
Farmer Apprentice		1		
Farmer Retired		1		
Footman			2	
Gamekeeper		1		
Gardener		1		
Gardener (Under)		2		
Gardener's Labourer	2			
Grocer		1		
Groom (of the Chamber)			1	
Groom (stable)			1	
Horsebreaker				1
Housekeeper			1	
Inn Keeper	1			
Joiner	3			1
Labourer (*from Norfolk)	26*	5		25
Laundress		1		
Leeds Duke of, plus family			5	
Maid (House)		1	3	
Maid (Kitchen)			1	
Maid (Lady's)			3	
Maid (Laundry)			1	
Maid (Scullery)			1	
Maid (Still room)			1	
Parish Clerk		1		
Piper			1	
Postillion			2	
Schoolmaster	1			
Servant (House)	8	7		2
Servant (Stable)			1	
Smith – Black	2			2
Steward (House)			1	
Steward's Boy			1	
Stonemason	5			1
Stonemason (Apprentice)	1			
Tailor				3
Tile maker				2
Valet			1	
Vicar		1		
Wife (when no other occupation listed)	19	9		27
Family members over 14 with no occupation listed, usually unmarried, sometimes 'retired'	10	7		11
Children (5s & under)	18	4		23
Children / Scholars (5 – 14 yrs.)	9	6		32
Visitor (Adult)	1	1		
Visitor (Child)		1	2	

290

Appendix 2 – 19th Century Census

OCCUPATIONS in 1861	No. employed from Hackforth Township (28 households)	No. employed from Hornby Township (17 households)	No. resident in Hornby Castle (1 household)	No. employed from Langthorne Township (31 households)
Brick Maker				1
Butcher				1
Butter Factor/Dealer				2
Carpenter	5			
Carter		1		1
Children's Nurse		1		
Clerk (Land Agent's)	1			
Cook		1		
Cordwainer/Shoemaker	2			1
Corn miller		1		
Dog feeder	1			
Dressmaker	1			
Farm / Agricultural Labourer	7	5		15
Farm Servant		3		
Farmer	4	4		5
Gamekeeper	1			1
Gardener	2	1		
Gardener's Labourer	1			
Governess/Teacher	2			
Grocer/Draper		1		
Horsebreaker				1
Housekeeper			1	1
Inn Keeper	1			1
Joiner	1			
Maid (House)		1		
Night Watchman (for Castle)		1	2	
Parish Clerk		1		
Piper				
Plough Boy		1		
Poor Woman		1		
Potato Dealer				
Schoolmaster	1			
Servant (House)	1	5		
Servant (General)	13	6	1	12
Shepherd		1		
Smith – Black	1			1
Smith - White	1			
Stonemason	6			1
Tailor				2
Vicar		1		
Wife (when no other occupation listed)	25	14		26
Woodman	1	1		
Family members over 14 with no occupation listed, usually unmarried, sometimes 'retired'	15	11		18
Children (5s & under)	35	14		19
Children / Scholars (5 – 14 yrs.)	40	15		36
Visitor (Adult)		1		

Appendix 2 – 19th Century Census

OCCUPATIONS in 1871	No. employed from Hackforth Township (28 households)	No. employed from Hornby Township (19 households)	No. resident in Hornby Castle (1 household)	No. employed from Langthorne Township (22 households)
Brick & Tile Maker				1
Butcher				1
Carpenter	3	1		
Cart Driver	1			
Clerk (Land Agent's)	1	1		
Coachman		1		
Cook		1		
Cordwainer/Shoemaker	1			1
Corn miller	1			1
Corn miller's man				
Dressmaker		1		
Farm / Agricultural Labourer	4	5		8
Farm Servant	5	3		9
Farmer	3	6		6
Gamekeeper/Gamewatcher		2		
Gardener	2	1		1
Gatekeeper	1	1		2
Grocer				1
Housekeeper	2			2
Inn Keeper	1			
Joiner	3			
Joiner (Apprentice)	1			
Laundress	1			
Maid (House)		1		
Night Watchman (for Castle		1		
Photographer				1
Rabbit Catcher				
Schoolmaster/Schoolmistress	2			
Schoolteacher (Assistant)	1			
Servant (House)			2	1
Servant (General)	4	7		
Shepherd		1		
Smith – Black (Master)	1			1
Smith – Implements				1
Steward (House)			1	
Stonemason	2			1
Stonemason (Master)	2			
Stonemason (Apprentice)	1			
Tailor				1
Vicar		1		
Washerwoman	1			
Wife (when no other occupation listed)	21	13	1	20
Woodman/Woodsawyer	2			
Family members over 14 with no occupation listed, usually unmarried, sometimes 'retired'	19	19		5
Children (5s & under)	24	7		15
Children / Scholars (5 – 14 yrs.)	46	16		19
Visitor (Adult)		1		
Visitor (Child)		4		3

292

Appendix 2 – 19th Century Census

OCCUPATIONS in 1881	No. employed from Hackforth Township (29 households)	No. employed from Hornby Township (20 households)	No. resident in Hornby Castle (1 household)	No. employed from Langthorne Township (27 households)
Bootmaker	1			
Brick Maker				1
Butcher				1
Butter Factor				1
Cabinet Maker	1			
Carpenter (House)	1			
Cart Driver		2		
Clerk (Land Agent's, Hornby Castle)	1			
Clerk & Nursery Gardener				1
Cook		1		
(Cordwainer)/Shoemaker	1			2
Corn miller	1			
Corn miller & Publican	1			
Cow Keeper	1			1
Dressmaker	2	1		
Farm / Agricultural Labourer	3	2		3
Farm Servant	10	6		7
Farmer	3	5		6
Gamekeeper/Gamewatcher		1		
Gardener (Head)	3	1		
Gardener				
Gardener (Under)		3		
Gardener's Labourer		3		
Gatekeeper/Lodgekeeper		1		
Grocer & Stonemason	1			
Grocer				2
Groom		1		
Housekeeper		1	1	1
(Innkeeper)/Publican				1
Joiner	6			2
Labourer (General)	6	2		11
Maid (House)		1	3	
Maid (Stillroom)			1	
Milliner		1		
Museum Keeper		1		
Night Watchman (for Castle)		1		
Parish Clerk	1			
Primitive (Methodist?) Local Preacher				3
Rabbit Catcher	2			
Schoolteacher (Certificated)	1			
Servant (Domestic)	8	4		3
Servant (General)				2
Shepherd (Hornby Park)	1			
Smith – Black (Master)	1			
Smith – Black				1
Smith – Black (Apprentice)	2			
Steward (House)			1	
Stonemason	4			
Vicar		1		
Wife (when no other occupation listed)	25	11		23
Woodman/Woodsawyer	2			
Family members over 14 with no occupation listed, usually unmarried, sometimes 'retired'	15	12		5
Children (5s & under)	15	11		17
Children / Scholars (5 – 14 yrs.)	42	9		29
Visitor (Adult)				2
Visitor (Child)		1		2

293

Appendix 2 – 19th Century Census

OCCUPATIONS in 1891	No. employed from Hackforth Township (28 households)	No. employed from Hornby Township (18 households)	No. resident in Hornby Castle (1 household)	No. employed from Langthorne Township (24 households)
Boot & Shoemaker				1
Bricklayer's Labourer	1			
Brick Maker	1			1
Carpenter (Estate)				
Cartman (for Castle)		1		
Charwoman	1			1
Clerk (Estate Office)		1		
Cook	1			
Cow Keeper				1
Dressmaker	2			
Farm / Agricultural Labourer	7	5		9
Farm Servant	9	4		7
Farmer	3	9		8
Gamekeeper	1	1		
Gardener (Foreman)		1		
Gardener		1		
Gardener (Journeyman)		1		
Gardener's Labourer	2	3		
Gatekeeper/Lodgekeeper		2		
Governess		1		
Grocer				1
Groom		1	1	
Housekeeper	1		1	
Innkeeper				1
Innkeeper/Miller & Farmer	1			
Joiner	2			
Joiner & Wheelwright				1
Labourer (General)	5			
Maid (House)		2	3	
Maid (Stillroom)			1	
Museum Caretaker		1		
Night Watchman (for Castle)		1		
Nurse (Hospital)		1		
Parish Clerk	1			
Rabbit Catcher	1			
Road Repairers' Labourer	1			
Schoolmistress	1			
Schoolteacher (Pupil Teacher)	1			1
Servant (Domestic)	3	2		5
Servant (General)	2	1		
Shepherd	1			
Smith – Black	1			1
Stonemason	1			
Stonemason's Labourer	1			
Vicar		1		
Wife (when no other occupation listed)	23	14		16
Woodman/Woodsawyer	1			
Family members over 14 with no occupation listed, usually unmarried, sometimes 'retired'	5	7		16
Children (5s & under)	11	8		10
Children / Scholars (5 – 14 yrs.)	28	14		22
Visitor (Adult)	1			2

294

Index

A

Adamson Family 38, 40, 41, 61
Ainderby Miers 21, 33, 287
Allan Family 221
Allen Family 225
Anderson Family 91, 247
Appleton, East & West..28, 34, 63, 126, 129, 157, 158, 188
Arbour Hill Farm 17, 18, 30, 39, 132
Armistice Day 66
Armstrong Family 231, 242
Arrathorne, East & West 63, 98, 99, 101, 144
Ashby, Mr Simon 248
Atkinson Family 118, 123, 126, 127, 131, 136, 142, 152, 165

B

Bardon Family 131, 139, 204, 206, 249
Barker Family 249
Beamish, Rev J. Forster 109, 110
Bedale Hunt 43, 198
Bishop Family 229
Blaisdon Publishing 2
Blanchard Family..... 231, 242, 243, 246, 252, 269, 272
Blenkiron Family 117, 131
Blows Family 247
Blundel, Rev Moss 107
Bolton Family 128, 247
Boultbee, Rev H T & Mary 25, 26
Bowe Family 144
Bowers Family 246, 247
Breeze Family 224, 231
Brigham Family 63, 89
Broadwith Family 255
Brown Family 18, 63, 109, 143, 161, 224, 246, 247, 248, 257, 272
Brunskill Family 185
Buck, Samuel – architect 13
Burrows Family 252
Bus Service 188, 233
Butler, Arnold 240, 256
Butler, Simon 256, 257, 272

C

"Capability" Brown 16, 17, 18, 19
Carmarthen, Marquis of (11th Duke of Leeds).............. 40
Carr, John – architect 14, 17, 18, 19, 30
Carruthers Family 131
Casey Family 208, 209
Chapman Family 143, 144, 211, 249
Christie, Rev. David 270

Church View, Hornby 26, 58, 236
Cinque Ports 13
Clay Pits 101
Clutterbuck Family 18, 87, 176, 192, 196, 255, 279
Cobshaws Farm, Langthorne 34, 36, 134
Commonwealth War Graves Commission 63
Conyers, Baron William 13, 15, 23, 25, 33
Corn Mill 140
Coulter Family 247
Cowley Family 252, 256
Cox Family 44
Coxson Family 243
Craggs Family 198, 224
Crate Family 247
Crawford, Rev B. 108, 144, 167, 194
Crown Inn, Langthorne 35

D

D'Arcy, 4th Earl of Holdernesse 13, 15
Danby, 3rd Earl of Holdernesse 13, 14, 15
Dawson Family 44, 45, 47, 64, 72, 130
Dean, Mrs. 21, 185
Deverill Family 20, 63
Diamond Hill Farm 26, 95, 99
Diana, Princess of Wales 217
Dobson, Brian 256
Dodd Family 221, 224, 231, 242, 243, 245, 246, 247
Domesday Book ~ 1985 .... 228, 277
Donaldson Family 247
Drury, Rev. W.F. 59
Duck Decoy 18, 47, 278

Duke of Leeds 17, 25, 30, 33, 38, 40, 41, 42, 43, 44,
                              45, 73, 89, 111, 240
Durrans Family 246, 247, 255

E

Easby Family 44, 269, 270
East Farm House, Langthorne 36
Edgecome, Rev. George S. 111
Elizabeth I, Queen 30
Elizabeth II, Queen 167, 205
Elizabeth, Princess 122, 156
Ellerton Family 107, 109, 117, 131
Errington Family 185, 279

F

Farnaby Family 185, 206, 209, 225, 229
Field Family 247
Fish Family 224
Flowers Family 206, 221, 224, 225
Forrest, Alex 104
Frost Family 209
Fullerton Family 185

G

Gargett Family 204, 208, 209, 221, 245
George V, King 59, 122
George VI, King 122, 167
Ghyll (Gyll) Hall 30, 91, 108, 112, 278, 283
Gibbens Family 209
Gibson Family 221, 224, 226
Godolphin, 11th Duke of Leeds 112, 113

Great War 62
Greaves Family 24, 91
Green Family 115
Greensit Family 208
Greetham, Rev & Mrs W 209
Gregg Family 203, 204, 208, 209
Greyhound Inn 30, 32, 45, 86, 115, 119, 120, 198

H

Hackforth Post Office 30, 32, 118, 187, 238
Hackforth School .30, 50, 59, 61, 62, 66, 67, 68, 91, 94, 109, 112, 115, 122, 123, 126, 129, 130, 137, 141, 142, 156, 167, 179, 180, 182, 184, 186, 203, 207, 216, 217, 221, 225, 227, 228, 229, 234, 240, 242, 245, 246, 248, 252
Hall Family 143
Hammond, John 87
Harrison Family 249
Hart Family 131
Hawkswell, Nicholas 111
Heeley Family ... 98, 100, 101, 107, 109, 110, 130, 131, 144, 148, 149
Hill, Mr Fred 90
Hillary Family 107, 135, 185
Hobson Family 88, 91
Hodgson Family 63
Holland Family 43, 143
Home Farm 17, 18
Home Guard (Hackforth/Hornby) ..130, 131, 132, 141, 151
Horn Family 246, 247, 257
Hornby Castle ... 13, 42, 48, 50, 63, 73, 86, 89, 91, 130, 132, 134, 150, 171, 192, 196, 211, 220, 278
Hornby Castle Auction 34, 77, 212
Hornby Castle Lodge 52, 182
Hornby Park Chase 212, 213
Hornby Spring 29
Howard Family 14, 201, 224, 226
Howe Family 255
Hulse Family 117
Hunt Family 68, 151, 185
Hurworth Family .. 52, 64, 103, 148, 159, 245, 247, 257
Hutchinson Family 26, 117, 234, 248, 250
Hutton-Squires Family 63, 150

I

Ice House, Hornby Park 27, 32
Ingledew Family .... .53, 54, 62, 68, 91, 103, 109, 111, 115, 117, 129, 131, 132, 133, 148, 149, 151, 204, 240
Iveson Family 242

J

Jackson Family 224, 231, 242, 243, 245
Jenkins, Mrs C. 242
Joblin Family 185
Johnson Family ..91, 115, 131, 132, 143, 156, 167, 182, 185, 203, 204, 206, 208, 209, 221, 247

K

Kennels, Hornby Castle 28, 38, 40, 43, 136
Kilding Family 131

Kirby Family 224, 242, 248
Knights Family 247
Knox Family .. 69, 93, 97, 107, 109, 110, 117, 131, 132, 139, 145

L

Land Army Girls 138
Langthorne Hall/House 34, 69, 70, 136, 143
Larby Family 247
Laundry Cottage 28
Leach Family 141
Leoni, Giacomo – architect 14
Lockhart Family 247
Lumley Family 143

M

Mableson Family 246
Maidment Family 68
Manor House Farm 31, 156, 158
Marshall Family 109, 115
McKinlay Family 221, 242, 243
McKnight Family 265, 269
Mellor Family 247
Metcalfe Family 107, 109, 131, 151, 185, 187, 204, 209, 221, 224, 231, 242, 246, 247, 270
Methodist Church 35, 143
Military Police 136
Mill Cottage, Hackforth 268
Mill House Farm 128, 140
Millennium Celebrations ... 3, 252, 254, 271, 272, 274, 275
Millward Family 242

Mitchell Family 246, 247
Moate Family 257, 272
Morley Family 44, 45, 47, 49, 117
Morris Family 107, 131
Moss, Mrs Kay 238
Mowbray Family 211
Murfin Family 115, 185
Myers Family 256

N

Newcombe Family 250
Nicol, Charles 63
Noone Family 242
Norman Family 135, 247, 257
North Road, Hackforth 31, 64, 186, 187, 238

O

OFSTED 248
Olivant Family 269, 272

P

Pace Family 250
Parker Family 221
Peacock Family 203, 242, 245, 257
Pearson Family 131, 151, 158, 250, 252, 265, 272, 274
Percival Family 224, 225, 272
Petch Family 131
Philips Family 131
Pierson Family 165
Pilkington Family 208
Plews, Audrey 238, 256

Pocklington, Jeff 127, 174
Point to Point, Hornby Castle 150, 175
Poole Family 242, 247, 255
Potter Family 247
Potts Family 131, 231, 242, 245, 246
Pounder Family 203, 208, 221, 225
Prime, Mr 89
Pringle Family 208, 209, 239, 252, 254, 272, 274
Pybus Family 202, 208, 269

Q

Queen Elizabeth II Silver Jubilee 204, 205, 209

R

Ramsay Family 131, 208, 218, 221, 224, 225, 226,
231, 242, 243, 255
Ramshay, Mrs Jean 249
Rawson Family 131
Remembrance Day 66
Reynolds Family 185
Riding School, Hornby Castle 58
Robinson Family 63, 131, 143, 204, 207, 208, 229, 242
Robinson, Frederick 107, 208, 218, 221, 224
Ross, Mrs. 128
Roundhill Farm 45, 50, 52, 62, 111, 129, 132
Rudd Hall & Farm . 50, 58, 91, 103, 123, 141, 161, 232
Rudd, David 185
Russell Family 209, 224
Ryans Family 221

S

Saw Mill, Hackforth 33, 140, 165
Scarf Family 100
Scott Family 131, 221, 224, 257
Scurr Family 131
Shaw, Jack 40
Silver Street 30, 31, 126, 140, 173
Smith Families .. 91, 106, 107, 108, 109, 115, 117, 131,
204, 225, 242, 246
Smith, Biddy 117
Snowdon Family 272
Spencer Family 248
Spirit Family 213, 221, 224
Sport, School & Village 70, 72, 244
St Mary's Cemetery 107
St Mary's Church .. 20, 34, 73, 104, 109, 110, 129, 135,
144, 164, 165, 194, 196, 220, 252, 270
St Mary's Church Choir 105, 109
St Mary Magdalene Church, Langthorne 35
St Quintin Family 25
Staniland Family 211, 234
Stirk Family 247
Stourton Family 17
Street House/Farm, Old/New 17, 30, 53, 54, 55, 62,
91, 111, 112, 129, 132, 141, 200
Stuart, James – architect 14, 15, 16

T

Taylor Family 208
Terry, George 63, 185
Thomas Family 221, 225

Thompson Family..50, 52, 56, 58, 62, 73, 86, 136, 143, 148, 151, 152, 159
Thwaites Family 208, 209, 221, 242
Todd, Mr John 73, 91
Towler Family 95, 102
Transport 154, 243
Tufty Club..203
Tunstall Family..30
Tyson Family......91, 109, 115, 117, 123, 129, 141, 161, 176, 232

V

Valks Family..109, 115
Vicarage, Hornby 21, 26, 28, 29, 109, 278
Victory in Europe (VE) Day 141
Victory in Japan (VJ) Day 141
Village Hall........30, 111, 115, 123, 129, 137, 141, 216, 217, 234, 239, 240, 243, 252, 254, 285

W

Walker Family 247, 256, 268
War Memorial, St Mary's 63
Ward Family 108
Ward, Thomas (Biddy Smith)............................... 108
Webb-Collins Family 247
Webster Family. 127, 131, 132, 203, 204, 208, 209, 225, 265
Williamson Family 247, 248
Willis Family 224
Wilson Family.. 185, 213
Winterfield 28, 41, 68, 134
Women's Institute...... 30, 117, 192, 211, 234, 249, 250
WW II Emergency Rest Centre 129

Y

Young, Arthur.. 14, 16, 17
Young Family 208, 221, 234